The Meaning of Communism

The Meaning of Communism

by
William J. Miller, *Staff Writer, Time Inc.;*
Associate, Columbia University Graduate School of Journalism

in association with
Henry L. Roberts, *Professor of History and Director of*
the Russian Institute, Columbia University

and
Marshall D. Shulman, *Professor of International Relations,*
Fletcher School of Law and Diplomacy, and Research Associate,
Russian Research Center, Harvard University

Published by
Silver Burdett Company / Time Incorporated

Book trade distribution by
Simon and Schuster, Incorporated

Library of Congress catalogue card number 63-10162
PRINTED IN THE UNITED STATES OF AMERICA

BOOK TRADE DISTRIBUTION BY SIMON AND SCHUSTER, INC.

CONTENTS

Introduction: Why Read about Communism? 7

1 The Idea: Karl Marx and His Revolutionary Theory 14

2 The Organization: Lenin and the Communist Party 30

3 The Result: Hardening of the Communist Dictatorship 66

4 The Goal: World Triumph of Communism 94

5 The Reality: Life under Communism 128

6 The Challenge: What We Can Do 170

Appendix

Chronology 184

Glossary 185

Bibliography for Further Reading 188

Index 189

Credits 192

ЛЕНИН
СТАЛИН

INTRODUCTION

Why Read about Communism?

Every thoughtful American senses the contradictory nature of today's world, so abundant in both danger and opportunity. It might be said of this world, as Charles Dickens wrote in *A Tale of Two Cities,* "It was the best of times, it was the worst of times."

The most hopeful and promising world in man's history is also the most dangerous.

It is the most hopeful and promising because in the six decades of this century alone science has made more progress than it has in the past history of man.

Man has unlocked the key to the atom, bringing the promise of fusion power, which would be as limitless as the energy of the sun.

Man has hurtled into space, defying the laws of gravity that kept him bound to the earth and its immediate atmosphere.

Man has penetrated the riddles of disease to such an extent that his life expectancy is being continuously increased. The answers to such remaining mysteries as cancer are gradually being assembled.

For the first time in all the history of man, through the desalting of ocean water, it may become possible to make the world's deserts bloom again—for many were once green. And with this great act of restoration, man may one day create abundance for that two thirds of humankind who are now undernourished.

The Shrinking World

Man seems to be expanding his potentialities and capabilities into entirely new dimensions, creating incalculable revolutions in his life, his thoughts, his hopes and his dreams. For example, Telstar, the first communications satellite put into orbit, has already enabled Americans to see events almost as they take place in Europe, and Europeans to attend a White House press conference. Soon it will be feasible for all men everywhere to witness other ways of life, share other peoples' problems or profit by their great variety of experiences. In such a shrinking world it will be far more difficult for totalitarian tyranny of any kind to wall off people from the truth

← COMMUNIST POWER ON DISPLAY AT LENIN'S TOMB IN MOSCOW

about events. And, as always, the truth will tend to make man free.

Why, then, is this world of hope and promise also the most dangerous?

The Forces That Divide. It is dangerous because the same power of the atom that promises boundless energy for peace also gives man the power to destroy the world by thermonuclear bombs. Moreover, the power of these destructive weapons is rapidly increasing on a seemingly limitless scale. The air burst of a 50-megaton bomb, for example, could start fires 45 miles in any direction from the point beneath the blast. Yet it is possible for both the United States and the Soviet Union to build bombs many times more powerful.

This explosive world is dangerous also because it is divided—by hate, fear, suspicion—as starkly as if a great stone wall were shutting off all those on one side from all those on the other.

There is such a wall. Both as a symbol and as a tangible fact, it is the essence of the meaning of Communism. It threatens our future because the force that raised it, Communism, is implacably dedicated to destroying the freedoms that the Free World cherishes: the freedom of every man to speak, write, worship as he pleases, and above all to choose his own rulers by "the consent of the governed." It is a wall deliberately reared to close man's mind to truth, to prevent him from knowing and understanding his neighbor, to deprive him of his freedom and to deny the very dignity of his humanity. It is reared to shut out the light, not to let it in; to instill fear and ignorance and hatred, not human compassion and fellow feeling. Wherever we look about us in the world, we can see the grim reality of this wall and the terrible importance it holds for our lives and our future.

A BOY DIES AT THE BERLIN WALL

The boy lying here, in the shadow of Berlin's "Wall of Shame," is 18-year-old Peter Fechter. On August 17, 1962, he and a friend tried scaling the barrier to freedom. Peter's friend escaped but Communist "Grepos," or border guards, gunned Peter down. For nearly an hour he moaned and called for help. But no help came. The Grepos made no move. While hundreds of onlookers watched, agonized, from each side of the wall, he slowly bled to death.

Where the Wall Exists. Here are some of the places and some of the ways in which this wall looms large:

▶ It is an uneasy line of truce, guarded on each side by hundreds of thousands of troops, along the 38th parallel in Korea. That line was broken by Communist aggressors when they swarmed across it in June 1950, and its restoration claimed the lives of 34,000 Americans and 3,000 other members of United Nations forces. Moreover, the truce agreement of 1953 that ended the fighting has been continuously and flagrantly violated by the Communists ever since—by reinforcing their troops, by sending in the latest planes and tanks, and in many other ways.

▶ The wall is a ring of Soviet tanks that encircle the entire city of Budapest, though hidden now in the peaceful countryside. In 1956 Soviet armor crushed out the life of a Hungary suddenly liberated by its own people in 13 days of spontaneous revolt that stirred the whole world. Men, women and children literally clawed their way to freedom with their bare hands. But a final massive onslaught of Soviet tanks smashed the uprising and freedom remains in chains today. So this wall is now a prison for the entire Hungarian nation.

▶ Another wall imprisons the whole vast Soviet Union itself and bars its 220 million people from any free acquaintance with the West. It is composed of thousands of miles of barbed wire, barricades, mine fields and guard towers which stretch from the deserts of Iran to polar Lapland. It keeps the people from learning what the rest of the world is really like—while Communism's controlled press and radio grind out a constant message of hate and fear.

▶ The most notorious wall of contemporary history is that which went up on August 13, 1961, around the free city of West Berlin, to shut off the wretched and oppressed people of Communist East Berlin from any contact with West Berlin's abundance and prosperity. It was built because since 1949 nearly three million Germans (the present East German population is 16 million) had used the escape hatch of West Berlin to flee to freedom in West Germany. Millions more would have followed if the Berlin gateway, with its air access to the West, had remained open. Many walls have been built to keep out invaders; the Communists are the first to build walls to keep whole nations from fleeing.

One Third of the World. In 1917, when the Bolsheviks overthrew the legal government of Russia, the extent of Communist control was measured by the city limits of Petrograd (now Leningrad). Today Communism reigns over the immense stretch of the earth's surface from East Germany through Russian Europe, across Siberia and China to the Pacific, extending as far as Tibet and North Vietnam in southern Asia. One third of the world's three billion people live under Communist rule.

Communism is confident that the remaining two billion people of the world will become its subjects. "Your grandchildren . . ." Soviet Premier Khrushchev has boasted to Americans, "will live under socialism."

All these things make it urgent for Americans to learn what Communism is, why it acts the way it does, the tactics and strategy it employs, the strengths it can muster and the weaknesses that make it vulnerable.

THE KILLERS REMOVE THEIR VICTIM

Not until young Peter became still in death did a jack-booted East German soldier march off with his body. This tragedy so outraged West Berliners that during late August they rioted and stoned buses taking Soviet troops to change the guard at the Soviet War Memorial in West Berlin. In the wake of this incident, the U.S. forces in Berlin were told to dispatch American ambulance teams into East Berlin should a similar event occur.

The Conquest Communism Seeks

The Communist rulers of the U.S.S.R. seek to sway the destiny of all the globe. Many times before, the world has felt the impact of savage or fanatic forces which have sought to conquer everything before them, only to break and recede. Communism seeks a similar conquest, but where others relied solely on the power of arms, Communism also uses the power of ideas in its pursuit of victory.

Ideas in Arms. Though Communism is armed to the teeth, and is prepared to use guns if need be, it puts words on a par with guns, and regards ideas with as much favor as bullets. These ideas have sometimes had an enormous appeal to the West because they are western in origin. Communism is not something alien to western civilization but a corruption that sprang from it.

It could well be defined as "Ideas in Arms."

In all its armories of ideas, the one it holds with the most fanatic conviction is this: *because history is on its side, Communism is certain to conquer the world and therefore Communists are justified in using any means to help reach their goal.*

▶ Everything that Communism does, the deceit and the treachery which so often baffle Westerners, flows from this obsession. Communism has no abiding interest in lessening the tensions in the world; regarding them as leading inevitably to its own triumph, it cheerfully worsens them.

▶ Communism has no interest in helping to create a stable world order, except where temporary stability enables it to prepare its next offensive against peace. Communism regards total disorder—lawlessness and revolution—as the necessary forerunner of its triumph. When it cannot win outright, Communism prefers chaos to compromise.

▶ Over the nearly 50 years of its existence, Communism has frustrated non-Communist statesmen with its policy of honoring only those agreements that served its interest. When non-Communists think they have settled a problem for good and all, the Communists are merely putting the problem aside until some new opportunity

Socialism and Communism Differentiated

Soviet Communists define the terms "socialism" and "Communism" in a manner confusing to the Free World. They deliberately blur the important differences that distinguish the two systems, both as political philosophies and as practical political doctrines.

The History. In political terms the word "Communist" refers to the Communist party created by Lenin. It is an outgrowth of the Russian Social Democratic Labor party founded in 1898. In 1903 this party split into so-called majority (Bolshevik) and minority (Menshevik) factions. Both sought to achieve "socialism" as defined by Karl Marx. But the Bolsheviks, under Lenin, fought for a small, secret organization and the immediate and violent overthrow of government. The Mensheviks were more like the Social Democratic parties in western Europe, which believed in bringing about socialism gradually and legally through ballot, trade unions and a large, open party.

In 1918 Lenin, to show his complete disagreement with the Mensheviks' policy, renamed his Bolshevik group the Communist party. Shortly afterward, the Communists began to persecute all opposition parties.

arises to reopen the whole question and to make the problem worse.

▶ Since Communists believe that any tactics are justifiable in the "class struggle," words do not have the same meaning to them as they do to others.

▶ Until very recently, Communism might have been dismissed as a distantly based threat. Now it has taken up an aggressive and menacing position in Cuba, only 90 miles from the Florida coast.

The Battle for the World. If the future held no hope that we should ever cease to face such total and merciless hostility, many Americans might well conclude it would be better to fight the Communists now and, for better or worse, have done with it.

But the cataclysmic nature of thermonuclear conflict makes major war something that both antagonists in this battle for the world have sought to avoid. And gradual evolutionary trends now taking place within the Communist world give grounds, as we shall see, to hope that Communism, extreme as it is in theory, may in time become something different in practice.

Because the peace of the world may well depend on how such evolutionary changes in Communism may develop, it is important for Americans to learn everything that they can about Communism, both as it is preached and as it is practiced, as idea and as fact. That is the purpose of this book.

Let us begin by seeing how the idea began in the mind of Karl Marx, the man who inspired the greatest mass movement of modern times and is one of the most influential figures in human history.

The Economics. In economic terms "socialism" means the public ownership and control of the essential means for the production and distribution of goods. "Communism," in its early sense, simply meant any system of social organization in which property is held *in common.*

The Social Democrats in Germany, France, Austria and the Scandinavian countries have largely contented themselves with pushing social reforms, such as publicly owned housing and unemployment insurance. In Great Britain the Labour party (sometimes also called Socialist) was voted to power and during its six-year term achieved some of its goals by nationalizing certain industries.

In the United States the major political parties have long since undercut American socialist programs by advocating measures such as collective bargaining, minimum wage and hour laws, social security and public power projects.

Soviet "Socialism." The Communists use the term "socialism" to describe the way of life in present Soviet society. Under it, practically every means of production and consumption are owned and operated by the state. However, some people are paid higher wages than others and some receive more goods than others. The Soviet Union is still far from Communism as Marx envisaged it many years ago: *"From each according to his ability, to each according to his needs."*

A World

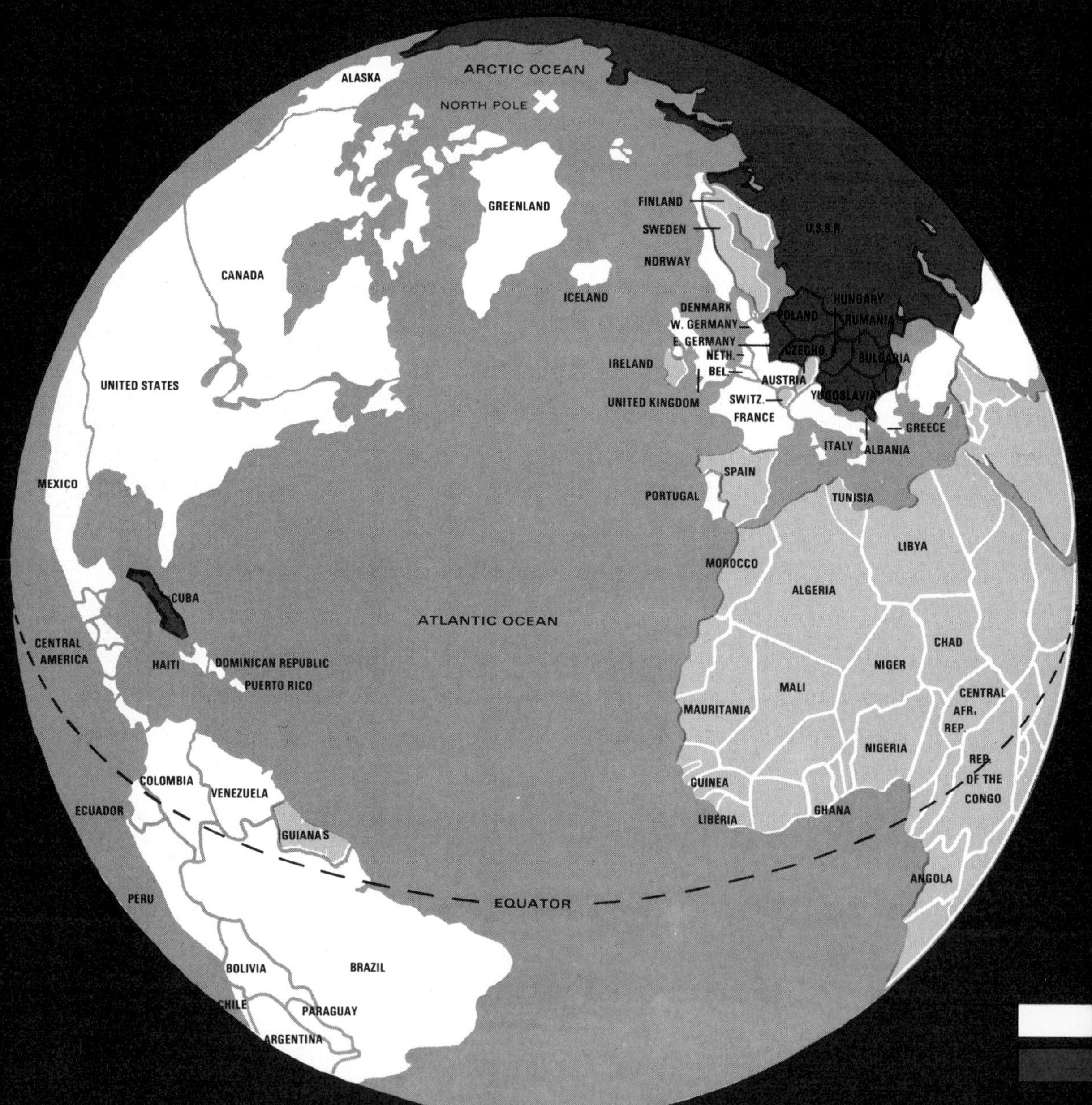

THE ATLANTIC COMMUNITY of nations, joined by Free World alliances (white), embraces most of the Western Hemisphere and western Europe. Communism's only serious inroad in the Americas has been in Castro's Cuba.

in Conflict

Free World alliances

Communist countries

THE COMMUNIST COUNTRIES are solidly set (red) in the strategic heartland of the immense Eurasian land mass. Yugoslavia has followed an independent Communist course. The nations colored gray are uncommitted.

KARL MARX

1 The Idea:

Karl Marx and His Revolutionary Theory

A specter is haunting Europe—the specter of Communism." These words of Karl Marx, father of revolutionary Communism, are truer today than when they were written in 1848. For today, the specter he invoked haunts the whole world.

In 1848 Marx, a brilliant, 29-year-old German journalist, issued the *Communist Manifesto* in collaboration with Friedrich Engels. They hoped that the *Manifesto's* eloquence would inspire a revolution all over Europe through which the workers would seize power, take the factories away from their owners and create a society free of class distinctions in which all property—land, buildings, machines and stores—would be owned by the state.

"The theory of the Communists," said the *Manifesto,* "may be summed up in the single sentence: Abolition of private property." The method it advocated—violent revolt—was summed up in these words: "The proletarians [workers] have nothing to lose but their chains. They have a world to win. Workingmen of all countries, unite!"

The revolution advocated by Marx and Engels did not take place until the next century—and then in a country, Russia, where their analysis did not predict it. But the world and the times in which they brought forth their *Manifesto* were certainly bursting with revolutionary ferment.

An Era of Painful Transition

Actually, there were two related revolutions going on at the same time during the 1840s, one industrial, the other political. The Industrial Revolution, the greatest economic change in man's history, was already well under way, having started in England in the 1700s. In the next hundred years machines would create abundance and prosperity beyond the wildest dreams of those philosophers who, since the start of history, had sought some way to create a good life for all. But industrialization was also creating poverty and misery as it changed men's traditional ways of living.

The Decline of Village Life. For centuries, children and grandchildren had lived in the same villages as their forebears. For generations, sons had followed family callings—a shoemaker's son made shoes, a baker's son baked bread. But great new inventions like Richard Arkwright's spinning water frame and James Watt's steam engine, both patented in 1769, disrupted the settled life of rural England. Independent craftsmen who had spun and woven wool in their own cottages began drifting away to the mills in burgeoning new factory towns like Manchester.

Watt's engine made possible the railroad, which further broke up the isolation of the farm countryside and brought new crowds to the cities hunting for factory jobs and places to live. Urban population was also swelled by people from rural areas forced to leave their homes by the Enclosure Acts. These acts allowed noblemen and country squires to consolidate their landholdings at the expense of the tenant farmer. The displaced farmers and craftsmen who crowded into the booming cities transformed large urban areas into grimy and miserable slums. New cities, similarly blighted, arose, and many villages became completely deserted.

Conditions have changed so much in the past century that it is hard for us even to imagine the life that early 19th Century workers lived. In their slum homes, they were herded like animals into human pigsties. At work, they labored from long before dawn to long after dusk in dusty, dimly lit factories. The wages that workers received for submitting to this wretched life were scarcely enough to sustain life—so little children had to work along with their parents to add a few pennies to the family's income.

The evils of the Industrial Revolution's early years must have seemed insoluble to those who had most to gain from reform. Popular government was practically unknown in the Europe of that time. England, however, was moving toward broadly based, representative government, and its elected parliament was tackling the problems through such laws as the Factory Act of 1844.

1848: A Continent in Flames. The long-brewing political revolution erupted in 1848. Industrialization in western Europe had begun before the people had thrown off the yoke of absolute monarchy. When Marx issued his call for a revolution, most Europeans did not yet have the basic human rights, civil liberties and constitutional government which Americans had proclaimed in 1776.

In 1848 all Europe was astir with demands for the "unalienable rights" of life, liberty and the pursuit of happiness asserted by Jefferson in the American Declaration of Independence. The example of free, prosperous, expanding America was itself a powerful spur to political change. Even more important was the French Revolution of 1789, with its slogan of liberty, equality and fraternity. Though its goals were not wholly realized before it gave way to the imperialism of Napoleon, the French Revolution did give other Europeans a vital hope: that revolution was indeed an effective way to bring on both political and social change.

In the Austrian Empire, the Hungarians and other nationalities chafed under the reactionary chancellor, Prince Metternich. Russia's

Seeds of Revolution: Inhuman Working Conditions

A WOMAN MINEWORKER crawls like a beast of burden, dragging a cartload of coal through a low, narrow passage. Marx argued that revolution was the only way to end such conditions. Instead, the British—spurred by pictures like this—legislated mining reforms in 1842.

FACTORY WORKERS' HOMES are jammed together in alleys and filthy streets *(right)*. City populations mushroomed as the Industrial Revolution lured workers from farm and village to jobs in mills and factories. As they crowded into cities, slums soon developed.

Tsar Nicholas I (1825-1855) ruled serfs who were hardly better off than slaves. Prussia's King Frederick William IV ran a state whose people had little personal liberty.

France was under the comparatively liberal and constitutional rule of King Louis Philippe. But the French factory system, like most in continental Europe, was extremely oppressive to its workers. Factory hands sang revolutionary songs as they worked. "Really," said the poet Heinrich Heine, "people in our gentle walk of life can have no idea of the demonic note which runs through these songs."

Revolt came in 1848 as the people of Paris barricaded the streets and seized the government, overthrowing the now ineffectual Louis Philippe. They set up a provisional government whose 11 members included four representatives of a workingmen's party. This government established the Second French Republic.

Revolts Spread. Similar revolutions were sweeping through Germany, Italy and Austria. Workers erected street barricades in Berlin, and King Frederick William IV of Prussia was forced to take off his hat to the dead—"the heroes fallen in the glorious struggle for social and political liberty." In Italy, a great popular hero named Giuseppe Mazzini swept to power, and for some months was the virtual ruler of a republic of Rome. The Hungarian patriot Louis Kossuth set off a revolution in Hungary which helped force Emperor Ferdinand I to

A CHILD WORKER is whipped by a foreman in a British cotton mill. Child labor was a major evil of early industrialization.

abdicate. Of the major European powers, only England (the most industrially advanced nation) and Russia (the least) were free of revolution that year.

All these revolutions were short-lived. Within little more than a year the revolutionary movement collapsed, and frightened rulers who suppressed the uprisings installed new tyrannies to forestall any recurrence of rebellion. But the revolts were indicative of Europe's yearning for political and social change. It was in this electric atmosphere that Marx and Engels rumbled the verbal thunder of the *Communist Manifesto,* whose lines were to become increasingly powerful with each passing decade.

The Education of Karl Marx

Karl Marx (1818-1883) came to the study of capitalism and Communism by the surprising route of religious philosophy. In the quiet Rhineland town of Trier, where his father was a prosperous lawyer, young Karl did well in high school.

A Belief in Goodness. Marx's father was a believer in the ideas of the French philosopher Condorcet, and Marx accepted his view that man is good by nature. Through his father, Marx also gained the belief that the triumph of man's innate goodness and reason was blocked only by social, political and religious barriers, and other artificially created rules. When these barriers disappeared, a new day would dawn for the human race. All men would be equal not only in law and politics but also in their social relations with one another.

Marx was deeply versed in art and literature, thanks to a neighbor, Ludwig von Westphalen. A distinguished government official, Westphalen was attracted by the boy's powerful intellect and eagerness to learn. He took young Marx for long walks, shared with him the delights of Cervantes, Dante, Shakespeare, Homer and the Greek tragedians, and loaned him books to read.

A Rebel at the University. At the age of 17, Marx went off to the University of Bonn, where he attended lectures on Homer's mythology, Latin poetry and modern art, and wrote poems of his own which in later years he considered rather juvenile. After a year at Bonn, he continued his studies at the University of Berlin.

In 1841 he was invited to contribute to a small newspaper published in Cologne. In less than a year he was its chief editor. Marx changed it from a somewhat liberal journal to a violently radical one —more opposed to the government than any other German publication. The government tried to censor it, but Marx usually outsmarted the censors. Finally, in April 1843, further publication of the newspaper was banned.

In the same month, Marx married Jenny von Westphalen, daughter of his mentor. Together, they decided to move to Paris, where he became the coeditor of a magazine. Earlier he had been introduced to Friedrich Engels, the wealthy son of a German cotton manufacturer. Now Engels sent Marx an article he had written. From this time onward, a lifelong friendship and close collaboration developed. The French government forced Marx to leave Paris in 1845, and he went to Brussels. But it was in Paris that Marx had formulated his guiding principle. "The philosophers," he noted, "hitherto have only interpreted the world in various ways: the thing is, however, to change it." To change the world! That would be Marx's driving force through all his life.

Marx and Engels were members, for a time, of a little-known and short-lived organization called the Communist League, for which they wrote the *Manifesto*. However, they had no other group to work with until 1864, when Marx became interested and active in the International Workingmen's Association. It fell apart in 1872, largely because Marx could not tolerate opposition to his own ideas. Although he could be mild and agreeable to his friends, Marx was capable of denouncing those who disagreed with him as louts, scoundrels and bedbugs, or charging them with a variety of scandalous crimes.

Marx spent the years between 1849 and 1883—virtually the rest of his days—in London, where he worked from early morning till late at night in the magnificent library of the British Museum. He was compiling notes for his monumental treatise, *Capital (Das Kapital)*, enlarging and expounding upon the *Manifesto's* outlined prediction of capitalism's doom. In *Capital*, Marx had little regard for anyone except the British factory inspectors who reported, with fearless honesty, the terrible conditions they found and the tricks owners used to evade the law. He drew most of his indictment of capitalism from these reports and parliamentary inquiries. Marx ignored the possibility that a society which could be so scathingly honest about its own shortcomings might find a way to remedy them. Ironically, no such public reports are, or could be, made by Communist inspectors today, nor could any foreigner use Soviet libraries as an arsenal of facts for an attack on Soviet society.

A REVOLUTIONIST'S LIFELONG FRIEND

Friedrich Engels, son of a prosperous German textile manufacturer, first saw the fate of the working class as a clerk in his father's mill in England. He was Marx's best friend, collaborator and main source of funds from the early 1840s until Marx's death in 1883.

Near-Starvation in the Slums. Marx, who spent nearly all of his time writing about the material shortcomings of society, neglected the material well-being of his own wife and six children, although he was unstinting in his love and affection for them. They often went hungry and would have starved if his friend Engels had not sent them money from time to time. One visitor to the Marxes' two-room apartment described it as follows:

> There is not one clean or decent piece of furniture in either room, everything is broken, tattered, and torn, with thick dust over everything and the greatest untidiness everywhere. In the middle of the parlor there is a large old-fashioned table. . . . On it there lie manuscripts, books and news-

papers, besides the children's toys, bits and pieces from his wife's sewing basket, cups with broken rims, dirty spoons, knives, forks, lamps, an inkpot, tumblers, pipes, tobacco ash—all piled up on the same table.

The grimness of the Marx family's life is also portrayed in one of Jenny Marx's letters to a friend, telling how they were evicted from their home. The landlord ordered two men to take

> possession of all my belongings: bedding, clothes . . . even the baby's cradle and the little girls' toys so that the children wept bitterly. . . .
>
> Next day we had to leave. It was cold and rainy. My husband tried to find a lodging, but as soon as he said we had four children no one would take us in. At length a friend helped us. We paid what was owing, and I quickly sold all my beds and bedding, in order to settle accounts with the chemist, the baker, the butcher and the milkman, who had heard [about our financial problems] . . . and had hastened to send in their bills.

Nor would their life ever be much better. Marx once wrote his friend Engels that he could no longer leave the house because he had pawned his clothes. He was arrested on suspicion of theft when he tried to pawn his wife's family silver. The silver bore the crest of the Duke of Argyll, from whom Jenny's grandmother was descended. "My wife cries all night," Marx wrote, "and that infuriates me."

Fairy Tales and Picnics. Marx loved children and they loved him. The children of the neighborhood called him "Daddy Marx." He would tell fairy tales to his children, take them on picnics to nearby Hampstead Heath, lead them to the first spring flowers.

But Marx's children were not to know continued happiness. Three of his six children, including his two sons, Guido and Edgar, died when young; two of his daughters committed suicide when they were grown women. When his tiny daughter, Franziska, died of bronchitis, there was no money even for a coffin. "Her small lifeless body rested in our little back room," Jenny Marx wrote in her diary, "whilst all went together into the front room, and when night came we made up beds on the floor." A friend finally lent a small sum for a cheap coffin. Amid such personal poverty, humiliation and bereavement, the relentless, aging revolutionist worked on at his task to change the world. Among other things, he suffered from boils. After completing a savage description of "The Working Day" he once noted: "I hope that the bourgeoisie [capitalists] as long as they live will have cause to remember my carbuncles." Indeed, they did.

How the Communist Idea Began

Neither Communism nor socialism (see definitions on page 10) were brand-new ideas that sprang full- grown from Karl Marx's mind. Throughout man's history, philosophers have searched for ways to

A Page from the Marx Family Picture Album

FATHER KARL at age 45 was living in London and sending articles on politics to journals in a number of countries.

WIFE JENNY, Marx's boyhood sweetheart, as a young girl was called "the enchanted princess."

SON EDGAR died when he was nine. Of the six Marx children, only three survived to maturity.

DAUGHTER LAURA wed a Cuban physician. A fine linguist, she spoke four languages with fluency.

IN LONDON the Marxes lived in poverty, harassed by creditors. This photo was taken in the 1870s.

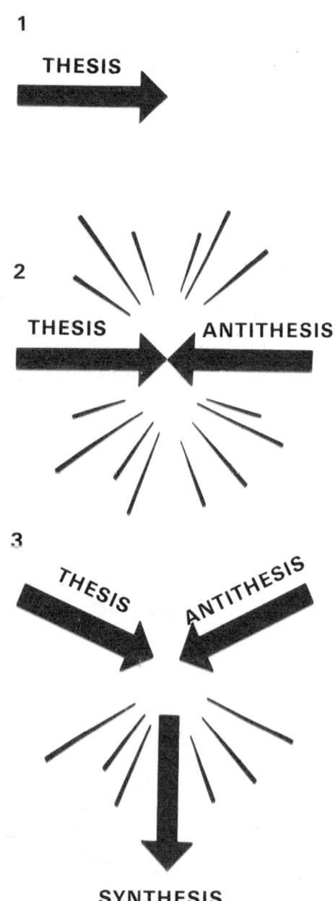

HOW MARXISTS SEE CONFLICT IN HISTORY

The diagram above depicts the opposition of historical forces as viewed by Marx in his concept of "dialectical materialism." In the development of history, a force comes into being called a thesis (1). In time, as the thesis outlives its usefulness, it is attacked by an opposing thesis which develops out of it. This is called an antithesis (2). Out of their opposing tension a new force emerges, called a synthesis (3). This, after it has lived its day, becomes a thesis to be opposed in turn by its opposite, or antithesis, to form a *new* synthesis and so on.

create a society in which there would be happiness and well-being for all. The problem of distributing man's wealth is discussed in the writings of Plato and Aristotle, in both the Old and New Testaments, and in such recently discovered manuscripts of Biblical times as the Dead Sea Scrolls. In his book, *Utopia,* published in 1516, Sir Thomas More described an imaginary, perfect island community with common ownership of property. In the early 1800s, such French philosophers as Saint-Simon (who fought on the side of the Americans in the American Revolution) and Charles Fourier proposed "utopian" societies in which production of all material goods—food, clothing, shelter—would be managed by the group itself, and the wealth thus produced be distributed among all the people according to some principle of an equitable nature.

Experimental Utopias. Attempts were made, both in France and in the United States, to establish little communities governed by Fourier's ideas for an equitable life. Fourier's admirers in the United States founded a radical newspaper, the New York *Tribune,* to advance his doctrines. Its managing editor, Charles Dana, who had met Marx and was deeply impressed by him, hired him to do one or two articles a week on European affairs. The English Socialist, Robert Owen, who created "model" cotton mills at New Lanark in Scotland, established a community at New Harmony, Indiana, where all property was owned by the group. Nathaniel Hawthorne, the famous American novelist, helped found a community at Brook Farm in New England, and wrote *The Blithedale Romance* about his experience. German refugees established communal villages in the Middle West in Zoar, Ohio, and Amana, Iowa.

These communities were established by good men with noble ideas, who hoped to eliminate the worst aspects of human society by sharing wealth and labor equally. But these so-called utopian systems had relatively short lives. What broke them up was the seemingly irrepressible human desire of every man to be his own master and, if possible, to own his own property. Marx scoffed at these small-scale experiments. In fact, he and Engels chose the term "Communism" to distinguish their ideas clearly from such utopian socialism. To Marx, complete social upheaval was both necessary and inevitable in order to achieve a new society.

Marx was not the originator of all the components of his theories. What he did was to take many men's ideas and set them into a totally new framework.

Hegel and "The Dialectic." To understand the theories of Marx, it is first necessary to learn something about the German philosopher Georg W. F. Hegel, whose writings had profoundly influenced Marx while he was at the University of Berlin. The key to Hegel's thought is what he called "the dialectic," a technical philosophical term meaning "argument," or "debate." Hegel's dialectic saw conflict or contradiction, as the moving force of all history, thought and existence.

To Hegel, everything in the world is constantly changing—something old dying, something new developing. One set of ideas (thesis) is violently opposed by another (antithesis) which has developed out of the first. From their clash arises a new combination (synthesis), containing the best elements of both. This synthesis becomes, as it develops, another thesis, again generating its own antithesis. Through the clash and struggle of thesis and antithesis, the world moves closer and closer to perfection. In applying this theory to life, Hegel thought in terms of the spirit. To him, all of man's history could be understood as man's conflict with his own nature—as man coming to realize that the spirit itself was reality.

Marx and "Dialectical Materialism." Marx approved of Hegel's method, but found its application mystifying. He thought Hegel had things right, but had them upside down. It was not man's spirit that creates its own world. Rather, Marx concluded, it was the world around man—his material surroundings and the way he adapts to them—which determined everything about man's life.

While men liked to believe that they created their laws and institutions according to their ideas and ideals of truth and justice, Marx felt it was the other way around. Every society's laws, politics, ideas of religion and morality have developed chiefly out of the ways by which its members produced and exchanged their food, clothing, shelter and other material goods. This is the first essential part of Marx's theories, and has come to be called dialectical materialism.

Workers against Owners—the Class Struggle. The second point in Marx's theories is that a conflict between the working classes and the owners is inevitable. "The history of all hitherto existing society is the history of class struggles," Marx said in the *Manifesto.*

In every era of the past, Marx wrote, a working class had struggled against an owning class—slave against master, feudal serf against lord and, with the coming of industrial capitalism in the 1700s, factory worker against capitalist owner. But capitalism, like feudalism and other earlier systems, Marx claimed, would inevitably destroy itself because it contains the seeds of its own destruction. It produces "its own gravediggers."

Why did he think this was so? Not because capitalism was inherently evil. On the contrary, says the *Manifesto,* capitalists have been the greatest revolutionaries of their day. Marx gives them credit for overthrowing the remnants of feudalism, for rescuing the peasants "from the idiocy of rural life," for making the more civilized cities the economic centers of a country, and for opening up backward countries to the civilizing effects of trade and culture. Says the *Manifesto:*

> In place of the old wants, satisfied by the production of [a single] country, we find new wants, requiring for their satisfaction the products of distant

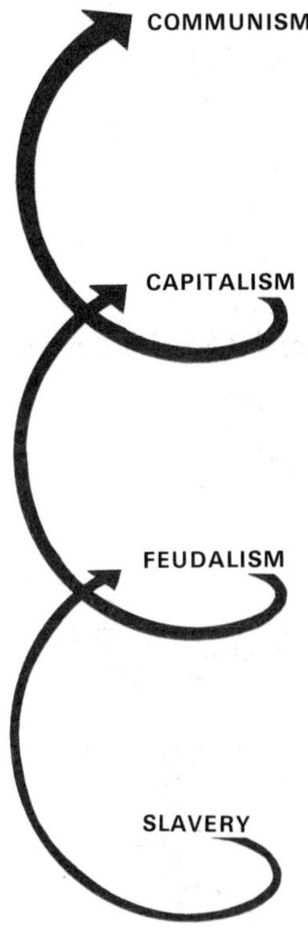

THE MARXIST VIEW OF HISTORY'S FLOW

As Marx saw it, society had grown in a series of upward spirals. Each stage, though adequate for its time, wore out its usefulness and was replaced by a newer stage. The catalyst responsible for these changes, he believed, was an endless "class struggle" between the oppressed and the oppressors in every age. Marx believed the growing misery of workers under capitalism would lead to revolution and force capitalism to be replaced by the stage he thought the highest—Communism. But, in practice, where the Communist way has triumphed, it has produced new forms of oppression.

lands and climes. In place of the old local and national seclusion and self-sufficiency we have . . . universal inter-dependence of nations.

Much of the *Manifesto* scarcely sounds as though an enemy of capitalism wrote it. It sounds like an admirer writing about its virtues and advantages. Capitalism, Marx says, "has been the first to show what man's activity can bring about. It has accomplished wonders far surpassing Egyptian pyramids, Roman aqueducts, and Gothic cathedrals; it has conducted expeditions that put in the shade all former migrations of nations and crusades."

"The bourgeoisie [capitalists] cannot exist without constantly revolutionizing the instruments of production, and thereby the relations of production, and with them the whole relations of society." But it is precisely this "inevitable" revolutionizing of society, he says, which makes capitalism self-destroying.

MARX'S TRIBUTE TO LINCOLN

A quirk of Marx's nature was his ability to see the profound greatness of Abraham Lincoln's personality but be blind to his own flaws. Right after Lincoln's assassination Marx wrote this eloquent tribute: ". . . he was a man, neither to be browbeaten by adversity, nor intoxicated by success, inflexibly pressing on to his great goal, never compromising it by blind haste, slowly maturing his steps, never retracing them . . . tempering stern acts by the gleam of a kind heart, illuminating scenes dark with passion by the smile of humor, doing his titanic work as humbly and homely as heaven-born rulers do little things with the grandiloquence of pomp and state; in one word, one of the rare men who succeed in becoming great, without ceasing to be good. Such, indeed, was the modesty of this great and good man, that the world only discovered him a hero after he had fallen a martyr." This tribute is startling when contrasted with an appraisal of Karl Marx's own character by one of Lincoln's friends, Carl Schurz *(opposite, far right).*

Marx and the Labor Theory of Value. Although classical economists had worked out the principles of the labor theory of value, Marx made it a foundation stone of his doctrine. From it arises the concept called "surplus value."

If, for example, a pair of shoes sell for $10, what gives them that value? According to Marx, ultimately nothing else but the amount of labor which went into them. Even the leather raw material and the tools used to make the shoes have value only because of the labor that was required to make them.

If you assume the capitalist who sells the shoes for $10 is making a profit, and that labor creates the *only* value, then where does the profit come from? Says Marx: from surplus value—the capitalist got more labor than he paid for. In effect, he "stole" it from the laborer. Marx concedes that the capitalist is not consciously a thief; rather it is that "stealing" is an essential element of capitalism. For under the factory system labor simply is another commodity, like the leather that went into the shoes. The value of labor is determined by what it costs to "produce" it—that is, to keep the worker alive and working, to pay his rent, feed him and his family and to buy needed clothes.

Say that it takes $50 a week to supply the worker's needs. Say that the worker's labor may be able to produce that amount of value in 30 hours. But he cannot work just 30 hours and quit. He has to work the hours set by the owner—in Marx's time, as much as 84 hours a week. So the extra hours of labor are "surplus value" to the owner, to pay for his rent, machinery and supplies, but also providing what Marx considered an unwarranted profit.

Modern economists have found Marx's labor theory of value an inadequate tool for economic analysis. Since this theory considers human effort and skill the only productive factor, it is impossible to figure the cost—and, consequently, a realistic price—of equally important *nonhuman* productive elements such as land and capital.

Depressions and Deepening Crises. Under Marx's application of the labor theory of value, factory owners have a supposedly "free ride" on labor, but this situation will not continue automatically. The owners are competing with each other. To continue to compete, they have to expand faster. To expand faster requires more workers, and to get them the capitalists have to compete against each other for workers. This, says Marx, will drive up wages and drive down the rate of profits. To meet the threat of rising wages, factory owners will introduce more and more labor-saving machinery. This creates unemployment, and the scramble of jobless workers for the smaller number of available jobs forces wages right back down again.

Since, according to Marx, labor is the source of all value, the more the capitalist reduces his need for labor by using machinery, the more his profits shrink. Only by getting ahead of his competitors can he hope to make a profit, so he will redouble his efforts to cut costs through new labor-saving machinery. But since other factory owners are also doing that, the rate of profit will continue to fall. Prices are cut until they fall below cost. The workers displaced by machines cannot afford to buy goods, so consumption falls too. All the capitalists scramble to dump goods on the market, and the smaller, weaker capitalists go bankrupt. The bigger, stronger factory groups then absorb the smaller ones, but the bigger they get, the bigger the smash when they fall. During these repeated crises, the workers—whom Marx called "the proletariat"—are forming protective associations, or unions, to try to make themselves stronger in relation to the owners.

From his analysis of how capitalism works, Marx theorized that the stage was set for the doom of capitalism. In its simplest form, his argument might be summarized this way:

Capitalism would destroy itself by bringing together enormous combinations of money, modern machinery and workers organized into units so vast as to be virtual armies. All of this would be a completely rational and efficient way of organizing production—except that the concentration of ownership in the hands of fewer and fewer coupled with the growth of the labor force inevitably would lead to economic conflict between the owners and the workers. Then, Marx predicted, "this [capitalist] husk is burst asunder. The knell of capitalist private property sounds. The expropriators are expropriated." If the workers took ownership from the few owners, the productive process would become completely rational and the periodic crises would not recur. Revolution, Marx therefore felt, was inevitable, for the capitalistic system itself made it so.

"The Dictatorship of the Proletariat." It is essential to note one other key point in Marx's theories, because of the great abuses to which it subsequently led.

This point is raised in his discussion of what would happen after

LINCOLN'S FRIEND ON MARX

Lincoln's good friend, Carl Schurz, who became a Union general in the Civil War, was a German who fled his country after the mid-century revolts. In 1848 Schurz had met Karl Marx, about whom he later said: "[Marx] enjoyed the reputation of having . . . great learning, and . . . I was all the more eager to gather words of wisdom from the lips of that famous man. This expectation was disappointed in a peculiar way. Marx's utterances were indeed full of meaning, logical and clear, but I have never seen a man whose bearing was so provoking and intolerable. To no opinion, which differed from his, he accorded the honor of even a condescending consideration. Everyone who contradicted him he treated with abject contempt . . . or with opprobrious aspersions. . . . I remember most distinctly the cutting disdain with which he pronounced the word 'bourgeois;' and as a 'bourgeois,' that is as a detestable example of the deepest mental and moral degeneracy he denounced anyone that dared to oppose his opinion."

THE TUILERIES PALACE BURNS AS COMMUNARDS WHO SEIZED THE CITY OF PARIS RETREAT. MARX SAW THE

the workers overthrew the ruling class, or capitalists, and their government, which he considered merely a "police force" to protect their property. Marx said there would be a "dictatorship of the proletariat," that is, a reign of the working-class majority, over the capitalist minority. This "dictatorship," however, would not be oppressive, since the conditions that created conflict and resulting oppression would have been removed. The state, in fact, would soon "wither away." Man would be free to develop all his latent capacities for good, his natural instincts for art, poetry, the beautiful. And life in this utterly new society would have as its golden rule: "From

1871 REVOLT AS A STEP TOWARD HIS "DICTATORSHIP OF THE PROLETARIAT" AND WARMLY ENDORSED IT

each according to his ability, to each according to his needs."

Many years later, these ideas of a benevolent "dictatorship of the proletariat" and of an ideally perfect distribution of responsibilities and rewards would be perverted by the Marxian disciples in Russia. These men would create a vicious dictatorship and a government which, far from "withering away," would become ever more powerful and concentrated in ever fewer hands.

Marxist Predictions in the Light of History. Marx's great revolution of the workers, inevitable in his theory, was not so inevitable after all. The only popular revolt in Marx's later life was the short-lived Paris Commune of 1871. In this revolt, workers did for a time seize control of Paris and its government. But in the process, the Commune executed hundreds of innocent people. While all Europe watched these events with horror and disgust, Marx decided that this was his "dictatorship of the proletariat" come to pass. He published an address in the name of the International Workingmen's Association warmly approving the Commune and all its acts.

FROM MARX TO KHRUSHCHEV

This is the cover page of Marx and Engels' *Communist Manifesto,* from an edition that was circulated within Germany during the 1848 revolts. At that time Marx wrote: "What the bourgeoisie [capitalist group] . . . produces above all are its own gravediggers. Its fall and the victory of the proletariat [workers] are equally inevitable." In 1962, Khrushchev was making the same prediction, although in slightly different words: "I am not a sorcerer . . . but I can tell you the day is not far away when capitalism will crumble, and I am as certain of it as the sun's rising tomorrow."

The Communards soon went down to defeat, and the political parties which based their goals on Marx's teachings began to turn their attention to political and legislative reforms instead of bloody revolution. Though he felt that reform measures had little permanent value, Marx himself had noted the possibility of such peaceful "revolutions." In the *Communist Manifesto* he conceded that political pressure had been able to reduce the legal British working day to 10 hours. Certainly reforms were needed, for workers did not even win the right to vote in Belgium and Sweden, for example, until after 1890, years after Marx's death in 1883. They won it then only through general strikes.

Most of Marx's basic assumptions were either wrong or vastly oversimplified. In the highly industrialized West, whose problems were Marx's chief concern, his prophecies of doom never came to pass. They were proved wrong by capitalism's ability to purge its worst evils without revolution. Indeed, Marx himself admitted the possibility: "We do not deny that there are countries like England and America, and I might add, even Holland, where the worker may attain his object by peaceful means." As history would prove, this one sentence contained more truth than his massive analysis of capitalism's downfall. Capitalism was destroyed only in Russia and China—two countries in which it never fully developed. And capitalism there was destroyed not by "inevitable" history, as Marx thought, but by the deliberate action of fanatics—with disastrous results.

Marx's Place in History. Karl Marx deserves to be remembered, but for reasons quite different from his prophecies. His method of looking at history—of looking at and analyzing every aspect of a society in terms of how people produce goods and earn a living—gave new tools to everyone who came after him. These tools are still being used by historians, political scientists, sociologists, psychologists, critics and creative artists. In this sense, Karl Marx made his contribution to western thought. Marx felt his insights would liberate man, not enslave him. It is history's irony that his Russian followers used these theories to fashion the most pitiless tyranny the world has ever seen.

2 The Organization:

Lenin and the Communist Party

LENIN

2 The Organization:

Lenin and the Communist Party

In 1883, the year that Karl Marx died, a 13-year-old boy named Vladimir Ilyich Ulyanov was living an uneventful life in the backwater Russian town of Simbirsk (now known as Ulyanovsk) on the Volga River. This quiet boy from this humdrum town would one day change the world more violently than even Marx's wildest dreams. The world now knows him by the revolutionary pseudonym he took in 1901, N. Lenin.

Within a red granite mausoleum in Red Square in Moscow, Lenin's embalmed body lies perpetually on view, an eternal light playing on his waxen face, reddish-blond beard and bulging, bald head. Each year, millions of people come from all over the Communist empire to view the man who created that empire through the force of his implacable will.

In doing so, Lenin turned Marx's theories upside down. For Marx thought the broad march of history determined events; Lenin proved that one man, ruled by a fanatic obsession, could alter history. Marx thought the inevitable tide of events would bring the working-class *majority* to power. Lenin proved that Marx's ideas could bring a ruthless, determined *minority* to power. Marx and Engels thought the state would "wither away" into classless Communism. Lenin made the Communist state all-powerful, a worse autocracy than that of the Tsars.

How Lenin Changed the World

Except for Lenin, Karl Marx might be chiefly remembered as a man who had a brilliant way of guessing wrong about the future, and Marxism might have no political meaning today, remaining merely an influence on the study of economics, history and sociology.

Almost every country outside the Communist bloc has a Communist party that seeks eventually to overthrow, by force or by subversion, the non-Communist government. Several such governments have already been overthrown. This worldwide conspiracy, under varying degrees of central control, is Lenin's creation.

The Methods of Communism. Each of these Communist parties uses the same methods. Its members are ready, when necessary, to cheat, lie, steal, spy, even murder, to reach the party's goals. Lenin's justification of the use of any means for a desired end supplied the philosophical support for these methods.

These parties, even those with few members, have proved that they can exercise a power and influence far beyond their numbers. Concealing their identities, working in secret, communicating in codes, they penetrate larger organizations, form "popular fronts" with temporary allies, whom they use, then destroy or discard. It was Lenin who taught them this technique by his own example.

Every true Communist is ready to go to prison, ready to give his own life, if need be, for the cause. Lenin set this example, too. He himself spent years in exile, months in prison, and eventually was wounded by a bullet fired by a political enemy. But he never spared himself, never flinched at danger, never wavered in his pursuit of his single, obsessive goal of violent revolution and merciless destruction of all enemies.

Lenin had a friendly smile and a hearty, ready laugh. Yet, without a quiver, he took responsibility for the deaths of thousands of men and women during the Bolshevik Revolution. "How can one make revolution without executions?" he calmly asked.

The Man and His Times

The extremes of violence that characterized the Russian Revolution had their roots in an old tradition of brutality and indifference to suffering that still governed Russian life when Lenin was born.

AN ARISTOCRAT WHO HATED SERFDOM

Ivan Turgenev, one of Lenin's favorite authors, was exiled to his estate in 1852 for condemning the evils of serfdom in his writings. He told the story of his partially paralyzed grandmother who, angry with a serf waiting on her, knocked the boy unconscious, placed a pillow on his head and, sitting on it, suffocated him. Turgenev's mother ordered serfs whipped, exiled to Siberia or enlisted into the army at her whim. "Over my subjects," he reported her saying, "I rule as I like and I am not answerable to anyone for them."

To Russians of the mid-19th Century, the kind of rights and freedoms Americans had enjoyed since their revolution were storybook tales with no relevance to their own existence. For centuries, Russia had known only autocracy under the rule of the Tsars.

It is difficult for Americans to comprehend how absolute the Tsar's power was. His right to rule was part of the unquestioned dogma of Russian life. There was no constitution, no congress, no right to vote. A few thousand nobles, the church and state owned most of the land. Until a decade before Lenin's birth, more than a third of the millions of Russia's people were serfs, bound to their masters and forbidden to leave the land where they worked as virtual slaves.

Nonetheless, serfs did exercise a certain responsibility. They maintained a form of primitive communal living in their village communes, in which they decided as a body such matters as time of planting, division of labor and lands, allocation of harvests and assessment of taxes. Once Alexander II came to power in 1855, he decided to liberate the serfs, and he did so in 1861. But they were charged such heavy prices for the tiny plots they got that to pay the full cost took decades. It was freedom in little more than name.

The Burden of Guilt. The only Russians fortunate enough to obtain educations were children of the nobility, of professional people, or of civil servants like Lenin's father. This educated class was known as the intelligentsia, or intellectuals.

Many of these young students felt weighed down with a sense of personal guilt at the sufferings of the millions of downtrodden serfs. They became attracted to the teachings of the Russian Populists such as Herzen, Chernishevsky, Bakunin and others who believed that Russia, because of its peasant communes, could lead the world in a peaceful transition to socialism. They hated capitalism as much as feudalism, and thought that socialism built around agriculture could save Russia from having to undergo the evils of western Europe's factory systems.

One of the leading influences on the young intellectuals was Mikhail Bakunin, a nobleman and former artillery officer. From exile he urged the abolition of hereditary property, the church and even the state itself. He favored giving the land to communes and the factories to the workers. He was the most revolutionary of those who encouraged the young intellectuals to "go to the people," to go into the villages and work among the peasants, and to rouse the villagers' social consciousness. Many young people did so. Dressed as peasants, they learned trades as shoemakers or carpenters, and lived in the villages. But the peasants themselves distrusted them, and often beat or drove out their would-be helpers. Moreover, the counterfeit peasants were easily spotted by the Tsar's police who sent them off to jail or exile in Siberia for their pains.

"Do Not Dream, but Act!" Another important revolutionist was

Peter Tkachev, a Populist theoretician. Since his words would have a profound effect on Lenin's later life, they are worth remembering. Tkachev called for a small, secret conspiracy of professional revolutionists. His program was bold and ruthless:

> On the banner of the revolutionary party, a party of action rather than a party of reasoning, may be inscribed only the following words: struggle against the government, struggle against the existing order of things, struggle to the last drop of blood—to the last breath....

On another occasion Tkachev wrote: "Do not dream, but act! Make a revolution and make it as fast as possible." According to Tkachev, not the people, but only a hard, organized minority could prevail against the Tsar:

> Neither now nor in the future will the common people by its own power bring on a social revolution. We alone, the revolutionary minority, can and should do that as soon as possible.

Later Lenin was to adopt this thought as his own, substituting only the Marxist word "proletariat" for Tkachev's "people."

Elsewhere, a secret, murderous conspiracy known as "The People's Will," an outgrowth of the Populist movement, had gone into action. On March 13, 1881, as Tsar Alexander II was returning to the Winter Palace in St. Petersburg, a young revolutionist threw a bomb at him. The Tsar was not hurt, but some of the Cossacks in his guard were wounded. Alexander got down from his carriage to speak to them. At that moment another revolutionist threw a second bomb, which exploded right between the Tsar's feet, mortally wounding him. He was carried into the palace to die. Among the many members of his family who came to bid him farewell was his 12-year-old grandson, Nicholas—a future Tsar who would one day die a similarly violent death and whose murder would end the long reign of the monarchy.

Lenin's Boyhood. Lenin, whose followers were to shoot down Tsar Nicholas and his family, was the son of Ilya Ulyanov, a man who served the Tsar well and faithfully. Papa Ulyanov was a provincial school inspector, a conservative in politics and a devout member of the Russian Orthodox Church. His wife, Maria Alexandrovna, the daughter of a physician, had taught herself German, French, English and how to play the piano. They had three boys and three girls. Lenin, who was named Vladimir, was the third-born. He wanted to do everything "like Sasha"—his brother, Alexander, who was four years older. They played chess, went skiing and skating in winter, and spent the summers fishing and swimming at their mother's family home, a pleasant rural estate. The family lived in modest comfort like the minor nobility—the father even had an honorary title because of his official position. In the evenings, the children would gather around their mother as she read to them from the great Russian

A FAMOUS AUTHOR SENTENCED TO DIE

Feodor Dostoevsky, a great Russian novelist, was the son of a doctor killed by his serfs for his drunken cruelty. In 1849 Dostoevsky was arrested with a group of friends who had met to discuss utopian socialism. A military court ordered 20 of them shot. When the men were standing in front of a firing squad they were told that the Tsar had commuted their sentences to hard labor in Siberia. Dostoevsky made use of this terrible experience in his book *The Idiot,* when he described the thoughts of a condemned man during the last moments of life.

classics. She taught them to play the piano and would lead them in singing melodies from operas.

She imparted to the children the same moral intensity and religious seriousness in which she had been reared. Papa Ulyanov would quiz the boys on their day's lessons. Papa also laid down one strict rule. From 1879—when Vladimir was nine—the father forbade all discussions of political or social problems, to safeguard the children from dangerous revolutionary ideas that were going around.

All thought or talk of violence was alien to the serious, industrious Ulyanov family, pursuing its quiet way in Simbirsk. From earliest childhood Sasha and Vladimir showed unusual intelligence, exceptional capacity for concentration, and remarkable memories. Sasha won the gold medal—mark of highest achievement—at the Gymnasium (high school), as Vladimir did four years later.

But the two boys had quite different personalities. Sasha was quiet, even-tempered, reflective. He was absorbed in the study of zoology and chemistry and enjoyed observing earthworms. Vladimir was loud, boisterous and bursting with energy. His tomfoolery disturbed his studious brother's homework. During summer vacations, Vladimir would scorn books to go swimming, fishing or horseback riding. Sasha became seriously concerned with social problems, reading the articles by Chernishevsky, a leading Populist, in old copies of *Sovremennik*, a journal to which Papa Ulyanov subscribed.

Chernishevsky had also written *Chto Delat? (What Is to Be Done?)*, one of the most popular novels of the day. This described a future socialist utopia which would be a land of milk and honey. It became a fundamental guide for young intellectuals, who saw themselves, in Chernishevsky's words, as "men of the new age." They considered themselves revolutionists who would build the new order, "strong personalities, who [would] impose their character on the pattern of events and hurry their course."

Vladimir did not read *What Is to Be Done?* until later. But a tragedy involving his brother Sasha was soon to occur that would cause Vladimir to read and reread it until it was seared on his brain.

In the fall of 1883, Sasha entered the school of physics and mathematics at the University of St. Petersburg, the capital of Russia, seemingly headed for a distinguished scientific career. In his third year, he was awarded the university's gold medal for a scientific paper on the anatomy of worms.

Although the university was a hotbed of revolutionary thought and discussion, Sasha did not become involved—not for lack of interest in social problems, but because he believed that such problems required deep, scientific study rather than impassioned oratory. In 1886 he did participate in a student political demonstration. Nothing happened to him, but he felt guilty when some of the students involved were arrested and expelled from the university.

A REVOLUTIONIST AND HIS CATECHISM

Sergei Nechaiev, a revolutionist admired by Lenin, was the son of an Orthodox priest. Together with Mikhail Bakunin, he wrote the *Catechism of a Revolutionist,* which seems to describe what Lenin later was to be: "The Revolutionist is a doomed man. He has no private interests . . . of his own. His entire being is devoured by one purpose, one thought, one passion—the revolution . . . he has severed every link with . . . the entire civilized world; with the laws, good manners, conventions and morality of that world. He . . . continues to inhabit it with only one purpose—to destroy it."

Sergei Nechaiev scared even his fellow revolutionist Bakunin, who recorded: "Nechaiev stops at nothing, and is as ruthless with himself as he is with others." To him, "all the members should serve as . . . tools in the hands of [the] leaders. It is permissible to deceive . . . members, compromise them in every way, rob . . . and even murder them if necessary." Before dying in prison, Nechaiev did turn to murder *(see note at far right margin)*.

Sasha Joins the Terrorists. The arrest of his friends convinced Sasha that it was his duty to act directly against the hated autocracy. He helped to organize a branch of the secret terrorist group, "The People's Will." Its student members plotted to assassinate Tsar Alexander III on March 13, 1887, the sixth anniversary of the murder of his father, Alexander II. The day before, one of the conspirators was arrested while carrying a large dictionary, its inside hollowed out to hold a crude bomb which Sasha had made. Sasha was also arrested, and on him the police found a codebook containing the names and addresses of other conspirators.

Under interrogation, one of the suspects revealed the key to the code. Within a few days, hundreds were arrested throughout Russia. Fifteen, including Sasha, were put on trial for their lives.

When the terrible word came to Simbirsk, Sasha's mother decided to go to St. Petersburg to plead for his life. (Papa Ulyanov had died a year before.) She knew many liberal people in Simbirsk, and hoped to find some friend to go with her. But now all turned their backs on her. She had to go alone. This made a lasting impression on young Vladimir, who developed a deep hatred for all middle-class "liberals."

In St. Petersburg, Sasha fell on his knees before his mother, begging forgiveness for the grief he had caused her. Although several of his friends avoided hanging by appealing for mercy, he stubbornly refused to do so. At the trial, he even took responsibility for the deeds of others. To a fellow defendant, he whispered: "Blame everything on me." He refused to engage a lawyer to defend him and defiantly cried, "There is no finer death than death for one's country's sake. Such a death holds no terror for sincere and honest men. I had but one aim: to help the unfortunate Russian people."

On May 20, 1887, at 3:30 in the morning, Sasha and four doomed comrades were taken from their cells in the Schlüsselburg Fortress. They embraced one another, knelt before the cross and, refusing the blindfold, walked unflinchingly to the hangman's noose. When 17-year-old Vladimir in Simbirsk read the newspaper telling of his brother's execution, he threw it to the floor and cried: "I'll make them pay for this! I swear it!"

A Revolutionist Is Born. Vladimir had thought of Sasha as a somewhat comical figure, bent over his microscope studying his worms. Now for the first time he realized that Sasha's devotion to his principles was so strong that he had been willing to give up his life rather than recant. Determined to discover the ideas that his brother believed in, Vladimir spoke to everyone who had known Sasha during that last year. Remembering the deep impression that *What Is to Be Done?* had made upon Sasha, Vladimir read it for days on end, studying every word with such intensity that many years later he could recall its least significant details.

It was from this book that Vladimir drew his vision of a Russian

A MURDER TRIAL AND A NOVEL

Feodor Dostoevsky based his book *The Possessed* on a murder organized by Nechaiev. The revolutionist told some Moscow students that he was a leader of a major revolutionary group. He persuaded them that a fellow student, Ivanov, was a police spy and had to be killed. The truth was, Ivanov had merely rejected Nechaiev's wild theories. In 1869 the students killed Ivanov and threw his body in a pond near the Moscow Agricultural Academy. The crime led to the arrest of hundreds of Nechaiev's followers. Nechaiev fled the country, but the trial of his student accomplices was a sensation all over Russia. Dostoevsky used the murder in his book to show how attempts at social change can be warped by people's willingness to employ evil means. "A new form of social organization is essential. . . ." says one of its characters. "[But] I am perplexed by my own data. . . . Starting from unlimited freedom, I arrive at unlimited despotism."

utopia. Above all, Vladimir envisioned a new order to be built by Chernishevsky's "men of the new age."

One friend in Simbirsk did not desert the family. He was Feodor Kerensky, director of the Gymnasium, who awarded the graduating Vladimir his gold medal in spite of Sasha's fate. Moreover, Kerensky suggested that Vladimir stay out of Moscow and St. Petersburg because of his late brother's notoriety, and he wrote a letter of recommendation to support Vladimir's application for admission to the University of Kazan, where Papa Ulyanov had studied.

THE PERSONALITY OF A REVOLUTIONIST

This fragment from Turgenev eloquently describes the harsh prospects of a revolutionist's life.

To you who desire to cross this threshold, do you know what awaits you?

I know, replied the girl.

Cold, hunger, abhorrence, derision, contempt, abuse, prison, disease, and death!

I know, I am ready, I shall endure all blows.

Not from enemies alone, but also from relatives, from friends.

Yes, even from them . . .

Are you ready even to commit a crime?

I am ready for crime, too.

Do you know that you may be disillusioned in that which you believe, that you may discover that you were mistaken, that you ruined your young life in vain?

I know that, too.

Enter!

The girl crossed the threshold, and a heavy curtain fell behind her.

Fool! said some one, gnashing his teeth.

Saint! some one uttered in reply.

Vladimir, however, did not last long at the University of Kazan. In December of that same year, 1887, following government repression of student activity, the students of Kazan met in assembly, drew up respectful petitions and sent a committee, including Vladimir, to present them to a local official. "Disperse!" he ordered them. When they refused, he demanded their identification cards. His eyes seized on the familiar name, Vladimir Ulyanov. *Ulyanov!* That very night Vladimir was arrested. He was quickly expelled from the university and ordered to leave Kazan.

Vladimir spent the next year at his mother's home, studying feverishly. He was twice denied permission to re-enter the university. His mother sold the home in Simbirsk and bought a small estate near Samara about 110 miles farther to the southeast, where Vladimir unsuccessfully tried his hand at being a country squire. When he was 20, his mother, after repeatedly beseeching the authorities, finally got permission for him to take the law examinations in St. Petersburg whenever he felt ready to do so. In little more than a year Vladimir read through the whole four-year university course in law so brilliantly that in the 1891 examinations he received the highest grade. He even managed to get the Certificate of Loyalty and Good Character that was required in order to become a lawyer. In 1892 Vladimir started the practice of law in Samara. In the year and a half he spent there, he defended 10 petty criminals, winning none of his cases. His only victory came when he brought a case at his own expense against a wealthy merchant who tried to force anybody who crossed the Volga at a certain point to hire his steam launch.

In Samara Vladimir discovered Karl Marx's works. Since some of these were available only in German, he mastered German. After studying these books, he applied the analytical methods Marx had used on British capitalism to Russian statistics. He also read all the reports and economic studies he could get hold of and all the writings of liberal economists.

Famines and Strikes. The times were ripe for the emergence of young revolutionists. In 1891, a terrible famine had swept Russia. Industrialization, although far behind that of western Europe, was advancing rapidly. Starving peasants were fleeing to the cities seeking factory jobs. Workers, whose living and working conditions were even worse than those of the England of Marx's time, began a wave of spontaneous strikes.

When Nicholas II, only 26, took the throne on Alexander III's death in 1894, it was hoped that the young monarch would grant the people a voice in government and that he would reform the intolerable working conditions. Nicholas soon ended any such dreams.

In the city of Tver, the *zemstvo,* or popularly elected local council, sent the Tsar the usual salutation. In it the council dared to make a veiled allusion to the need for a constitution. Nicholas warned them they were "carried away by senseless dreams . . ." and declared, "Let everyone know that I, who am dedicating all My strength to the welfare of the people, will preserve the principle of autocracy as strongly and undeviatingly as did My lamented late Father."

When violent strikes broke out in the city of Yaroslav, an army regiment shot down the strikers. The Tsar sent a telegram of congratulations to these "brave" troops. With this, the last hopes of the young intellectuals for reform from above died. The strikes also heralded the appearance of the new social force—the workers or proletariat—that Marx had described. Many of Russia's intelligentsia, at last convinced that progress could not be achieved by working with the villagers and that the monarchy would never reform itself, turned enthusiastically to Marx, whose predictions seemed more and more to have a ring of truth.

The new wave of revolutionary sentiment found a Russian spokesman in George V. Plekhanov, a brilliant young engineering student who had abandoned his career to become a revolutionist. In 1883 in Geneva, Switzerland, he founded the first Russian Marxist organization, the League for Emancipation of Labor. He began publishing Marxist pamphlets that were shipped to Russia, where young Vladimir, among others, devoured them. Like many of his contemporaries, Vladimir admired Plekhanov without limit—as he later wrote, with "respect . . . reverence . . . infatuation."

ROYAL COUSINS IN YEARS OF PEACE

Two royal cousins who led widely differing lives were King George V of Britain *(right)* and Tsar Nicholas II of Russia. In 1918, just a few years after this picture was taken, the Tsar was executed by the Bolsheviks, and the Romanov dynasty came to an end. George V died in his bed in 1936, and his granddaughter reigns today as Elizabeth II.

The Bolshevik Party Emerges

Vladimir arrived in St. Petersburg in 1893, and immediately began playing a leading role in its Marxist circle. Something about him—his bright, penetrating glance, the ability of his mind to cut straight to the heart of an issue—made everyone give him a respectful ear. At 23 he was getting bald and he seemed older than his years in his laugh, voice and manner. His associates called him *starik*—the old man—half in affection, half in awe.

Vladimir made no attempt to conceal his contempt for what some of them were doing to advance the revolution. For, influenced by Populist theories, there were those who felt that education of the workers was the first step toward emancipation, and that a vital educational task was teaching illiterate workers to read. Nadezhda Krupskaya, who later became Vladimir's wife, lifelong companion and closest aide, was working for the Committee for Literacy. She first met Vladimir at a pre-Lenten pancake party, where he gave a laconic laugh when someone praised the importance of her committee. "Well," he said sarcastically, "if anyone wants to save the fatherland in the Committee for Literacy, we won't stop him."

Vladimir was just as scornful of the attitude, basic in Marx's writings and general among the Marxists, that a revolution was inevitable and thus nobody had to do anything to bring it about. Vladimir kept pounding away at the idea that only a strong, tightly organized, secret party made up of professional revolutionists could hope to overthrow the government. Action was needed. Moreover, he lashed out at those who thought the workers themselves would become revolutionary leaders once they learned about the class struggle. Not the workers, but the professional revolutionists, he argued, would make the revolution. While it was necessary to keep the revolutionary party small and secret, its members should propagandize as much as possible among the workers to convince them, too, of the necessity for revolution.

Marx's writings were available in Russia. The Tsar's censors had found his *Capital* so dull and technical that they had allowed it to be translated into Russian, thinking nobody would read it. They also began to allow Plekhanov and others to publish boringly academic

Lenin: From Middle-Class

A YOUNG LAWYER, Lenin at 22 had recently passed his law examinations.

WITH ALL HIS FAMILY, Lenin *(lower right)* sat for this formal photograph in 1879, at age nine. His ill-fated, bookish brother Sasha, 13, is at top center.

articles on economics. The censors thought that such solemn stuff was harmless compared to the terrorism preached by the old "People's Will" assassins. Vladimir welcomed this but was angered at the way some of the Marxists watered down their writings to pass the censors. For that reason, he became active in printing illegal leaflets for distribution among the workers. He was about to bring forth an underground newspaper, "The Workers' Cause," when in December 1895, the Tsar's police—who had been shadowing Vladimir for months—arrested him.

"I Ate Six Inkwells." Vladimir served 14 months in jail. He was allowed all the books he wanted, and sent coded messages to Krupskaya and to other Marxists. Long before, he had learned from old hands of the "People's Will" the various methods of secret communication they had used. One of his favorite "inks" was milk, which became invisible when it dried but turned brown and readable when heated by the recipient of the letter. He kept his milk in little inkwells molded out of the prison bread, so that he could swallow both ink and well if anybody approached. "Today," he wrote a friend, "I ate six inkwells."

While in prison, he became recognized as the real leader of a local Marxist organization, the St. Petersburg League of Struggle for the Emancipation of Labor, and he wrote many of its pamphlets in his cell, using various pen names. The signature "N. Lenin" eventually became his hallmark, and he was to be known only by this name. He

Schoolboy to Veteran Rebel

HIS FUTURE WIFE, Krupskaya, seen as a girl, was two years Lenin's senior.

EN ROUTE TO EXILE in 1897, the bald, 26-year-old Lenin and a group of radical friends stared hard at the camera just before being sent to Siberia.

was so active in prison that he was rather sorry when the police ordered him off to exile in Siberia for three years.

Lighting "The Spark." The exile life was not bad at all. Lenin had plenty of hunting and fishing. Soon Krupskaya, who had also been banished, was allowed to join him and they were married in Siberia. He began working out a plan for an official Marxist newspaper to be published outside of Russia to direct Marxist political action inside Russia. At the same time, he began developing his ideas for a secret, tightly knit party of professional revolutionists. In 1900, shortly after he was allowed to leave Siberia, Lenin was off to Switzerland and Germany to confer with Plekhanov, win his blessing and launch the new Marxist party newspaper, *Iskra (The Spark).*

"If we have a strongly organized party," Lenin wrote for *Iskra's* first issue, "a single strike may grow into a political demonstration, into a political victory over the regime. If we have a strongly organized party, a rebellion in a single locality may spread into a victorious revolution."

From an editorial office in Munich, Germany, *Iskra* shipped instructions to hundreds of Marxist cells throughout Russia. And though the revolutionists were only beginning to organize their political party, the doctrines formulated in *Iskra* were to serve as the future battle program for party members everywhere.

A Bible for Communists. Two years later, Lenin published a book pulling together all his earlier thoughts on how to organize the kind of party that could create a revolution, overturn the government and seize power. He gave it the same title as Chernishevsky's book which had so impressed him in his youth: *Chto Delat? (What Is to Be Done?).* This book became a bible for all his followers. Its tactics and techniques are still the fundamental doctrines that guide Communists all over the world.

Although it was not generally realized at the time, Lenin in this

SUNK IN A SURPRISE ATTACK by the Japanese navy, two Tsarist warships rest in the harbor of Port Arthur, then a Russian base in Manchuria. This sneak attack in February 1904 launched the Russo-Japanese War, which brought disaster to Russian arms, misery to the Russian people and helped bring on the revolt of 1905.

book had presented—hard and clear as a diamond—the basic issue which would eventually split the whole Marxist movement. According to Lenin, uninstructed workers could progress in their political development only to the point of organizing trade unions. Their spontaneous reaction to oppression would be insufficient to carry them any further on the path to revolution. And the trade unions that they might form would be no match for the capitalists. Therefore, he concluded, professional Marxists would have to fight the tendency of workers to limit their activities to trade unions, for unless workers were diverted from such organizations, they would be headed for "ideological enslavement" by the capitalists.

When the Russian Revolution came, Lenin's position would be of critical importance. The crucial issue would be: *Would Marxism emulate the democratic procedures of the great legal labor parties and trade unions of the West, or prepare for armed uprising under the leadership of a self-chosen, rigidly controlled secret conspiracy?*

We can see the question in even simpler terms: *Democracy, or dictatorship?*

Lenin never lost sight of this issue. It was the one great central theme he hammered at again and again. In 1903 it dominated the Second Party Congress of what was then the major Russian Marxist movement, the Social Democratic Labor party. This meeting met at Brussels, then moved to London because of police interference. During the congress, Lenin fought for a highly centralized party with tight discipline imposed from above—in short, an out-and-out dictatorship.

Lenin won, but only by a narrow, and temporary, majority. For many years after, his followers were known as the Bolsheviks, from the Russian word *bolshinstvo*, or "majority." They did not long remain the majority faction of the Social Democrats, but they continued to call themselves Bolsheviks.

A U.S. PRESIDENT NEGOTIATES PEACE

In 1905 President Theodore Roosevelt helped extricate Russia from its disastrous war with Japan. Suspecting that both sides wanted to end the clash, he offered to act as intermediary if each would send a representative. Each did and Roosevelt brought them together on the presidential yacht *Mayflower* at Oyster Bay, Long Island. Then Roosevelt sent them on to the naval base at Portsmouth, New Hampshire, where they concluded the Treaty of Portsmouth on September 5, 1905. For his efforts, Roosevelt won the Nobel Peace Prize in 1906.

The Revolution of 1905

Lenin had preached that the people, by themselves, were incapable of making the kind of revolution he wanted. But in 1905, the Russian people did revolt—without his help.

Lenin had also preached that workers were incapable of determining political events in a scientific manner. But when the workers took up arms in 1905, they created their own "governments" and shook the foundations of the throne. Lenin at first took no part in this process. Living in Switzerland, he was just a spectator, trying to catch up with events.

The revolts of 1905 were set off by Russia's humiliating defeat in the war with Japan, into which the Tsar blundered in 1904. He lost most of his navy, and the Japanese took Port Arthur, a great Russian base on the South Manchurian coast. The disaster revealed the incredible ineptitude of the Tsar's government and encouraged vigorous protests by the people.

Bloody Sunday. On a Sunday in January 1905, a large group of workers in St. Petersburg made a peaceful march on the Winter Palace, carrying placards demanding an improvement in working conditions and a constituent assembly. Thousands of these unarmed men were accompanied by their wives and children.

When the people tried to present their pleas, the troops were ordered to block their way and to keep them out of the Winter Palace square. The soldiers opened fire on the helpless people. Hundreds were killed. Thousands of wounded were left behind on the bloody square as the crowd fled. This horrible day would live in Russian history as "Bloody Sunday." It destroyed the people's last shred of faith in the Tsar. A wave of protest strikes broke out all over Russia.

APPRENTICE YEARS OF A REVOLUTIONIST

When Lev Bronstein, shown in this early police photo, came to London in 1902, he had spent four years in exile and prison. While working with Lenin in England, he settled on his permanent pen name, Leon Trotsky. As Trotsky he would lead the first Soviet in the 1905 revolt when just 26, and win Bolshevik fame in 1917.

Meanwhile, the old "People's Will" had been transformed into a new political group, the Socialist Revolutionary party, which was busily forming secret cells among the peasants. Less than a month after Bloody Sunday, one of its terrorist bands assassinated the Tsar's uncle, Grand Duke Sergei, Governor General of Moscow. In August, the Tsar agreed to call a representative assembly. But this Duma, as it was called, would be given only "advisory" powers. This made the people all the angrier.

In September, the printers' union of Moscow went on strike, then the bakers, and the telegraph and postal operators. When in October the railway workers' union joined in the general strike, trains, essential services and industries ground to a halt; the government was paralyzed.

The First Soviet. Now something strange and new arose on the Russian scene, something that startled Lenin almost as much as it shocked the Tsar. It was a Soviet (council) of Workers' Deputies formed by Lenin's enemies, the Mensheviks. Menshevik comes from the Russian word *menshinstvo,* or "minority." This was the group opposed to Lenin's ideas of tightly disciplined, autocratic party control, and they urged the St. Petersburg workers to elect a kind of "proletarian parliament" in order to give representative political control to the general strike.

On October 26, forty delegates representing 20,000 workers met in the Technological Institute and elected three leaders—among them a fiery young Menshevik called Leon Trotsky—and called for a general strike. Overnight the Soviet generated tremendous popular enthusiasm all over Russia, for this was the first time that the people controlled an institution wielding political power.

The Soviet got quick results through the strikes. On October 30, 1905, the Tsar issued the October Manifesto, granting freedom of speech, conscience and assembly, and he increased the number of those eligible to vote in the elections for the Duma. But these concessions were not enough to satisfy the people. Thousands of workers in St. Petersburg marched with red flags, singing revolutionary songs. Sporadic protest strikes continued for some time.

Lenin, who had finally left Switzerland, reached St. Petersburg in November. He had opposed the Soviet because it was a spontaneous, undisciplined body, which his "professional" revolutionists could not control. Discovering that the Soviet had become virtually a second government, he quickly shifted his tactics and began to support it. Indeed, he demanded that it expand to become the nucleus of a provisional government for all Russia. From the outset Lenin had urged that the strikes be transformed from a workers' demonstration into an armed uprising. He had earlier told his Bolshevik wing of the Social Democrats:

> Go to the youth. Organize at once and everywhere fighting brigades among students, and particularly among workers. Let them arm themselves immediately with whatever weapons they can obtain—rifles, revolvers, bombs, knives, brass knuckles, clubs, rags soaked in kerosene to start fires with, rope or rope ladders, shovels for building barricades, dynamite cartridges, barbed wire, tacks against cavalry. Let the squads begin to train for immediate operations. Some can undertake to assassinate a spy or blow up a police station, others can attack a bank to expropriate funds for an insurrection. Let every squad learn, if only by beating up police.

The Soviet, led by Trotsky, called for the overthrow of the government, but popular fervor had begun to subside. On December 16, the entire Executive Committee of the Soviet was arrested.

The Collapse of the Revolt. From St. Petersburg, Lenin turned his hopes to Moscow, where the strike did turn into armed revolt. Fighting brigades of workers threw up barricades across important avenues. Lenin drew on his studies of past revolts and sent out leaflets containing tactical instructions: fight in groups of three and four, attack suddenly, disappear fast.

To quell the Moscow revolt, the Tsar sent crack Guards' regiments and artillery from St. Petersburg. The workers fought desperately, but on December 31, the Revolution of 1905 ended. Just as quickly as he had granted "freedom," the Tsar revoked most of the people's new rights. The collapse of the revolts brought strong opposition to Lenin into the open even among the Bolsheviks themselves. He was accused of deliberately sacrificing lives to prove his theory. This accusation gained support from Lenin's words to a colleague who had doubted that the workers could win. "Victory? What do we care about victory?" Lenin exclaimed. "Let no one believe that we shall necessarily win. We want the uprising to shake the foundation of the autocracy and set the broad masses into motion. Our task

ANGRY STRIKERS HALT TRANSPORT

Trains ground to a stop in Russia during the revolts of 1905, when the powerful union of railway workers joined the general strike. The strike's crippling effect on the whole economy had a large share in causing the Tsar to offer reforms. This painting by Paul Thiriat depicts the seizure of a locomotive by the strikers in the outskirts of Moscow.

will then be to attract those masses to our cause. That is the main point! *The uprising is what matters!"*

Lenin in Exile Again. Lenin's influence dwindled, both among the Russian people and in the Social Democratic party itself, as a pro-Tsarist reaction set in throughout Russia after the 1905 revolt. In the long years from 1907 until 1917—years Lenin spent entirely abroad, living a lonely life in Geneva, Paris and Zurich—it often seemed that all his dreams were in vain. He chafed in idleness, worried about finding money for a cheap apartment, had little to do but go to the movies in the evening. In Paris, he bicycled to the library each day to compile new essays or treatises. One day a minor disaster struck him. Somebody stole his bicycle. Such were the humiliations suffered by a man who had thought to make kings tremble.

A Futile Forum. In Russia, the Tsar no longer trembled as he must have when the 1905 uprising was at its height. However, he was disappointed when the first Duma produced a reformist majority. When it met in May 1906, the largest bloc of votes, 179 seats representing nearly 40 per cent of the chamber, belonged to the Constitutional Democratic party, called the Cadets. Their sober program calling for a constitutional monarchy, land redistribution to the peasants and an eight-hour day gave promise of real and needed reforms. But the Minister of the Interior, Peter Stolypin, who favored land reform to strengthen peasant loyalty to the Tsar, was nonetheless a determined opponent of the Duma. Soon promoted to Prime Minister, he dissolved the legislature.

A new Duma was elected in 1907. Despite every sort of pressure by Stolypin, the voters once more chose representatives who favored reforms. After three months, the Duma was again dissolved. A third Duma, convened in November 1907, was to last for a full five-year term. But this time the vote had been carefully rigged and Stolypin at last had a majority. However, it really made little difference to the throne whether or not it had the support of the Duma. Absolutism still held sway. The fourth and last Duma was elected in 1912, and was in existence when rebellion broke out in 1917.

The Dumas were in the main ineffectual bodies that might have accomplished some good had they been given a chance. At least they gave the opposition an opportunity to express the country's grievances. The pity is that the Tsar and his coterie were too obtuse to realize that the modern age had caught up with Russia.

The End of the Tsars

Russia's entrance into World War I in 1914 was followed by a series of humiliating defeats and devastation. In 1917, as in 1905, the misery of wartime life touched off the Revolution. But this Revolution overthrew the Tsars. Once more, the long-awaited event caught Lenin by

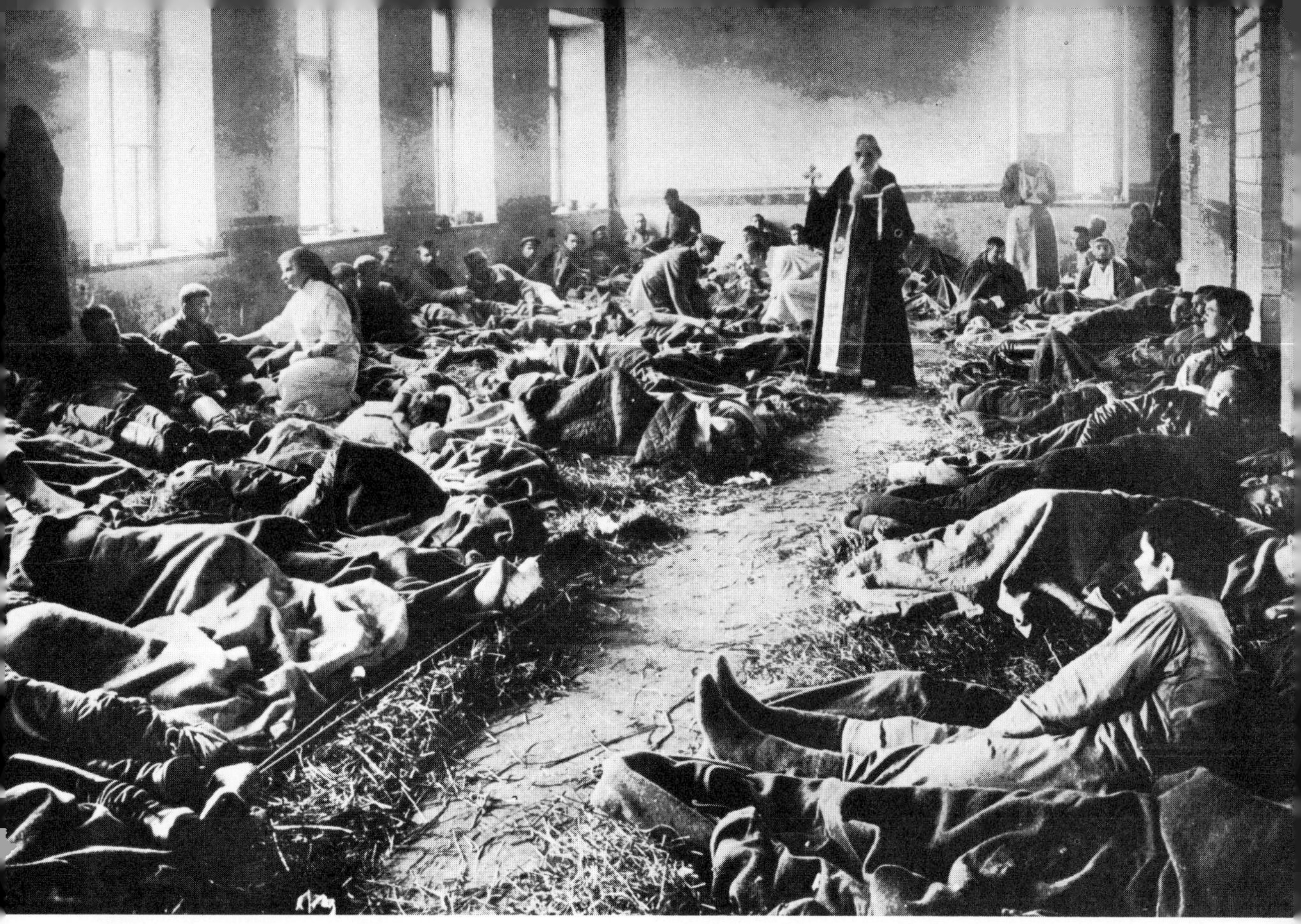

RUSSIAN WOUNDED lie on the straw *(above)* in a World War I field hospital in Poland. Estimates of Russia's shocking losses range as high as nine million casualties.

RUSSIANS AT HOME stand in line *(below)* as civil war curtails food and clothing stocks. By 1921 prices were 16,800 times higher than they had been in prewar 1913.

surprise. As late as January 22, 1917, he expressed doubts that he would live to see another revolution. Again, Lenin had nothing to do with it—at first.

In part, the Revolution was touched off by the millions of losses the ill-equipped Russian army suffered in World War I. The dead were never even counted accurately. "In the great war ledger," the German commander Von Hindenburg wrote afterward, "the page on which Russian losses were written has been torn out. No one knows the figures. Five or eight millions? We, too, have no idea . . ."

A TSAR'S UNCONCERN AMID UPHEAVAL

Nicholas II always seemed indifferent to the violent currents that moved about him. During the hectic year of 1905, the 37-year-old Tsar wrote in his journal: "Pretty doings! . . . Was quietly busy until dinner and all evening. Went paddling in a canoe. . . . Got dressed and rode a bicycle to the bathing beach and bathed enjoyably in the sea. . . . The weather was wonderful."

"Give Us Food or Stop the War." On the home front, things were not much better. Because of the demands of the mobilization, the transportation system failed. Trains broke down, food supplies fell off to a trickle and long lines of people formed in every Russian town—only to find no food. People began to cry: "Either give us food or stop the war."

But the Tsar paid little attention, for he spent most of his time away from the capital at the army's general headquarters. The country was actually being governed by the Empress Alexandra and a succession of half-mad or totally incompetent ministers. The Tsarina appointed and fired them depending on the whim of a semiliterate, vile-smelling, self-proclaimed "holy man" named Rasputin, who held a hypnotic influence over her.

The Empress, born in Germany, had been a princess of Hesse before her marriage, and the ordinary people suspected her of betraying Russia to the German enemy. The results were much the same as if she had. While the Tsar's whole empire crumbled around his head, he himself seemed totally unable to act.

On December 30, 1916, with the complicity of the Tsar's cousin, Grand Duke Dmitri, Rasputin was lured to the home of Prince Yusupov, one of the high nobility. Rasputin was given poisoned wine to drink. When it had no effect on him, he was shot and killed. The elimination of Rasputin, however, came too late to help Tsar Nicholas regain control of his kingdom.

The Tsar's Final Duma. On February 27, 1917, the Tsar called another session of his almost powerless fourth Duma in Petrograd, as the capital was now called (St. Petersburg sounded too German). At the opening, a leader of a socialist peasant party spoke. He was Alexander Kerensky of Simbirsk, whose father had given the young Lenin a gold medal on graduation from school. "The Tsar himself must be removed," cried Kerensky, "by force if there is no other way. . . . If you will not listen to the voice of warning now, you will find yourself face to face with facts, not warning. Look up at the distant flashes that are lighting the skies of Russia."

On March 3, 1917, workers in a branch of the Putilov Steel Works —at that time one of the largest in the world—went on strike to protest the dismissal of some employees. When their demands were refused, workers in other branches joined them. The owners answered by locking out all 30,000 workers. These men went off to other factories asking for support. Five days later, thousands of women in Petrograd's textile factories stopped work for "Women's Day."

"Stop the disorder in the capital at once," wired the Tsar to his Petrograd commander. The Tsar might as well have tried to sweep back the ocean.

His Empress still did not understand. She wrote to the Tsar: "Youngsters and girls are running around shouting they have no bread. They do this just to create some excitement. If the weather were cold, they would probably all be staying at home."

"Dissolve the Duma!" wired the Tsar, but the Duma continued to meet. No one listened. No one cared. Suddenly, everything came apart. All remaining traces of discipline disappeared. The troops refused to shoot at the people. Soldiers shot their own officers and joined the civilians. On March 12, workers began assembling to hold some kind of election. Remembering the Soviet of 1905, they were choosing another such council—the Soviet of Workers' Deputies. It moved into one section of the Tauride Palace. The Duma had ignored the Tsar's order to dissolve and was holding an emergency meeting in another wing.

That evening, in the course of a tumultuous meeting of the Soviet, a group of soldiers asked for the floor. One by one they named their regiments, pledging their participation in the Revolution. With a tremendous burst of enthusiasm, the assembled delegates united soldiers and workers in one Soviet of Workers' and Soldiers' Deputies, and elected an Executive Committee, heavily Menshevik in composition but including a few Bolsheviks, none in top positions. The chairman of the Soviet was the leader of the Social Democrats, and Kerensky was one of the vice-chairmen.

On March 14, a committee of 12 chosen by the Duma appointed a Provisional Government with a liberal noble, Prince Georgi Lvov, as its chairman. Kerensky, as minister of justice, was the only socialist member.

The Tsar Steps Down. On March 15, the Tsar abdicated in favor of his brother, Grand Duke Michael, who on the following day refused to accept the supreme power. Russia was without a Tsar, and two rival groups were seeking to fill the governmental vacuum. The Provisional Government had little real authority, for the other government—the Soviet of Workers' and Soldiers' Deputies—could block any action to which it objected. Under the Soviet's pressure, the Provisional Government issued its first decree, which called for release of all political, religious and military prisoners; free speech and press; the right of workers to unionize and to strike; an end to discrimination based on social, religious or national origin; and honest elections for a constituent assembly, with a vote for everyone.

A TSARINA'S TROUBLED ARROGANCE

Just before Tsar Nicholas was forced to step down, in March 1917, the Empress sent this note to him at his army headquarters in the field: "Things are rotten. I don't know where I can reach you but I firmly believe, and nothing can shake my belief, that everything will be all right. . . . It is clear that they are trying to prevent you from seeing me before they make you sign some paper, a constitution or some other horrid thing, I suppose. . . . It is the greatest meanness and vileness, unheard of in history, to detain someone's Emperor."

REBELLIOUS SOLDIERS refuse to obey orders to fire on rioters as the 1917 Revolution nears its climax. Instead, as dramatized in this scene from a Russian film, they fired their guns in the air and joined the uprising. This defection was part of the general breakdown in discipline and helped to assure the Revolution's success.

Note well the demand for a constituent assembly. It had been the chief demand of the revolts of 1905. It was the slogan which, more than any other, ran through every great revolutionary upsurge in Russia. It was the universal cry of every party—right, left or center. The story of the life and death of this idea is the central tragedy of the Russian Revolution.

The second government, or Petrograd Soviet, consisted of 2,500 workers and soldiers chosen without any formalities by the factory workers and members of army units. The largest political group in it was the Socialist Revolutionaries, direct descendants of the old "People's Will." Next largest was the Menshevik faction of the Social Democratic party, the moderates who always opposed Lenin's hard, ruthless line. Third came the Bolsheviks, who formed a small minority. Similar Soviets sprang up in Moscow and all over Russia.

Lenin's Return to Petrograd. At this moment, the Germans, figuring correctly that Lenin's influence would help to knock Russia out of the war, permitted his passage from Switzerland across Germany in a sealed train, along with his wife, several other Bolsheviks and other political exiles. On April 16 as dusk fell, a great crowd of workers, soldiers and sailors waited outside the Finland Station in Petrograd. Many carried red banners. The headlight of

A NEW SOVIET, patterned after the one suppressed in 1905, meets in the Tauride Palace in March 1917, as members of the Duma meet in the same building. Worker and soldier delegates made up the Soviet, and at this stage both Bolshevik and non-Bolshevik leaders, including Kerensky, were able to work together effectively.

the locomotive lit up the rails and a bell clanged as the cars, brilliantly lighted, came into the station. Lenin, wearing his familiar worker's cap, stepped out. For the first time in 10 years, he was on Russian soil. A group of workers carried him on their shoulders to the station's former royal waiting room. Someone handed him a bouquet of flowers.

"Comrade Lenin," cried the chairman of the Petrograd Soviet, "we welcome you to Russia in the name of the Petrograd Soviet and the Revolution. . . . The chief task of the revolutionary democracy at present is to defend our revolution against every kind of attack both from within and without. . . ."

But Lenin had other ideas. As soon as he was alone with his own Bolshevik leaders, he began bitterly attacking them for even conditionally supporting the Provisional Government in his absence. He cried: "No support for the Provisional Government!"

In his absence, the Bolsheviks had not only been supporting the Provisional Government, but one of the editors of the Bolshevik paper *Pravda*, a man named Joseph Djugashvili but already known as Stalin, had even favored a complete political union of the Bolsheviks with the left wing of the Mensheviks. "As members of one party our small differences will fade away."

Not so, said Lenin. He insisted the Bolsheviks must regard the whole non-Bolshevik majority in the Soviet as their enemy.

Lenin Seizes Power. While other political groups decided that the war effort should take priority, Lenin argued for an end to the war and action on social issues. From the moment of his arrival, he turned all his energies toward seizing the powers vested in the Provisional Government. In his famous "April Theses," Lenin appealed to soldiers all over Europe to end the war by starting civil wars in their own countries. He demanded immediate distribution of the land to the peasants. He pounded home the powerful slogan of "Peace, land and bread!" He spurned all talk of uniting with the Mensheviks. Soon many of the workers' delegates to the Soviet were supporting Lenin. He gained strength among the troops, particularly the fiery revolutionary sailors from the Kronstadt naval base.

In May, the Provisional Government was reorganized, this time with six socialists in the cabinet, including Kerensky as Minister of War and Marine. He was, in fact, its actual leader.

Kerensky began a July offensive against the Germans, but as a result of its failure and staggering losses an uprising began back in Petrograd, the "July Days" crisis. Angry workers and sailors began converging on the Tauride Palace where the government sat. Lenin

FIRING ON STREET CROWDS during the disorder of July 1917, Bolshevik sailors from the Kronstadt naval base strike at Kerensky's Provisional Government. The sailors drove a tank to an important intersection in Petrograd and shot at civilians and unarmed Cossacks because they could find no suitable governmental target.

had not directly instigated this and hesitated to urge the mobs to overthrow the government. But while he hesitated, the tide broke. The Provisional Government ordered Lenin's arrest on charges of incitement to armed insurrection with financial aid from the Germans. Again Lenin went into hiding, shaving off his mustache and beard and wearing a wig, sleeping in haystacks until he reached safety in Finland.

The Trend to the Bolsheviks. Soon, however, everything began to go Lenin's way. In August, Kerensky (who by then was prime minister) called a national political conference in Moscow, with representatives of the main political and economic groups of the nation. The conservatives all supported General Lavr Kornilov, Kerensky's military commander in chief. Only the socialists stuck by Kerensky. Expecting a coup by the general, Kerensky dismissed Kornilov from his command. Kornilov refused to leave his post and ordered troops to move against the government. All the left-wing groups of the Soviet temporarily joined Kerensky in preparing to fight Kornilov. Railroad workers refused to move Kornilov's troops, and the troops began going over to the socialists. Kornilov was arrested.

Kerensky apparently had won. But actually, his power was gone. With the alliance among the Provisional Government, the conservative forces and the army leadership broken, Kerensky was at the mercy of the Petrograd Soviet. The Soviet, for its part, was leaning more and more toward Lenin's militant Bolsheviks, for it had become apparent that Kerensky was unable to control the forces around him. Kerensky's only hope, then, was to hold out until the national elections—called for November 25—could choose the long-awaited constituent assembly. But Lenin had no intention of giving Kerensky time. Lenin secretly returned from exile and called an all-night meeting of the Bolshevik Central Committee to plan Kerensky's overthrow. This group, after 10 stormy hours and much violent opposition, approved Lenin's plans. Trotsky, who had only recently left the Mensheviks to join Lenin, vividly recalled the scene: "Hastily, with a stub of a pencil, on a sheet of graph-paper torn from a child's exercise book, [Lenin] wrote: 'The Party calls for the organization of an armed insurrection.' "

Trotsky had become president of the Petrograd Soviet, in which the Bolsheviks were now in the majority. He was put in charge of organizing the military side of the insurrection. His Military Revolutionary Committee, which included some left-wing Socialist Revolutionaries as well as Bolsheviks, sent a "commissar" to every army unit in Petrograd, telling the troops to obey only the Revolutionary Committee's orders.

Before dawn on November 7, armed detachments of Red Guards occupied the central telegraph office, the post office and a large number of other government buildings. Other armed squads surrounded

A TEMPORARY PREMIER REVIEWS HIS TROOPS

Alexander Kerensky *(above at right)*, who had been the Provisional Government's minister of war, became prime minister as well soon after the "July Days" crisis. When the Bolsheviks overthrew his government in November, Kerensky escaped to western Europe. He has lived in the United States since 1940.

the Winter Palace and the military district headquarters. Showing cool courage, Kerensky went to headquarters and then left in an open automobile, driving right through the soldiers, who snapped to attention from habit and let him pass. He tried and failed to get the support of any troops. He was unable even to return to Petrograd. Meanwhile, an all-Russian "Congress of Soviets" had begun to meet in the Smolny Institute, a fashionable girls' school where Lenin had his headquarters.

Out in the Neva River, the guns of the cruiser *Aurora* boomed. As planned, Communist sailors were firing on the Winter Palace. Communist troops burst into the palace. The remaining members of the Provisional Government were arrested and marched off to the Fortress of Saints Peter and Paul.

"The Revolution . . . Has Come to Pass." At the meeting of the Congress of Soviets in the Smolny Institute, Lenin was wearing his wig and his face was half hidden by a dirty handkerchief. He removed his handkerchief to speak. His companion whispered to him: "Take off your wig."

He did so, then moved onto the rostrum, hands in pockets, head bowed. Welcomed with thunderous applause, he spoke:

"Comrades, the workers' and peasants' revolution, whose need the Bolsheviks have emphasized many times, has come to pass."

Years of Violence, Capped by Revolution

The Revolution of 1917 had been centuries in the making. But it was not until the early part of the 20th Century that the Tsar's long-repressed subjects moved to overthrow the monarchy. On Sunday, January 22, 1905, two hundred thousand workers, wives and children marched toward the Tsar's Winter Palace in St. Petersburg (now Leningrad) with peaceful intent. They wanted to present a petition asking for a constituent assembly and better working conditions. The order was given to bar the people from the palace square, and horsemen like the Cossack shown on the opposite page slashed at the crowd to turn it away. Panicky troops opened fire, killed 500 and left thousands wounded in the snow. This "Bloody Sunday" led to the 1905 revolt and ultimately to the violence of 1917. Paintings on the pages that follow show some high points of this epoch.

Lawless Acts of Retribution

Here carousing peasants loot valuables of a landowner whose mansion they have set afire. In this way the impoverished and oppressed peasants took vengeance on

their wealthy masters. The practice was called "letting loose the red rooster" because of the fiery look of flames against the night sky. Sporadic outbursts of this kind had been known in Russia for centuries, but the autumn of 1905 saw a great increase in burnings; at least 2,000 landowners' homes were razed in that wild year.

Terrorist Raids for Funds and Murders for Revenge

ROBBERY of a post office shipment in Tiflis, Georgia *(above)*, in 1907 was planned by a 27-year-old revolutionist. This daring venture enriched the Bolshevik coffers by over $30,000. The young mastermind would later become world-renowned under the name of Joseph Stalin.

ASSASSINATION in Kiev *(right)* in 1911 of Prime Minister Peter Stolypin was a terrorist act. The Tsar's ablest premier, Stolypin was hated both by royalists and revolutionists. He was ruthless toward terrorism, but nobles resented his efforts at badly needed land reforms.

АНТА

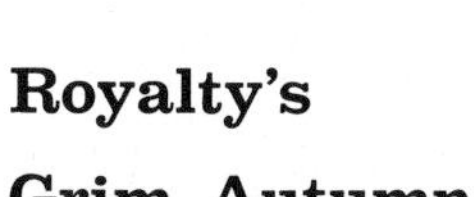

Royalty's Grim Autumn

REGALLY ALOOF, a Russian noblewoman *(opposite)* is helped from her carriage as she attends an evening at the ballet. Right through the autumn of 1916, the upper class in Russia kept up a pretense of normal life despite the fact that the ravages of the war meant bread lines for the poor people and workers of the hungry land.

VIOLENT ACTION against the "monk" Rasputin is taken in late December 1916 by Prince Yusupov, seen at far right. Appalled by the unhealthy influence wielded by Rasputin on the Empress, this high noble is about to shoot him. Rasputin's death, however, came too late to improve the way that affairs of state were conducted.

The End of the War for the People of Russia

LENIN'S HOME-COMING is welcomed by soldiers and workers *(above)* at Petrograd's Finland Station on April 16, 1917. He had been in Switzerland and France for 10 years. The Germans, hoping that he would help take Russia out of the war, were glad to send Lenin back.

FRATERNIZATION between German and Russian soldiers *(opposite)* reflects the dissolving discipline of the weary front-line troops. From March 1917 until the armistice in December of that year, Russian Marxists often distributed propaganda leaflets to German troops.

The Last of the Tsars

After being held captive for 16 months, Tsar Nicholas II, with his wife, children and several servants, was finally executed by the Bolsheviks on the night of July 16, 1918. The Tsar had abdicated in March of the previous year.

3 The Result:

Hardening of the Communist Dictatorship

JOSEPH STALIN

3 The Result:

Hardening of the Communist Dictatorship

The two decades between the Bolshevik Revolution and the outbreak of World War II comprise an era of enormous violence and enormous change.

This era saw Communism's newly won power shakily survive three years of battering by civil war and economic upheaval. In the collapse of Communist revolutions in Germany and Hungary, it saw the death of Lenin's hopes for world revolution in his own lifetime. It saw the turning, by his successors, to the building of "socialism in one country"—an effort which, at tremendous cost of blood and agony, lifted backward Russia into the first ranks of industrial and military power.

The Communists Remake Russia. With the Bolsheviks ruling Russia after 1917, Lenin had to make up his mind what he would do with the power he now possessed. He had never thought this question through adequately. The seizure of power itself and the ruthless destruction of the old order had been his lifelong obsession. "Its political task," he had said, "will be clarified after the seizure."

He was Marx's disciple, yet he had already departed from the master's teachings by trying to achieve Communism without going through the capitalist period Marx had predicted. But Lenin could justify this by his "discovery" of a new phase of capitalism—he called it "imperialism"—which Marx did not foresee. In essence, Lenin saw imperialism as capitalism's ability to ward off its "inevitable" decay and disintegration by aggressive expansion into undeveloped colonies. This made "imperialistic wars" a certainty and also made it possible for Communists to use the war to take over in Russia, the weakest link in the imperialistic chain. Thus, Lenin justified immediate exclusive power for Bolsheviks rather than going through a "capitalist" phase in collaboration with other Marxist parties.

"Only the dictatorship of the proletariat," he asserted, "is able to establish democracy for the *poor*." He failed to see what Trotsky had warned long ago in fighting Lenin's theory of party organization—that it would end with the party bureaucracy taking the place of the party itself, the Central Committee taking the place of the bureaucracy and "finally the dictator [taking] the place of the Central Committee." This is precisely what did happen.

The Road to Dictatorship

Peace, land and bread—this was the slogan that brought Lenin to power. On the day after the Bolshevik success, Lenin strode before the Congress of Soviets, meeting in the Smolny Institute, with decrees to make the slogan real.

▶ *Peace.* He called on all the warring powers to arrange an immediate armistice, for not less than three months, in order to negotiate a final peace "without annexations or indemnities."

▶ *Land.* He proclaimed that the "landlord's right of property in land is abolished immediately without any payment" and ordered hundreds of thousands of acres of land "turned over" to the peasantry, which had already in fact seized much of it. He also nationalized all natural resources including oil, coal and other minerals.

▶ *Bread.* Lenin had none to give. He could only announce the formation of a new government that would promise to provide bread. This would be the first "Soviet Government."

Naming the New Government. Earlier, in talking with Trotsky, Lenin had insisted that the new government officials be called "anything but ministers . . . a vile, hackneyed word." Trotsky had an idea. "We might call them commissars [commissioners]," he said. "But there are too many commissars. Perhaps supreme commissars? No, supreme does not sound well. . . . What about People's Commissars?"

"Well, that might do . . ." said Lenin. "And the government?"

"A Soviet [council], of course—the Soviet of People's Commissars."

"Splendid," said Lenin, "it savors powerfully of revolution!"

And so it became. And so it remained until 1946, when Joseph Stalin changed the name to Council of Ministers and the "vile, hackneyed word" was restored. The state itself was called the "Russian Soviet Federated Socialist Republic."

The Soviet of People's Commissars included:

- ▶ Chairman, N. Lenin.
- ▶ Foreign Commissar, Leon Trotsky.
- ▶ Nationalities Commissar, Joseph Stalin.

A Comic-Opera Government. As it began from scratch, this totally new form of government was frequently comic. In the middle of a revolution that shook the world, its drably dressed leaders wandered through the corridors of the Smolny Institute looking for a place to sit. One Communist volunteered to find an office for Stalin's new department. He located an empty table in a large room, tacked over it a sign that read "People's Commissariat of Nationalities," then spent his last funds for a rubber stamp with the same name. He told Stalin he needed 3,000 rubles for office expenses. "Borrow it from Trotsky," said Stalin. "I hear he found some money in the [old] Ministry of Foreign Affairs."

An agent Lenin sent to the state bank for 10 million rubles to stock the treasury came back with two bags stuffed with money. He put them in a closet guarded by a semicircle of chairs and a sentry. This was the first Soviet treasury.

"Hand Over Your Weapons!" The comedy soon turned deadly for anyone that Lenin's hard, ruthless band of Communists decided was an enemy. Lenin's onetime mentor, the revered pioneer Marxist George Plekhanov, discovered this. Three days after the Bolshevik seizure of power, Plekhanov wrote an "Open Letter to the Petrograd Workers" warning them that the proletariat was not yet ready and that if they tried to govern now they would bring on civil war.

On November 13, Red guards invaded Plekhanov's house. One put a pistol to his head, crying, "Hand over your weapons! If I find them without you, I'll shoot you on the spot." Plekhanov replied quietly: "Killing is easy enough—I have no weapons." The next morning, his friends whisked him away in an ambulance to safety.

What of the constituent assembly, for which so many Russians had yearned and died over the decades? Lenin had often accused Kerensky of postponing the election of deputies. Now he faced the prospect of elections scheduled for November 25—a date set by Kerensky.

Russia's Only Free Election. "We must postpone the election," Lenin now said. Trotsky told him it would not look right. "Nonsense," said Lenin, "it is facts that are important, not words." However, against his instincts, he allowed the election to be held. The Bolsheviks lost decisively. Nearly 42 million Russians went to the polls; some 16 million, or 38 per cent, cast their votes for the

THE END OF THE PRESS

David Shub, who was personally acquainted with Lenin, tells this incident in his *Lenin: A Biography:*

"On November 10, 1917, the Soviet Government published a decree curtailing . . . the press, with the assurance that the repressive measures were only temporary. . . . [The official explanation was that] 'the simple return of printing offices and paper to capitalists, poisoners of the people's conscience, would be an unpardonable . . . counterrevolutionary measure.'

"But it was just as important for Lenin to gag Socialist opinion. From the first days . . . he insisted on shutting down the Socialist Revolutionary and Menshevik papers. . . . At [a] Congress of the Soviets, to the outcries of the Socialists, *'Our papers have been closed,'* Lenin replied: 'Of course, unfortunately not all of them! Soon all of them will be closed. . . .'

"The freedom of speech and press for which generations of Russian revolutionists had fought since the days of the Decembrists [1825] was completely destroyed within a matter of months."

It stayed destroyed.

HARANGUING THE PEOPLE in 1918, Lenin addresses the first May Day celebration under his new regime. At this period, the Bolsheviks were still consolidating their gains following the Revolution. And as Lenin told a companion while watching the crowd: "The most important thing is not to lose constant contact with the masses."

Socialist Revolutionary party. Another two million voted for the leading nonsocialist party, the Constitutional Democrats, known as the Cadets. Fewer than 10 million, or 24 per cent, voted for Bolshevik candidates. In the only free election Russia has ever had, for every Bolshevik who won, the opponents elected three.

Communism had its chance to win power legally, legitimately, at the polls. It lost. It never took that chance again.

Lenin immediately outlawed the Constitutional Democrats. He also postponed indefinitely the December 11 convocation of the assembly that Kerensky had scheduled when he called the election. But the elected deputies began drifting into Petrograd anyway, and they insisted on convening the assembly despite Bolshevik opposition. On the afternoon of January 18, 1918, the long-sought constituent assembly finally met at the Tauride Palace.

To intimidate the assembly, Lenin had summoned Red sailors from nearby Kronstadt to swarm outside the building. The cruiser *Aurora* and battleship *Republic* were brought up along the banks of the Neva River. Lenin ordered a detachment of sharpshooters from Latvia brought to Petrograd. "We cannot depend on the Russian peasant," he said. "He is likely to join the other side."

The oldest deputy present, a veteran of the old People's Will, called the meeting to order. Bedlam broke out at once, for Bolshevik deputies, soldiers and sailors began to raise a racket in the hall. The Bolshevik deputies sought to vote "all power to the Soviets," which they now controlled, and then to disband the assembly on the ground that it was no longer needed. The other deputies, however, insisted on acting like an elected congress.

Whistles, Howls, Jeers. The Bolsheviks made a farce of the proceedings. Every speech was interrupted by Bolshevik whistles, howls and jeers. Lenin lolled about on the steps to the platform, then curled up on a bench and pretended to sleep. Around midnight the Bolshevik deputies walked out. The rightist Socialist Revolutionaries and a handful of Mensheviks stayed on, passing resolutions to create a federated republic, voting to give the land to the peasants and to end the war. They passed a host of measures as revolutionary as any the Bolsheviks had decreed. But they would not accept a Communist dictatorship that had no legal sanction.

Victor Chernov, the elected chairman of the assembly, was still trying to speak in the early dawn when Bolshevik soldiers and sailors tried to force the delegates out of the hall. They had been in session for over 12 hours. Next day, guards blocked the doors and would not admit deputies. Illegal though it was, the Bolshevik dictatorship was now complete. The only right by which this dictatorship acted was the right of naked force. And Lenin commanded that force.

THE MAN BEHIND THE TERROR

Felix Dzerzhinsky was the first chief of the Cheka, Lenin's secret police. A personally unselfish bleak ascetic with a friendly smile, he was utterly merciless to political opponents.

Lenin at a meeting once scribbled a note to Dzerzhinsky asking how many prisoners the Cheka had in jail. "About 1,500," the chief replied. Lenin read it, muttered something, jotted an "X" beside the figure and returned the note. This signified that he had noted the figure, but Dzerzhinsky mistook the meaning. Silently he got up, left the room and had all 1,500 shot that night.

Lenin Turns to Terror

With dictatorship, Lenin also openly established the instrument that all dictators require: Terror. He believed terror was needed to bring order out of chaos and protect the Revolution from its enemies.

Lenin had already set up an official agency to direct the terror, the Extraordinary Commission for Combating Counter-Revolution and Speculation. This long name was shortened to "Cheka," from the Russian initials for its first two words. When his comrades objected to the terror, Lenin asked, "Do you really think that we shall be victorious without using the most cruel terror?" At another time he demanded: "If we cannot shoot a man who sabotages . . . what kind of revolution is that?"

The Cheka's Victims. Felix Dzerzhinsky, the sinister commissar of the Cheka, sent his squads on after-midnight prowls of apartment houses, rounding up anyone even suspected of being an enemy of Bolshevism. Endless numbers of captives were hustled to the old police station not far from the Winter Palace, stood against the wall and shot. The sounds were muffled by the roar of truck motors kept going for that purpose.

Early in 1918, fearing that the Germans might reach Petrograd, the Soviet government moved its headquarters to Moscow and took over the ancient fortress called the Kremlin. The Cheka installed itself in an old stone building on Lubianka Street. That soon became—as it remains—the most fearsome address in all Russia. Its dark and spacious cellars were ideal for secret executions in the dead of night.

The Tsar Executed. Among the early victims of the terror were Tsar Nicholas II and his family, who since his abdication had been held under guard in Ekaterinburg (now Sverdlovsk). At midnight on July 16, 1918, the royal family was awakened, told to dress and go down to the cellar. Not only was the Tsar executed: his wife, his son, four daughters, doctor, cook, chambermaid and waiter were shot, too. To make sure that no possible loyal Tsarists could ever find a trace of the remains the bodies were hacked to pieces, burned, then scattered in a swamp and covered with dirt and leaves.

The pace of the terror became frenzied after Lenin himself was wounded. This happened on August 30, 1918, when he spoke at a labor rally in Moscow. As he left the hall, a woman named Fanya Kaplan came up beside his car and asked him a question. About to enter the car, Lenin turned to answer. She produced a pistol and fired three shots point-blank. She shot him, she said, because she believed Lenin was "a traitor" to the Revolution. One bullet pierced his neck, another his collarbone. Though badly wounded he insisted on being driven to the Kremlin and on walking up the stairs.

"We Kill Whole Classes." Lenin soon recovered, but in reprisal, 500 "bourgeois" hostages were killed in Petrograd. Red Army bands combed the streets in search of suspects. "The bourgeoisie kill separate individuals but we kill whole classes," cried Grigory Zinoviev, party head of Petrograd. The Bolshevik newspaper *Pravda* (Truth) announced: "From now on the hymn of the working class will be a hymn of hate." When people complained about the shooting of innocent persons, Lenin was surprised. The important thing, he said, was to put teeth into the dictatorship: "Outside of force and violence, there is no way to suppress the exploiters of the masses."

A GIGANTIC LIFESAVING MISSION

Soviet leaders never cease accusing the U.S. of having tried to overthrow the Communists during the Russian civil war. Every such accusation pointedly ignores some $70 million of American relief which Herbert Hoover, as head of the American Relief Administration, distributed in Soviet Russia during the famines of 1921 and 1922 caused by severe drought and the economic distress left from the civil war.

Former President Hoover has told about a 1924 banquet in the Kremlin at which Communism's leaders credited the American relief with saving 20 million lives. They presented Hoover with a scroll that thanked the U.S. "in the name of the millions . . . saved. . . . The people . . . will never forget the aid rendered to them by the American people, holding it to be a pledge of the future friendship of the two nations." The people did not forget, but the Soviet leaders did.

Civil War and Intervention

Lenin's promise of peace and of an end to Russia's participation in the World War was part of the slogan with which he seized power. Accordingly, his government signed a humiliating and costly peace treaty with Germany at Brest-Litovsk, in western Russia, on March 3, 1918. The Bolsheviks agreed to give up a great deal of territory including the Russian "breadbasket," the Ukraine.

Peace with Recent Enemies, War against Former Friends

COSTLY PEACE for the new Communist state is sought by Trotsky *(center)*, seen arriving to negotiate with the Germans at Brest-Litovsk in early 1918. The treaty's terms were so humiliating that Trotsky would have no part of it.

CIVIL WAR that followed peace was complicated by conflict with the Czech Corps, seen advancing on a Bolshevik-held town.

A Party Congress, the Seventh, was quickly convened later in March to ratify the treaty. The delegates did so. They also officially adopted a new name for the party: "All-Russian Communist (Bolshevik) Party." Since then the "(Bolshevik)" has been dropped, and in any case in common usage it is simply "the Communist party."

Despite the treaty, Russia was not yet to know peace. A civil war now began that bled the country for three years. In May 1918, the anti-Bolshevik Don Cossacks were campaigning against Red troops. Also in May, the Czechoslovakian Corps began fighting the Bolsheviks. This corps had been recruited partly from anti-German prisoners of war, partly from former members of Czech colonies in Russia who longed to see their homeland free of Austro-Hungarian rule. Oddly, the collapse of the Russian army after Brest-Litovsk left the Czech Corps the most powerful organized force inside the country. Some 40,000 members of the corps were seeking to leave Russia to join the Allies on the western front. They were headed for Vladivostok, the far eastern terminus of the Trans-Siberian Railroad, and were strung out along 3,000 miles of the railroad, all the way from the Volga River to Irkutsk in Siberia.

By mid-May some 15,000 had reached Vladivostok, when some of the corps farther west got into a fight with the Bolsheviks in the Ural Mountains. Soon fighting broke out between the Czechs and the Bolsheviks all along the railroad. This fighting encouraged anti-Bolshevik

Best-armed unit in Russia, the corps' fight to escape via Vladivostok encouraged the White forces in their war with the Reds.

WRECKED LOCOMOTIVES, derailed by the Bolsheviks along the Trans-Siberian Railroad, block the Czechs trying to reach the Pacific. In this confused struggle, 40,000 Czechs were strung along some 3,000 miles of track.

Russians all over central Russia to rise in arms. Some were fighting for a constitutional monarchy, some for independent republics, some for socialism, some were just fighting. All the troops making up the military opposition to the Bolsheviks were loosely referred to as the "White Army" forces.

The United States in Vladivostok. More than 800,000 tons of war supplies were stored in the port of Vladivostok. Some 800,000 German and Austro-Hungarian prisoners of war were also in the area, and the Allies feared they might be released and try to seize the valuable stores. In July, President Woodrow Wilson decided to send United States troops to safeguard the matériel and the railroad long enough to evacuate all the Czech Corps. He had no intention whatever of intervening in Russia's civil war. Allied troops were also landed at Archangel and Murmansk in the far northwest to protect Allied supplies there against possible seizure.

However, British and French forces did get into some active fighting with the Red troops. Britain sent troops and arms to bolster a White Russian government set up by Admiral Alexander Kolchak in Omsk, Siberia. In southern Russia, other British forces landed in the Caucasus, and the French made a naval landing on the Black Sea. American troops themselves had only one brief and accidental skirmish with Bolshevik forces. In 1920, the Poles, unhappy with the Curzon Line, which the Allied Supreme War Council had proposed as the eastern frontier of the newly re-established Polish state, sent troops into the Ukraine. Eventually the Red Army, under Mikhail Tukhachevsky, drove the Poles out.

The Phase of War Communism

AMERICAN SOLDIERS IN RUSSIA'S NORTH

Three members of America's "Polar Bear" regiment based in Archangel, in Russia's far north, are shown above. After Lenin took Russia out of World War I in 1918, President Wilson sent American soldiers to protect huge Allied stores of arms from possible seizure and use against the Czech Corps. But Wilson limited the troops' activities to this mission and he made it clear that there was to be no meddling in Russia's internal affairs.

The Communists emerged from the civil war shaky but still in power. They ruled a starving land. Part of the cause was their attempt to impose Communism in the midst of war. This three-year period of "war Communism" (1918-1921) brought such disaster that the Communists came very close to being overthrown by unorganized, dissident Russians.

By turning industry over to the control of the workers, the Communists had plunged production into total confusion. The workers spent most of their time settling scores with old bosses, or scrounging what they could to feed their families amid the prevailing chaos. Everything went to pieces. Factory production virtually ceased. Industrial production by 1920 fell to only 13 per cent of its prewar level. The Communists nationalized all industry and attempted to restore some order by setting up a one-man—rather than "workers'-committee"—management system for factories.

The government had tried to obtain food supplies for the cities from the farms. At the same time it attempted to extend the "class war" to the rural areas by creating so-called "committees of the poor" in the villages. These committees were ordered to seize the grain of wealthier peasants, or *kulaks,* and ship it to the cities. The poorer peasants responded by killing many *kulaks* and seizing their grain. Many kept the grain for themselves, while the cities starved.

Lenin thereupon sent out "food detachments" of city workers on a crusade for bread. These workers did succeed in seizing enough grain to feed the cities. But the peasants, forced to deliver grain at the point of machine guns, simply stopped working. By 1921, farm production had fallen to about half the 1913 level. Everywhere peasant uprisings broke out, directed primarily against the food detachments. They had one simple slogan: "Down with the Communists!"

A Workers' Strike against Communism. In February 1921, the workers of Petrograd began throwing down their tools and going on strike. If the Communist dictatorship was for the "working class"—as all of its theories claimed—why was the working class striking against it? Mainly because the people were hungry.

Something even more ominous now happened. The revolutionary sailors of the Kronstadt naval base, who had been so helpful to the Bolsheviks in 1917, turned against the Communists to support the striking factory workers.

On February 28, 1921, the crew of the battleship *Petropavlovsk* met to vote for a series of demands. These demands boiled down to one simple word: Freedom. They called for freedom of speech and the press, freedom for peasants to do what they pleased with the land, and for the liberation of all political prisoners. And "in view of the fact that the existing Soviets do not express the will of the workers and peasants," they demanded secret elections to reorganize the Soviets. The next day, 12,000 angrily shouting sailors and members of the garrison jammed a mass meeting in the main square of Kronstadt. They endorsed the resolutions and chose a provisional revolutionary committee.

In Moscow, the Communist government was flabbergasted. How could the "unguided" people stage a revolution of their own, in violation of all of Lenin's theories, and against the Communists at that? The government ordered the revolutionary committee to disband. The committee refused. Confident that the justice of its demands would soon spread revolt all over the country, the committee also refused to fight, except in self-defense.

EFFICIENT RELIEF FOR HUNGRY PEOPLE

An American Relief Administration truck stands near a supply center in Russia. The ARA brought in over 700,000 tons of relief goods during Communism's most crucial period and helped millions of Russians, some of whom are shown below at an American health and food center in Petrograd.

A Retreat from Communism. Perhaps there would have been a widespread rebellion if the Communist 10th Party Congress, which began meeting on March 8, 1921, had not taken quick action to placate both workers and peasants. Under Lenin's guidance it voted some measures to retreat partially from Communism and to restore some aspects of capitalist-style free trade. The sudden about-face came to be known as the New Economic Policy (NEP).

But allowing some individual enterprise to exist did not mean surrendering Communist power or permitting the rebels of Kronstadt to escape reprisals. War Commissar Trotsky sent the Red Army under Tukhachevsky to storm the fortress of Kronstadt. Some regiments of Red soldiers were reluctant to fire on fellow Russians, and many of the soldiers had to be driven at gun point to attack the rebels. After Kronstadt fell on March 17, hundreds, perhaps thousands, of the rebels—Communist and non-Communist alike—were executed in merciless retribution for daring to question the justice of the Communist dictatorship.

Lenin was willing to kill even Communists to keep the power he thought essential to transform the old social order and to improve the country's backward economy. "Communism," he said, "is the Soviet government plus the electrification of the whole country." In his grim view, the grand goal was worth the cost in blood.

The End of Toleration. One reason Lenin had turned his back on the Mensheviks was that they contended Marx's analysis called for capitalism to precede socialism. Now that disaster had come, Lenin seemed to be moving in the direction of the Menshevik position with his economic reforms. One might think this would logically lead to inviting the Mensheviks in to help run the program. Not so. That would mean sharing power. Lenin gave his answer, cold and ruthless: "When the Menshevik says, 'You are now retreating! I was always in favor of retreat, I agree with you, let us retreat together,' we say in reply: 'Permit us to put you up against the wall for saying that.'" Which is what he did. The Mensheviks and Socialist Revolutionaries, who had been tolerated during the civil war, were now imprisoned, shot or exiled.

The Fight for Power inside the Party

LENIN: A MAN WITHOUT VANITY

"No dictator in history was less vain," David Shub wrote of Lenin. "On his 50th birthday he refused to listen to the eulogizing speeches. . . .

"The fulsome praise constantly heaped on him by the Soviet newspapers disturbed him even more. . . . 'I consider this completely un-Marxist emphasis on an individual extremely harmful,' he told a deputy."

Lenin's friend, author Maxim Gorky, said: "He could with equal enthusiasm play chess, study . . . the *History of Dress,* debate . . . with his comrades, fish, walk along the stony paths . . . admire the golden colors of the furze bush and the dirty children of the fishermen. . . . He enjoyed fun, and when he laughed, his whole body shook . . . ."

But Lenin could reduce ideas to merciless formulas: "Whoever is not with us is against us. . . . Everything is moral which is necessary for the annihilation of the old exploiting social order. . . . We do not believe in external principles of morality."

It was not long before the party's leaders began fighting each other for power. The rivalries and disputes of the party leaders were kept within peaceful bounds as long as Lenin could decide them. He was the unquestioned leader whose word was revered. All stood in awe of him. Moreover, Lenin did not exact revenge from his colleagues when they disagreed with him. He held no petty grudges, and he made them abandon their own. He believed that they could work together selflessly for the party—so long as he was the supreme leader who directed everything.

In 1922, however, when Lenin suffered a stroke, the rivalries among his lieutenants began to come into the open. He had some partial recoveries, but he never really fully regained his health. The most important question for his lieutenants now became, as the Russians say, *"kto-kovo?"* (who does what to whom?).

Who Would Succeed Lenin? At that time, Stalin still seemed most unlikely to emerge on top. He had been ever-present but inconspicuous in the party—a sort of "gray blur," as he was once described. Stalin was always on hand, always brave and dependable, but never a leading orator or Marxist theoretician. He was more the silent listener and the quiet doer in the party, while the dynamic giants—Lenin, Trotsky, Kamenev—captured the public eye.

Throughout the civil war all these men—including Stalin—had shared power with Lenin as members of the all-powerful Political Bureau, or "Politburo," of the party. Stalin was the Politburo's liaison with the highly important Organization Bureau, or "Orgburo," which handled party personnel. Later, as general secretary of the party, Stalin had closer day-to-day touch with all its affairs than other Politburo members. But the crucial importance of the general secretary's job was not completely evident as long as Lenin overshadowed everything and everybody.

After Lenin became ill, Stalin's job clearly became more important. He supplied the agenda for each session of the Politburo. He transmitted its decisions to the lower bureaus. He was in daily contact with the thousands of party workers in the capital and provinces. He was responsible for their appointments, promotions and demotions. His years of devoted fulfillment of thankless party tasks were finally giving him a path to power.

Stalin's Boyhood and Early Life. Stalin's connection with the

Bolsheviks went back a long time. He had become a disciple of Lenin as early as 1904.

Stalin, born Joseph Djugashvili, was the son of a shoemaker, who himself had been born a slave under serfdom. As a boy, in the province of Georgia, Stalin was a star pupil of his local school, the acknowledged leader of all his classmates for his agility and daring. At 14, Stalin entered the Tiflis Theological Seminary on a scholarship. His extraordinary memory—he learned his lessons almost without effort—encouraged the monks who taught him to think he might become an outstanding priest of the Russian Orthodox Church. But in five years at the seminary he became interested in the nationalist movement in his native province, in Darwin's theories and in Victor Hugo's writings on the French Revolution. As a nationalist he was anti-Tsarist and joined a secret socialist society.

Stalin was also one of the best debaters in the seminary, but he became fretful whenever his arguments were effectively challenged. He nursed grudges and took revenge by spreading gossip and slander—habits which stayed with him all his life. He resented the searches the monks made of students' rooms and was marked down as "generally disrespectful and rude towards persons in authority."

Expelled in his fifth year at the seminary, Stalin soon began working in the socialist underground. He was helping write and distribute illegal leaflets when he was arrested in 1902. Deported to Siberia in 1903, he escaped and a few months later joined the Bolsheviks in time to take part in the revolts of 1905.

In 1912, Lenin put Stalin on the Bolsheviks' Central Committee and also made him one of four members of the bureau which ran the Bolshevik party's affairs inside Russia during Lenin's long exile. He began to use the somewhat theatrical pseudonym of Stalin, meaning "made of steel." In 1913 he was betrayed by a Tsarist secret police agent who was on the Bolshevik party Central Committee and whom Lenin trusted. Friends tried to spirit Stalin to safety dressed as a woman, but the police caught him again and exiled him to Siberia for four years.

This time he got out only when the Revolution in March 1917 effected an amnesty for many political prisoners. He reached Petrograd and was editing *Pravda* when Lenin came home from abroad.

Stalin's Rivals. Easily the most outstanding of Lenin's lieutenants on the mighty Politburo was Lev Davidovich Bronstein, known as Leon Trotsky ever since he forged a jailer's name to his passport. He had caught Lenin's notice as a contributor to *Iskra* as early as 1902. Before that he had been living in Siberia, where he had been exiled as an underground revolutionist. He became known to Socialists the world over as leader of the St. Petersburg Soviet in the violent strikes of 1905, when Stalin was still an unknown. True, he had voted against Lenin's Bolshevik "majority" in 1903 and opposed

STALIN:
RULED BY VANITY

Stalin "was a man dominated . . . by an insatiable vanity and love of power, coupled with the keenest sort of sense of his own inferiority and a . . . jealousy for qualities in others which he did not possess. He had . . . an inordinate touchiness, an endless vindictiveness, an inability ever to forget an insult or a slight, but great patience and power of dissimulation in selecting and preparing the moment to settle the score. . . . At the same time . . . he was a man with the most extraordinary talent for political tactics and intrigue, a consummate actor, a dissimulator of genius, a master not only of timing but of . . . the art of 'dosage'—of doing things gradually . . . a master, in particular, of the art of playing people and forces off against each other, for his own benefit. . . .

"This was a man of incredible criminality . . . a man in whose entourage no one was ever safe; a man whose hand was set against all that could not be useful to him at the moment."

—George F. Kennan
Russia and the West under Lenin and Stalin

that dictatorial faction of the Social Democrats for 14 years thereafter. But he had come over to the Bolsheviks in the summer of 1917 and had led the October uprising. He had created the powerful Red Army out of an undisciplined mob and led it to victory in the civil war. His name was known the world over.

There were other important Communists who formed the party's inner circle. Lev Kamenev, Trotsky's brother-in-law and the man who helped recruit Stalin as a Bolshevik, had taken Stalin's place as editor of *Pravda*. He later became boss of the Moscow Soviet. Grigory Zinoviev, leader of the Petrograd Soviet, had served with Lenin (as had Kamenev) on the editorial board of the *Social Democrat,* a leading Marxist journal, in 1909. Zinoviev and Kamenev, Lenin's closest comrades before 1917, had opposed the October Revolution, but Lenin forgave them.

Finally came two younger men: Mikhail Tomsky, the leader of the trade unions, and Nikolai Bukharin, a brilliant economic theorist.

Like Trotsky, both Kamenev and Zinoviev were better known than Stalin. Together with Trotsky they could have ousted Stalin from the Politburo and sent him into obscurity. Instead, they joined with Stalin to block Trotsky, whom they feared most because his military exploits made him a possible Napoleon.

A Conspiracy against Trotsky. As Lenin lay dying in 1923,

From Scholarly Piety to Godless Power

AS A RELIGIOUS SCHOLAR, young Stalin *(top center)* is pictured with fellow students and instructors of the church school in Gori, his home town. In 1894 he went to a theological seminary on a scholarship but was expelled in 1899.

AS A CONVICT sentenced to exile for his political activities, a youthful Joseph Stalin is shown in profile and front view

Kamenev, Zinoviev and Stalin formed a conspiracy against Trotsky.

What provoked the showdown with Trotsky in 1923 was a sudden outbreak of strikes and Trotsky's open letter criticizing "the bureaucratic degeneration of the party leadership." Russia had been recovering under the New Economic Policy and its restricted "capitalism," but heavy industry was still crippled. Hundreds of thousands of workers were unemployed. Low wages and hunger drove the proletariat to despair.

Even Communists began demanding more freedom of discussion, more democratic procedures in the party. Trotsky led the cry. He demanded the removal from party positions of "those who at the first voice of criticism, of objection, of protest, are inclined to demand one's party ticket for the purpose of repression."

Zinoviev proposed that Trotsky should be arrested. But Stalin would not agree to this suggestion. Then, as later, he gave the impression of being the most moderate and peace-minded member of the Politburo. He called a national conference—made up almost entirely of his own appointed local officials—to meet in January 1924 to consider this controversy.

During a meeting at the end of December, Stalin lashed out—not at Trotsky directly—but at extreme "democrats" of the opposition. He reminded them of Lenin's rule banning "factions"—opposition

on his 1910 police dossier. His long record included not only inciting strikes and uprisings but also highway robbery.

AS A RISING COMMUNIST LEADER, Stalin visits Lenin at his home in 1922, the year in which Lenin suffered two strokes and had to give up much of his power. Shortly before Lenin's illness, Stalin had become the party secretary.

groupings—inside the party. Did they want Lenin's rule abolished? Having endorsed the rule originally, Trotsky could not now change his position. He was driven to the defensive.

Stalin ended the January conference with a great democratic show. He proclaimed a "Leninist call-up" of 200,000 workers "from the [factory] bench" to join the Communist party and considerably enlarge the "proletarian spirit." Then he revealed a previously unpublicized rule of Lenin's which authorized the Central Committee to *expel its own members* for creating "factions." He asked to have it reaffirmed.

The conference thundered its approval of all of Stalin's proposals. He had hardly mentioned Trotsky. But he had cut the ground entirely out from under him.

Lenin's Startling Will. Three days later, Lenin died. Trotsky, who was ill and had gone off for a rest, failed to come to the funeral. He claimed later that Stalin wired him the wrong date. But Stalin was there, from start to finish. He stood in the guard of honor at Lenin's coffin and helped carry it into the improvised crypt which became Lenin's tomb. And it was Stalin who addressed the memorial meeting next day.

Four months later, Lenin's widow forwarded to the Central Committee Lenin's so-called "testament." It included the startling request that Stalin be removed from his post of general secretary.

> Comrade Stalin, having become General Secretary, has concentrated enormous power in his hand, and I am not sure that he always knows how to use that power with sufficient caution. . . . Stalin is excessively rude, and this defect, which can be freely tolerated in our midst and in contacts among us Communists, becomes a defect which cannot be tolerated in one holding the position of the General Secretary. Because of this, I propose that the comrades consider the method by which Stalin would be removed from this position and by which another man would be selected for it, a man who, above all, would differ from Stalin in only one quality, namely, greater tolerance, greater loyalty, greater kindness and a more considerate attitude toward the comrades, a less capricious temper, etc.

Instead of following Lenin's instructions, however, Stalin's colleagues kept him in the job. It was Zinoviev who made this possible by saying: "Comrades, every word of Lenin is law to us. . . . We have sworn to carry out his every behest. . . . But we are happy to say that in one point Lenin's fears have proved groundless . . . the point about the General Secretary. You have all witnessed our harmonious cooperation in the last few months. . . . Lenin's fears have proved without foundation." Kamenev echoed this sentiment. The Central Committee decided to suppress Lenin's testament. It was not officially made public in the Soviet Union until 1956.

Now Stalin was strong enough to keep the whole Communist party from heeding the gravest warnings Lenin had wished to give it.

A COMMUNIST'S LITANY

In his funeral oration for Lenin, Stalin used terms that smacked of his years at theological school. The speech sounds like a litany:

"Comrades, we Communists . . . have been cut out of peculiar stuff. . . . There is no loftier title. . . .

"In leaving us, Comrade Lenin ordained us to hold high and keep pure the . . . title of member of the party. We vow to thee, Comrade Lenin, that we shall honorably fulfill this thy commandment. . . .

"In leaving us, Comrade Lenin ordained us to guard the unity of our party. . . . We vow to thee, Comrade Lenin, that we shall fulfill honorably this thy commandment, too. . . .

"In leaving us, Comrade Lenin ordained us to guard and strengthen the dictatorship of the proletariat. We vow to thee, Comrade Lenin, that . . . we shall honorably fulfill this thy commandment, too. . . .

"In leaving us, Comrade Lenin ordained us to strengthen with all our might the alliance of workers and peasants. We vow to thee, Comrade Lenin, that we shall fulfill honorably this thy commandment."

What was Stalin like? Isaac Deutscher, a historian who lived in Poland for 32 years before emigrating to Britain, has described him:

> What was striking in the General Secretary was that there was nothing striking about him. . . . His bearing seemed of the utmost modesty. . . . He was more accessible to the average official or party man than the other leaders. He studiously cultivated his contacts with the people who in one way or another made and unmade reputations, provincial secretaries, popular satirical writers and foreign visitors. Himself taciturn, he was unsurpassed at the art of patiently listening to others. Sometimes he would be seen in a corner of a staircase pulling at his pipe and listening, immovably, for an hour or two, to an agitated interlocutor and breaking his silence only to ask a few questions. . . .

Stalin Eliminates His Co-Conspirators. Once, when Trotsky and Zinoviev threatened to resign over an argument, Stalin told them: "The party could not possibly dispense with the services of two such important and beloved leaders." Stalin would ultimately dispense with them both. But he let them knock out each other first.

Though the contest between Trotsky and the other three was actually a struggle for power, it was waged around a question of policy. Trotsky argued that socialism could not be established with any lasting success as an isolated phenomenon in one country alone. Therefore, he reasoned, the Communists had to work for a world revolution. Stalin, however, was convinced that "socialism in one country" was feasible and that it was important first to secure Communism at home before attempting worldwide revolt. Stalin began to sway the Politburo to his view.

Within a year of Lenin's death, Stalin, Zinoviev and Kamenev forced Trotsky to resign as war commissar. In 1926 Stalin forced him off the Politburo and later into exile, first in the U.S.S.R. and Europe, and finally in Mexico. There, in 1940, hunted down by a Stalinist agent, Trotsky was bludgeoned to death with a pickax.

After dealing with Trotsky, Stalin then turned his full attention to getting rid of Kamenev and Zinoviev. He resurrected Trotsky's charge against them—that they had opposed the Bolshevik Revolution—and saw that it was well aired. He attacked them as "left-wingers" for their attitude towards the New Economic Policy. In the end he joined with the "right-wingers"—Tomsky, Rykov and Bukharin—to expel them from the Politburo, then from the party.

When Stalin had got rid of the "left-wingers" he put trusted men of his own on the Politburo, then got rid of Tomsky and Bukharin.

CREATOR OF THE RED ARMY

War commissar Leon Trotsky is shown in 1924. He had created the Red Army and led it to victory. Considered a leading possibility to succeed Lenin, Trotsky lost to Stalin, who later had him assassinated.

The "Good" Years of NEP

During the seven years from 1921 to 1928—the period of the New Economic Policy—the Soviet Union knew peace and increasing prosperity. Allowed to trade freely, the peasants planted and harvested

MARCHING TO THE FIELDS, Soviet peasants smile for this propaganda picture. But brutally enforced farm collectivization from 1929 on was anything but pleasant. Peasants fought with guns and pitchforks, slaughtered cows and horses, and left the land untilled rather than submit. For this, five million were annihilated or exiled.

so effectively that food production quickly came back up to prewar levels. Small businesses were allowed to flourish in private hands, and foreign capitalists were even brought in to run state "trusts." It was a limited kind of capitalism, watched over by Communist overseers who for the most part kept hands off.

The system had its critics. Before his expulsion, Trotsky, for one, thought that the trend towards capitalism was a betrayal of Lenin's hopes for quick industrialization. Trotsky drew up a Five-Year Plan to show how a shift could be made from NEP to a forced-draft build-up of heavy industry. Stalin mockingly denounced this scheme as "superindustrialization."

With Trotsky, Kamenev and Zinoviev gone, Stalin felt free to change course and set up a Five-Year Plan of his own for industrialization. It began in 1928 as a tremendous program to convert the backward Soviet Union into a major industrial power in a decade, and to turn the land farmed by peasants under private ownership into collective farms which would be "great factories of grain." The reason for the farm program was twofold: (1) to provide food for the industrial workers in the cities; (2) to provide exports which would bring in capital to help finance the build-up of industrial power.

What the Five-Year Plan really became was a new war—against

COLLECTIVIZED WORKERS eat a drab meal at a state-owned factory. As part of the industrial speed-up of the first Five-Year Plan, labor had to work where the party ordered. Determined to close the U.S.S.R.'s 50-to-100-year gap "behind the advanced countries," Stalin used the harshest regimentation to expand production.

the Russian people. It would kill millions upon millions of them. Even those who sympathized with Stalin's desire to lift the Soviet Union by its bootstraps in this tremendous program could never understand why he deliberately decided to make his methods so bloody and violent.

A Man-Made Famine. The peasants, particularly the relatively well-to-do *kulaks,* resisted the orders to merge their holdings into collectives, whereupon Stalin applied force against them.

The local Communist party leaders were ordered to "apply all necessary measures in the struggle against the *kulaks,* including total confiscation of their property and their banishment [to Siberia]." To make sure they did their job well, 25,000 trusted party workers were sent into the countryside to "help out." They may have even gone further than Stalin intended in their zeal to show how ruthless they could be. Poor peasants as well as *kulaks* were arrested out of hand and packed off to exile. Within nine months, 13 million peasant households had been forced, willy-nilly, into collectives—which meant in many cases the victims had simply been robbed of their property and herded together at gun point by the party brigades. The result was a total disintegration of the peasant economy and the onset of a man-made famine. Over five million people are believed to have starved to death. Another five million peasants were herded into exile or simply exterminated.

The peasants fought back with guns and pitchforks. Whole regions rose up and began guerrilla warfare. The Red Army surrounded villages and attacked them with tanks, artillery and bombers, or laid them waste by burning them. "Districts were stripped of their stocks of grain and seed, then cordoned off to die of famine and plague," writes historian Bertram D. Wolfe in a graphic account. "Lands, tools, animals were confiscated. . . . The entire independent peasantry . . . was destroyed or enserfed under the monstrous slogan of 'the liquidation of the *kulaks* as a class.'"

A HUMANE COLLECTIVIZER

The mystery of Stalin's incredible cruelty in collectivizing agriculture is only deepened by the following story. "His name was Betal Kalmykov . . ." recounted Maurice Hindus in *House without a Roof*. "He told me that during the collectivization campaign he had always assured the peasants, which Stalin's agents rarely did, that they would be allowed, in private ownership, their gardens and orchards, a cow and calf, a sow, six head of sheep, and all their fowl. . . . He gave [the kulaks] the choice of remaining in their homes with gardens and orchards of their own . . . or suffering confiscation of all their property and banishment in the North. Naturally they chose the lesser punishment.

"Betal Kalmykov was acclaimed as the most successful collectivizer in the country—the 'Peter the Great' of his region. He was idolized in the press, and a never-ending stream of journalists and authors . . . wrote glowing tributes to his person and his leadership.

"In 1938 Stalin executed him."

Forced Labor in the Factories. In the parallel campaign to industrialize the U.S.S.R., the workers suffered almost as severely as the peasants. Wolfe describes what it involved: "The highest sales tax in human history, forced loans . . . export of needed foodstuffs to buy machines and technicians; change of diet from meat, milk, fats to bread, and even that scarce and rationed . . . decreeing of imprisonment and the death penalty for stealing state property, for 'wrecking' and other industrial crimes."

As the shortages in all important foods grew more stringent, rationing got tighter and tighter. The privilege of eating in the commissaries and restaurants operated by factories and shops became increasingly important. Since discharge from a job meant loss of this privilege, the implicit threat undoubtedly had a strong influence in forcing men to work harder and harder. Forced labor was introduced, and squads of police roamed the cities rounding up men for national construction projects. All over Russia the suffering was so great that Stalin's own wife denounced it at a gathering of leading Communists. Later that night, in their suite in the Kremlin, she shot herself in despair.

Looking back over this terror, students of history have wondered how Stalin possibly could have waged this merciless war upon the whole Russian people without himself being destroyed in the process. One reason was that the Red Army was generally pampered throughout it all. The troops were well fed and new recruits were attracted by the prospects of swift promotions. Thus the army remained loyal to Stalin.

Not so the Communist party. Mutterings against Stalin began to grow. The secret police uncovered so many small plots to remove or overthrow Stalin that he asked the Central Committee for authority summarily to execute Communists as well as ordinary Russians. It refused to give him that authority.

In December 1934, a prominent Communist was killed, and this event set off an endless and ever-spreading blood bath. During the following years Stalin killed more Communists than the Tsars had ever even arrested. There was only one thing more dangerous than being a Communist in Communist Russia during those days. That was to be an *important* Communist.

Stalin's Great Purges

The Communist whose death set off the purges was Sergei Kirov, chief of the Communist party in Leningrad (formerly Petrograd). On the afternoon of December 1, 1934, he was shot to death in his office in the Smolny Institute. The assassin was Leonid V. Nikolaev, a young party member and former government worker who had been dismissed from the Leningrad party organization.

Why Was Kirov Killed? The events surrounding this murder are so mysterious that as late as 1961, Soviet Premier Khrushchev reported that a new investigation was being made to get to the bottom of it. The Leningrad NKVD, as the secret police was then called, knew that Nikolaev was plotting to kill Kirov. They had stopped him, found a gun in his briefcase and a diary allegedly stating his intention. Yet they gave him back the gun—and released him! When Nikolaev came to Smolny on that fateful December 1, the NKVD guards were curiously absent, except for Kirov's own bodyguard, Borisov. And Borisov was killed in an automobile accident the next day. In making these details public years later, Khrushchev said the automobile was deliberately driven into a building. Presumably Borisov was killed because he knew too much.

There is much to suggest that Stalin himself may have arranged Kirov's murder. Kirov had been urging a "relaxation" of the party purges during which Stalin had expelled 700,000 members (out of 2.7 million) the year before. In any event, the death of the Leningrad chieftain was to be useful to Stalin. He rushed to Leningrad to lead the mourning.

That same night Stalin got the Central Executive Committee to issue an extraordinary decree which gave him at last the total powers he had sought. He now got the full authorization of the Politburo to execute any "terrorist" without the right of appeal. This literally gave him the power to execute almost anybody he chose. This he soon began to do.

The Show Trials. He struck first at Zinoviev and Kamenev, arresting them on December 16, 1934, with 13 other "members of the former Zinoviev group." At first they were merely sent to prison, after Zinoviev obligingly took the "responsibility" for the murder of Kirov. In August 1936, Zinoviev and Kamenev were brought back for a second, and this time public, trial. With 14 other defendants they confessed to the most outrageous and murderous plotting, spying and treason. The trial was a worldwide sensation and created controversy that has not yet died out. Could the confessions have been true? If not, why would men calmly make them in public without

A BIG LAUGH IN THE KREMLIN

The God That Failed is a report by a group of honorable and sensitive men who were briefly attracted to Communism, then turned away from the party in disgust and revulsion.

One of the authors, Italian writer Ignazio Silone, tells about a Kremlin meeting in which a British delegate asked what the British Communist party could do about a Trade Union Congress decree ordering its local groups not to support Communist-led factions. A Russian answered: Pretend to comply with their decree while secretly violating it. "But that would be a lie!" cried the Englishman. The other delegates broke into uproarious laughter. When Stalin was told the story, he too laughed at this naïve man who thought decency and integrity had a place in the Communist movement.

any indication of having been forced to fabricate the confessions?

Khrushchev has since revealed part of the reason: The prisoners had been tortured, and promises had been made to some to spare their families if they admitted to preposterous crimes. *Moreover, only those who confessed saw a courtroom—the others were simply shot.*

The real defendant was absent. It was the exiled Trotsky. Charges were made that Zinoviev and the others had sought to betray the Soviet Union to Nazi Germany. The true aim of the charges was to destroy Trotsky's reputation. To link the "plotters" up with Trotsky, the prosecutor, Andrei Vyshinsky, introduced "facts" that have since, outside the U.S.S.R., been shown to be utterly false. For example: A supposed meeting with Trotsky took place in a Copenhagen hotel which had in fact been demolished years before; a foreign airplane supposedly arrived at a Norwegian field whose records showed that no such plane had landed at that time, and so on. Yet all the defendants were shot.

Within two days of the trial, *Pravda* was demanding that this group's "connections" with Bukharin, Tomsky, and other old friends and disciples of Lenin be "investigated." Tomsky killed himself. Stalin announced that "charges would not be pressed" against Bukharin and Rykov—but they both were shot within two years.

Stalin's "Democratic" Constitution. In the middle of the purges, a new constitution for the Soviet Union was promulgated in 1936. (Ironically, Bukharin drafted much of it before Stalin had him shot.) This Constitution caused many Soviet sympathizers in the United States and elsewhere to conclude that Stalin was really a "democrat" at heart. After all, on the surface the document guaranteed free speech, free press, free elections, freedom of religion, public trials by

REVOLT IN HUNGARY brings volunteer marchers into Budapest streets in 1919. But Communist Béla Kun was overthrown when he tried to keep huge manors intact as state farms instead of dividing them among land-hungry peasants. Lenin's hopes for immediate world revolution died when Hungarian and German revolts failed.

jury—nearly all of the treasured protections guaranteed to Americans by the Bill of Rights. The favorable stir created by its preachments helped cover up the fact that Stalin, in actual practice, was shooting one of the Constitution's authors by dictatorial decree.

Stalin summoned the 17th Party Congress to meet in 1934 as the "Congress of the Victors." The "victory" referred to the impressive strides in industrialization which the first of the Five-Year Plans had achieved. But this triumphant meeting was soon followed by a wave of purges of officials high and low who were accused of the most shocking crimes, including espionage. Marshal Tukhachevsky, chief of staff of the Red Army, and seven high officers were executed, supposedly because they were agents of Germany and Japan.

These revelations did not make democratic countries in the '30s rate the U.S.S.R. very highly as a possible ally against the rising tide of Nazi aggression. They seemed to prove one of two things: Either Stalin's regime was the most corrupt in all history because it had produced such an incredible number of traitors in high places; or else it was the most corrupt regime in all history because it had murdered such an incredible number of innocent and loyal servants.

The facts, so far as they are known, seem to bear out the second conclusion. In the war with Hitler, the Allies captured vast numbers of German secret records, but nothing pertaining to Red Army officers in German pay.

The Purge Widens. Once Stalin embarked on this campaign of slaughter, he was apparently compelled to make it ever bigger and wider. Each slain man had friends and relatives who loved and trusted him, each executed general had the loyalty of companion officers whom he had sponsored. After the chiefs were liquidated, the sub-

IN GERMANY, Communists in Berlin engage in vicious street fighting in an abortive attempt to gain control of the city during January 1919. In Munich, Communists actually succeeded in establishing a Soviet state but the new government was soon overthrown. Its leaders were executed by regular troops of the German army.

ordinates had to be slain, after the subordinates, *their* subordinates.

There was some method to all this madness. After Stalin had decided to industrialize and collectivize swiftly and forcibly, a repressive police apparatus became a necessity. After men were set to spy on and betray one another, it was only a matter of time before the punishment of genuine laggards, or "wreckers," would veer over into the denunciation and arrest of mere bystanders. Moreover, by repeatedly purging even the most loyal Stalinists, Stalin set his own henchmen trying to outdo one another in order to survive and in this cruel way he brought new talent to the top.

TWO GENERATIONS OF CHINESE LEADERS

The George Washington of modern China, Sun Yat-sen *(seated above)*, is shown with his disciple and successor, the then youthful Chiang Kai-shek. Dr. Sun had high hopes for the Russian Revolution and sent a congratulatory cable when Lenin seized power. Chiang, Sun's heir apparent, was sent to Moscow for military and political training. But in 1927, after Dr. Sun's death, Chiang turned on the Communists and thereafter fought them.

The Communist Party and the World Outside Russia

What had happened to Communism's goal of world revolution? Lenin had never believed that Communism could long survive if its power were confined to Russia. When World War I ended in 1918, Lenin was sure that defeated Germany would be the next to succumb to revolution and thus fulfill the Marxian prediction, and a long-held tenet of socialist faith, that highly industrialized Germany would be the *first* country to adopt a Marxist government. Indeed, revolution did break out in Germany amid the post-armistice chaos. Communist governments even triumphed briefly in Bavaria and also in Hungary. But both these regimes quickly fell.

In 1919 Lenin established the Comintern (short for Communist International) in Moscow to maintain liaison with Communist parties overseas and direct them to follow Russia's lead. In 1922 a new name, the "Union of Soviet Socialist Republics," was adopted. It no longer included the word "Russian," so that any foreign country which might go Communist could join it. But it became clear that Lenin's lonely Communist outpost would get no help from kindred revolutions anywhere in Europe. The Comintern met in Moscow to work hopefully for world revolution, but Stalin was already organizing on the basis of "socialism in one country"—meaning that Russian Communism had to build a firm foundation at home before it could expand abroad. He began placing more emphasis on developing trade with western governments through normal diplomatic channels, rather than on attempting to overthrow those governments through their own local Communist groups.

In the United States the tiny United States Communist party was attractive chiefly to the so-called "Wobblies," members of the old anarchistic Industrial Workers of the World, whose traditions of bomb-throwing and other violence resembled the Bolsheviks' own. "Big Bill" Haywood, leader of the Wobblies, fled to the Soviet Union to avoid imprisonment for sedition, and when he died he was buried next to one of the walls of the Kremlin.

Communism in Asia. It was not in the highly industrial West, but rather in feudal Asia that Russian Communism made its first major impact. Sun Yat-sen, the leader of China's own national revolution, which deposed the monarchy, had sent a congratulatory telegram to Lenin in 1917 on his seizure of power. For their part, the Russians issued a manifesto to the Chinese people solemnly renouncing former Tsarist claims to Chinese territories and property. Hundreds of Chinese students arrived in Moscow to study, among them in 1923, Chiang Kai-shek, Sun's military adviser. At Sun's request, the Russians sent political and military advisers to China. A Chinese Communist party was founded in 1921 by 12 men, including a 27-year-old teacher named Mao Tse-tung.

The Soviet Union pursued a policy of collaboration with nationalist Chinese forces. Chinese Communists were ordered to co-operate with Sun's nationalist movement, the Kuomintang, or Peoples' Party, and—after his death in 1925—with Generalissimo Chiang, who became the Kuomintang strong man. But in 1927 Chiang broke with the Chinese Communists and smashed them in showdown street battles in Shanghai. Mao then formed a Communist army that continued to fight Chiang's forces, except for an uneasy truce period when both armies fought the Japanese during World War II.

Secret Collaboration with Germany. In 1922, during an international economic conference at Genoa, Germany and the U.S.S.R. were treated like stepchildren by the other powers. The Soviet and German ministers responded by going off to nearby Rapallo and signing a treaty for trade and cooperation. As a consequence, Soviet-German relations, which had been improving, became even closer. While some German officers were already being secretly trained by the Red Army, their numbers were to be increased. War materials, which Germany was forbidden to make under the Versailles Peace Treaty, were now made in the Soviet Union by the Germans. From Germany the Soviets got technical advisers and industrial plants.

Stalin Underestimates Hitler. Despite all his foreign activities, Stalin kept his main attention throughout the early 1930s on building "socialism in one country." In fact, when Hitler first threatened to take power in Germany in 1932, Stalin badly underestimated the nature of the threat. The Communist party by then was a strong political force in Germany and—if it had collaborated with the Marxist but non-Communist Social Democrats—it could have kept Hitler out of power. But Stalin, emulating Lenin's 1917 refusal to collaborate with Mensheviks or Socialist Revolutionaries, ordered the German party to stay out of coalitions. He thought Nazism would create a chaotic situation in Germany and thus foster ideal conditions for a Communist revolution. As a result of his decision, the Communists actually helped Hitler to succeed.

Hitler immediately set about killing and imprisoning Communists until they were destroyed as an effective force in Germany. Only

CHALLENGER OF MOSCOW'S AUTHORITY

Communist China's chief, Mao Tse-tung, is one of the 12 founders of the Chinese Communist party. At first he opposed affiliating his party with the Communist International dominated by Lenin. This heresy proved prophetic, because in later life he has become the chief Communist thorn in the side of international Communism's present leader, Nikita Khrushchev.

after Hitler began to rearm Germany and proclaim his intention to destroy Bolshevism did Stalin come to realize that Nazism was his greatest single enemy. Then the order went out to the world's Communist parties to form "popular fronts" with all anti-Nazi and anti-Fascist forces for the purpose of "defeating Fascist aggression." A typical "popular front" group which sprang up in the United States at that time was called "The American League Against War and Fascism." Organized and run mostly by secret Communists, it nevertheless succeeded in enlisting wide support for such causes as boycotting German-made goods.

A TOTALITARIAN GET-TOGETHER

Wartime collaborators, Nazi leader Adolf Hitler and dictator Francisco Franco of Spain, meet in October of 1940. During the Spanish civil war, Hitler had sent airplanes to help Franco overthrow the democratic government of Spain. During World War II, Franco reciprocated by letting German submarines refuel in supposedly neutral Spanish ports. Franco also sent a division to take part in Hitler's invasion of the Soviet Union. But today Franco aids in the defense of the West by granting America military bases.

Communists and the United States Labor Movement. In 1933, when America accorded diplomatic recognition to the U.S.S.R., the Soviets were able to set up ambassadorial and consular offices to help direct other Communist fronts inside the United States.

This period, when America was struggling to come out of the Great Depression which had struck in 1929, made some Americans give credence to Marx's theory that capitalism was doomed. Thousands of banks had failed and millions of people had lost their savings. Farmers were being driven to the wall. More than 12 million men were unemployed by 1933. Aided by all this misery, Communist agitators could occasionally get a sympathetic hearing.

A new phenomenon, the "sit-down strike," arose, which, since it suggested seizure of private property, smacked of revolution. In Akron, Ohio, in 1936, rubber workers simply sat down inside the factories and refused to work or to leave until their demands were met. Detroit's auto workers soon did the same; even Woolworth clerks sat down in New York. These people were fighting for—and soon got—the right to form unions, which negotiated with their employers for better wages and working conditions.

The union victories were not gained easily. Many United States employers had fought unions, even to the extent of hiring their own private police to keep union organizers out of the factories. For a short time, during the sudden surge of unionizing in America, Communists gained an influence out of all proportion to their numbers because their training made them useful in teaching the newly organized workers how to gain a lot through the determined actions of a few.

John L. Lewis, president of the United Mine Workers, created the Committee for Industrial Organization to organize unions for the first time in all the mass-production industries, like automobile and steel. Lewis first set out to organize the steel industry. Communist veterans of labor strife volunteered and turned out to be the hardest workers. A Republican most of his life, John L. Lewis did not hide the fact that he used Communists to organize unions. He considered them useful but temporary tools for achieving a goal.

It was true that the Communists, by virtue of having organized

ATTACKING FRANCO'S FASCISTS, young Spaniards loyal to the republican government advance through Toledo. But Franco won, aided by quantities of military supplies from Italy and Germany and by the democracies' decision not to intervene. Soviet aid to the republic was relatively small and had vicious political results.

some of the unions, often rose to high office in them. As a general rule, however, they were not able to stay in power very long. The workers at first trusted the Communists because of what appeared to be their total dedication to the workers' own welfare in the bitter struggles of the organizing movement. But later, when the Communists began using their union offices to promote causes which the workers did not even understand, much less support, the motives of the Communists became so easily recognizable that all but a few were soon voted out of office.

The Rise of Fascism. A foreign event which, for a time, gave Communists increasing prestige and influence was the tragic Spanish civil war of 1936 to 1939. Spain, which had known little progress under monarchic rule for centuries, had become a republic in 1931. Five years later, left-wing parties gained control of the government. Their Popular Front included Communists, but the cabinet did not. Soon afterward, several army units led by General Francisco Franco rebelled and began fighting to overthrow the government.

Several of the great powers undertook to see that the Spanish civil war did not spread to the rest of Europe. To do so, they agreed

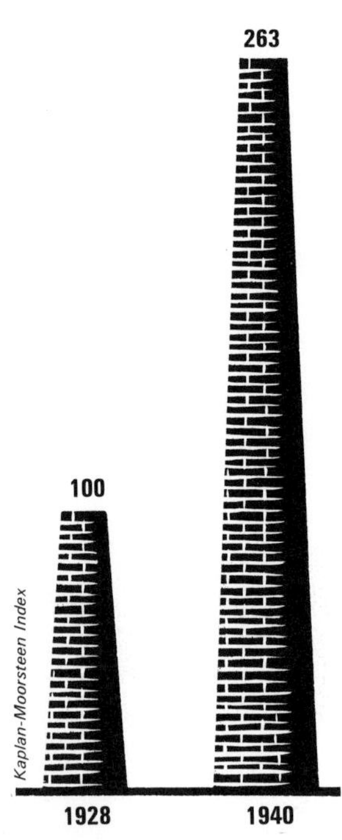

INDUSTRY'S SURGE UNDER STALIN

Total Soviet industrial production in 1940, as this diagram shows, was more than two and a half times what it had been in 1928. Enforced industrialization that took place in the U.S.S.R. during Stalin's various Five-Year Plans set a record pace —but at a vast cost in money, personal freedom and human life.

to an embargo on arms shipments or other aid to both belligerents. Accordingly, France, Britain and the United States effectively kept the Spanish republican government from securing arms aid. But Hitler and Mussolini, out of ideological sympathy for the rebels, blatantly circumvented the embargo. Italy sent tanks and over 100,000 troops to Franco. German planes and pilots, attacking Republican forces, destroyed the ancient Basque city of Guernica and badly damaged other cities and towns. Only Soviet Russia among the world's great powers sent aid to the Spanish republic. But in addition to sending arms, the U.S.S.R. was playing its own vicious political game in which the goal was a powerful Spanish Communist party strong enough to dominate the Loyalists. At a time when it seemed that democracies everywhere were cowering before Hitler's threats, the Soviet Union was applauded by many who thought that Fascist Germany was the greatest danger to humanity.

This feeling about Russia deepened during the Munich Conference of 1938, when Britain and France weakly abandoned Czechoslovakia to Hitler in the hope of "peace for our time." Stalin, however, had given the impression that he would fight with the Czechoslovaks against Hitler, and the Soviet Union at that point seemed to be the only nation encouraging a firm stand against Germany. Events would soon prove how little credit was deserved by the U.S.S.R., but the emotional climate of the late 1930s in many countries was anti-Fascist and pro-Soviet.

Stalin the Builder. Another reason for pro-Soviet feeling was Stalin's impressive achievements in lifting the U.S.S.R., in a single decade, to the first rank of great industrial powers. What his admirers did not know—or forgot—was *how* he did it. As we have seen, he did it literally with the blood of the Russian people.

He squeezed the capital needed for building industry out of regimented peasants and out of deprived industrial workers. A whole generation of Russian workers built blast furnaces while they could not buy so much as a razor blade or a safety pin. They paid huge taxes and the strength of their labor unions was utterly destroyed.

Stalin was inexorable in his drive for industrialization during the 1930s. He declared the U.S.S.R. must accomplish in 10 years what other nations had in 100, or be crushed. In that decade he shoved the Russian people forward overnight into the modern age at the cost of millions of lives. He reared a whole great system of new industry far beyond the Urals where invaders could never reach it. It was well he did, for Hitler would shortly launch a massive onslaught against him that would threaten the existence of the Soviet Union.

4 The Goal:

World Triumph of Communism

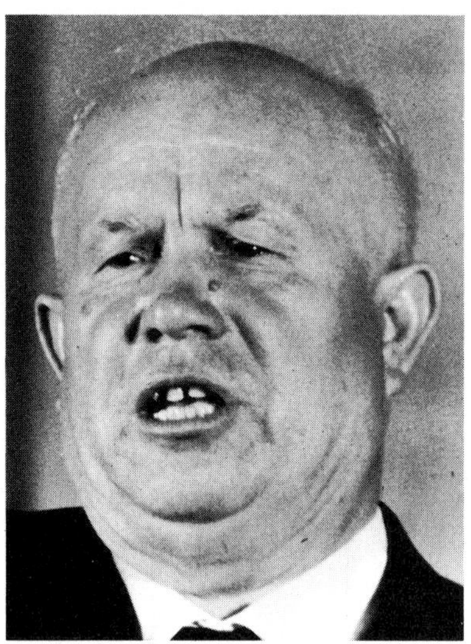

NIKITA KHRUSHCHEV

4 The Goal:

World Triumph of Communism

In the two decades following the outbreak of World War II in 1939, the Soviet Union emerged as an aggressive, expansionist powerhouse of Communism, bent on domination of the world. Seldom has there been a period filled with such earth-shaking events and upheavals, with so much triumph and tragedy.

This fateful era saw Stalin join with Hitler in the 1939 Soviet-German pact which helped unleash World War II. Two years later it saw Hitler betray Stalin and invade the Soviet Union. It saw the West's own attitude toward Communism seesaw from revulsion at the Soviet-German pact to blind admiration and friendship when the Russian people rose to throw back the German hordes. In 1941 it saw the treacherous attack on Pearl Harbor by the Japanese, which resulted in a grand alliance of the United States, Britain and the U.S.S.R. In 1945 it saw Adolf Hitler—and with him Nazi Germany—die in an underground shelter in blazing Berlin, and Japan's defeat completed by atomic bombs.

These crowded years also saw the beginning of the cold war when the U.S.S.R. turned against its allies of World War II and expanded its domination over eastern Europe. And countering this, the Free World finally united in a successful policy of resistance to further Communist expansion in Europe. But the period also saw Communism win China, then turn to open aggression against the West in Korea.

It saw Stalin's death in 1953, the struggle for power among his heirs which led to the ascendance of Nikita Khrushchev, and the startling revelation of Stalin's crimes—all of which set the stage for the valiant but vain struggle for freedom in East Berlin and in Hungary. It saw Communist science leap ahead in space by hurling the first satellite—and later the first man—into orbit. And it also saw Communist power overleap its immediate borders to threaten the peace in the Congo, to offer its arms and influence to Egypt and Algeria, to airlift arms and puppet troops to threaten Laos and South Vietnam in Southeast Asia. It saw world peace threatened over Berlin. It saw Khrushchev pursue his strategy of "wars of national-liberation"—insurrection by Communist-led guerrilla warriors. Finally, it saw the U.S.S.R. win a new base for Communist expansion on America's very doorstep, 90 miles away in Cuba.

The Stalin-Hitler Pact

Early in the morning of August 24, 1939, Joseph Stalin raised a glass to toast Joachim von Ribbentrop, foreign minister of Nazi Germany, who less than three years previously had signed an Anti-Comintern Pact that pledged Germany, Italy and Japan to a relentless fight against Communism, that is, against the U.S.S.R. Stalin, whom the world had regarded as Hitler's most determined enemy, toasted the Führer's health. Von Ribbentrop drank to Stalin's. In the course of that long night, the Nazis and the Communists had signed a secret protocol that ruthlessly divided the lands that lay between them and had agreed on a nonaggression pact. Von Ribbentrop had told a joke current in Berlin: "Stalin will yet join the Anti-Comintern Pact."

Stalin had done just about that. An Anglo-French mission was even then in Moscow hoping to align Stalin with the democracies. Stalin had been suspicious of Britain's intentions ever since Munich, which he had appraised as an attempt to turn Hitler's aggression against Russia. On August 22, 1939, Hitler had wired Stalin that "the tension [with] Poland has become intolerable . . . Germany is determined . . . to look after the interests of the Reich with all the means at its disposal." Stalin knew that meant war, and Hitler went to war with Poland on September 1, 1939, just eight days after the pact. Britain and France declared war on Germany in Poland's defense. World War II was on.

Hitler's Lightning War. Soon after Hitler took western Poland.

BITTER ENEMIES NOW BECOME BRIEF ALLIES

Stalin congratulates his ally, Foreign Minister Von Ribbentrop, in late September, 1939. A year later, in Nazi Germany, Von Ribbentrop assured visiting Soviet Foreign Minister Molotov that Britain was already defeated. During the discussions, a British air raid on Berlin forced the Nazis and Molotov into a shelter. Molotov asked, "If [England is finished] why are we in this shelter, and whose are these bombs which fall?" A month after he left, Hitler formally ordered preparation of Operation Barbarossa—the invasion of the Soviet Union.

Stalin took eastern Poland under the secret provision of the nonaggression pact with Germany. He also moved into neighboring Finland, ostensibly in order to make Leningrad and the Soviet Arctic more secure against possible attack. The Soviet army's performance against its vastly outnumbered Finnish opponent was miserable, but Finland finally capitulated after 105 days. Finland's brave struggle aroused so much sympathy that Britain and France were preparing to send troops to help. They could consider fighting both Hitler and Stalin because the land war in the west at that time was little more than skirmishing—the so-called "phony war." Then, in the spring of 1940, Hitler took Norway and Denmark with lightning swiftness. He smashed through the Low Countries, pushed the British into the sea at Dunkirk and forced France to its knees by June 1940.

Stalin now found himself facing a Hitler able to command continental Europe's tremendous resources and manpower. Stalin grabbed what he could while he could. He seized the tiny Baltic states of Estonia, Latvia and Lithuania. From Rumania he took Bessarabia and northern Bucovina, notifying Hitler only at the last moment. Hitler, on his part, alarmed Stalin by rearranging the borders of Rumania and Hungary with no notice to the U.S.S.R., and then moving German troops into Finland. When Stalin's Foreign Minister Vyacheslav Molotov bitterly protested these acts, von Ribbentrop invited him to Berlin to discuss a bigger deal with Hitler himself—dividing the whole world. The Nazi dictator spread before Molotov the alluring prospect of sharing the vast British Empire, but the U.S.S.R. was more concerned with getting the Balkans.

Hitler Turns on Stalin. On December 18, 1940, a month after Molotov left Berlin, Hitler sent out top secret orders to complete the preparations for an attack on the U.S.S.R. no later than May 15, 1941. As the troops began to gather, Winston Churchill, the British prime minister, warned Stalin that a German attack was imminent. But Stalin, stalling for time, faithfully continued to ship grain and oil to Germany to help in the war against England.

The Grand Alliance against Hitler

Then on June 22, 1941, Hitler struck. Within hours of the surprise attack, Churchill said that Britain would "give whatever help we can to the Russian people." Two days later, President Roosevelt announced that the United States, still at peace, would give all possible aid to the U.S.S.R. That December, after Pearl Harbor made the United States an ally of Russia and Britain, American soldiers on Bataan felt bound in a joint struggle with the Soviet soldiers who were dying in battle against a common enemy. General MacArthur later sent a cable paying tribute to "the courageous Russian army."

Courageous indeed the stand was. The Russian people fought with

FIGHTING FOR STALINGRAD in 1943, Russian soldiers advance through the smoking rubble to break the five-month German siege. This was a major turning point in the invasion of the Soviet Union and in World War II itself. As part of Khrushchev's program of downgrading Stalin, the city was renamed Volgograd in 1961.

incredible sacrifice and dauntless bravery, and the world hoped that the crimes and conspiracies of Communism were a thing of the past. Churchill voiced the general sentiment:

> I will unsay no word that I have spoken [against Communism]. But all this fades away before the spectacle which is now unfolding. The past, with its crimes, its follies and its tragedies, flashes away.

Leningrad was under German bombardment for 900 days, often at the mercy of a single perilous supply line. About one fifth of its 3.2 million people died—but the city would not surrender.

The Great Decision at Stalingrad. Even more inspiring was the battle of Stalingrad, the city on the Volga against which Hitler hurled division after division all through the fall of 1942. In the blackened shells of the buildings, remnants of Soviet divisions fought on, defending every ruin to the death. Germany threw some 350,000 troops into the onslaught but as winter came, Marshal Georgi Zhukov closed pincers around them north and south until the Nazis were surrounded and annihilated.

By January 1943, only 91,000 frozen, shell-shocked German survivors were left to surrender. This great battle marked the turn of the tide against the Nazis. At the conference of Allied chiefs at Teheran, Iran, in November 1943, Churchill presented a special Stalingrad Sword of Honour to Stalin, who lifted it and kissed it with reverence, while President Roosevelt, deeply moved, looked on. Such were the days and deeds that stirred men's blood.

The Teheran Conference was one of several discussions on strategy, war aims and post-war settlements. In May 1942, Stalin's Foreign Minister Molotov had gone to London, thence to the White House, to press for a "second front" in the west to draw German troops away from their campaign against the U.S.S.R. The United States promised a landing, but Stalin did not regard the invasion made that November 1942 in North Africa as a genuine second front. As time went on he voiced suspicion that the Allies were holding back to give Hitler free rein against the Soviet Union. The Communists welcomed the new landings in Italy in 1943, but still clamored for a "real" second front. At the meeting in Teheran in the fall of 1943, the Allies pledged that they would launch a major invasion of France. It came on June 6, 1944.

The Teheran Conference also discussed the question of what to do with Poland when the war was over. One formula proposed was that Poland's eastern border would follow the so-called Curzon Line discussed after World War I. This would allow the U.S.S.R. to keep most of the Polish territory seized in 1939; Poland presumably would be compensated with German territory. But the question of Polish freedom—for which Britain had gone to war in 1939—continued to trouble the grand alliance.

The Katyn Forest Murders. A Polish government-in-exile had been functioning in London since early in the war. It had insisted that Stalin divulge the whereabouts of over 10,000 Polish officers who had been captured by the Russians during their drive into Poland in 1939. Nothing had been heard from them since April 1940. In the spring of 1943, German troops occupying Smolensk found some 4,000 Polish officers buried in a mass grave in the nearby Katyn Forest. Charges and countercharges as to who was responsible for the deaths of the officers gave Stalin an excuse to cut off all relations with the exiled Polish government in London. One year later, as Soviet forces returned to eastern Poland, a Communist-sponsored Committee of National Liberation was formed as a provisional government of Poland.

In August 1944, the Polish underground army in Warsaw, loyal to the exiled government in London, rose to fight the retreating Germans. Russian troops, on the other side of the river, halted their advance and waited while the Germans slaughtered the Poles. The British tried to help the doomed underground army with air drops, but Stalin refused to cooperate in this supply task until it was too late.

When Churchill, Roosevelt and Stalin met again in February 1945 at Yalta, in Russia's Crimea, the western leaders got Stalin to agree to "free and unfettered elections" in Poland and to promise to broaden the provisional government by including Poles from the London group. The details were to be worked out by conferences in Moscow.

THE BETRAYAL OF HEROIC WARSAW

On July 29, 1944, Moscow Radio broadcast an appeal to the people of Warsaw to rise against the Germans, saying that liberation was near. After the Polish Underground began to fight on August 1, the Soviet radio went silent and so did the Soviet guns. Stalin kept his army idle until the Polish heroes were annihilated. One of Warsaw's last broadcasts said: "Your heroes are the soldiers whose only weapons against tanks, planes and guns were their revolvers and bottles filled with petrol. Your heroes are the women who tended the wounded and carried messages under fire, who cooked in bombed and ruined cellars to feed children and adults, and who soothed and comforted the dying. . . . These are the people of Warsaw. Immortal is the nation that can muster such universal heroism. For those who have died have conquered, and those who live on will fight on, will conquer and again bear witness that Poland lives when the Poles live." In their death struggle they cost the German army 10,000 killed, 7,000 missing, 9,000 wounded.

A Flood of Allied Aid

British tanks are loaded on a Russian merchant ship in late 1941. Though hard-pressed, the U.S. and Britain poured enormous quantities of supplies into the U.S.S.R. to help beat the Germans. U.S. aid alone totaled $11 billion.

A Fateful Meeting

Churchill, Roosevelt and Stalin meet in the Russian resort city of Yalta during February 1945 to discuss postwar policy. At the meeting, the Big Three pledged free elections in liberated nations—a promise that Stalin never kept.

The Allied leaders also pledged free elections to form representative and democratic governments in all liberated nations.

However, Stalin was soon violating the Yalta agreements. On February 27, the Soviet diplomat Andrei Vyshinsky appeared in Bucharest, Rumania, and ordered King Michael to dismiss his coalition government. On March 6, a Communist puppet regime was installed. At the meetings on Poland in Moscow, Molotov continued to veto all suggestions made by the United States and British ambassadors, while the Soviet-backed provisional government in Poland began executing or deporting hundreds of potential opposition leaders. In March, 16 Polish underground leaders who had accepted a Soviet pledge of safe conduct to Moscow were accused of espionage and—as Churchill complained to Stalin—simply "disappeared." Later, after a "show trial," 13 were executed, three imprisoned for life.

Meanwhile, the western Allied troops under General Dwight D. Eisenhower crossed the Rhine, and the Soviets pushed through Poland into Germany. By April, American troops were at the Elbe River, near Berlin, and virtually at the gates of Prague. Churchill and Roosevelt had become concerned about Stalin's intentions toward Germany, for the Soviet army, having captured Vienna, was denying Allied access to the city despite the Yalta pact, which called for joint Anglo-American-Soviet occupation and control of Austria.

Roosevelt and Churchill had never definitely agreed between themselves on post-war plans for Germany nor had they drawn Stalin into a firm pledge for joint policies. There was agreement only on zones of occupation: Soviet in the east, American in the south, British in the north and joint control of Berlin. Subsequently the French were also assigned a zone.

The Fateful Decision on Berlin. Actually, the United States troops broke through Germany so fast they could have taken Berlin before the Soviet army. Instead, they waited on the Elbe until Soviet troops took Berlin and then linked up with them at the river. On May 8, when Germany surrendered, American forces were far inside the Soviet zone-to-be and holding northwest Czechoslovakia.

Churchill urged that the Allies stand firm where they were until the U.S.S.R.'s good faith could be better tested. But the United States ordered its troops to withdraw to their own zone on June 24, and Churchill reluctantly agreed. American troops turned over such major German cities as Dresden, Leipzig and Magdeburg to the Soviet army and pulled out of Czechoslovakia completely. No guarantee of access to Berlin was sought. All this was done in good faith and in the belief that it was worth risking high stakes to keep the Soviet Union's confidence and friendship in the post-war era.

Roosevelt had been deeply troubled in his last days by the Soviet Union's violation of the agreements on Poland. And Churchill had greeted victory in Europe with these prophetic warnings:

THE ALLIES JOIN UP IN GERMANY

American and Russian soldiers welcome each other joyously as they meet at the Elbe River on April 25, 1945. U.S.-Soviet relations were possibly at their best during this period when the twin drives across Germany, from east and west, ended in victory.

I wish I could tell you tonight that all our toils and troubles were over. [But] we have yet to make sure that the simple and honourable purposes for which we entered the war are not brushed aside or overlooked in the months following our success.... There would be little use in punishing the Hitlerites for their crimes if law and justice did not rule, and if totalitarian or police Governments were to take the place of the German invaders.

The Wartime Pledges Betrayed. Churchill's fears were well grounded. As in Poland, Stalin slowly began extending Communist rule to those sections of Europe occupied by Russian troops. In Rumania, Bulgaria, Hungary, Poland and Czechoslovakia the pattern, with slight variations, was much the same.

At first, the Communists joined with non-Communists in coalitions. In Poland, for example, Stanislaw Mikolajczyk, leader of the London Poles, entered the government. Land-ownership reforms and other popular measures were begun. Then the leaders of the non-Communist parties were either jailed—as Iuliu Maniu was in Rumania—or forced to flee for their lives. The Communists meanwhile extended their iron control over the police, army, press and radio, and all centers of power and propaganda. Eventually, Communist tyranny became complete. These transition phases were not needed in Yugoslavia and Albania, where local Communist dictators

A Short Dictionary of Communist Jabberwocky

"When I use a word," Humpty Dumpty says in "Through the Looking Glass," "it means just what I choose it to mean—neither more nor less...." Communism's spokesmen over the decades have shown that they decide what certain words mean, even if they reverse usual meanings. Here is some of the confusing Jabberwocky used by the Communists.

Aggression. Communists state this can be committed only by capitalist or "imperialist" powers. The *Dictionary of the Russian Language* defines aggression as "The armed attack by one or several imperialist countries against other countries with a view to . . . their forcible subjugation and the exploitation of their people." Since Communist countries refuse to believe that they can be aggressors, no military action *they* take can be so defined. Thus, when Communist North Korea invaded South Korea, it contended that South Korea had committed aggression. Similarly, when the U.S.S.R. violated treaties with its attack on Poland and the Baltic states, the invasion was brazenly described as protective.

Democratic Centralism. This is the theory under which every local party cell, unit branch

Josip Broz Tito and Enver Hoxha, who had led Communist guerrilla armies—"Partisans"—against the Germans and Italians, were already in power at war's end. In 1948, however, Tito was to break with Stalin and his country was to become the first Communist nation not completely subservient to Moscow.

The Tragedy of Czechoslovakia. More than any other event, the Communist takeover in Czechoslovakia awakened the American people to Stalin's aim of world domination. Czechoslovakia had been born a democracy. Its founder, Tomáš Masaryk, proclaimed the independence of the republic in Washington, D.C., in 1918.

In the postwar election Czechoslovakia held in 1946, the Communists got the largest vote (38 per cent) because the Czechs remembered that, at the time of the Munich agreement in 1938, the U.S.S.R., unlike England and France, had sounded as though it were prepared to defend the Czechs against Hitler. Communist leader Klement Gottwald became premier. So far this was all legal and constitutional.

Gottwald then tightened his control of the police and army. With new elections approaching in 1948, he forced Czechoslovakia's President Eduard Beneš to accept a cabinet entirely Communist except for Foreign Minister Jan Masaryk, a non-Communist, who two weeks later either jumped, fell or was pushed to his death. Beneš, broken by Masaryk's death and the emerging tyranny, resigned and died the

---

and district committee is supposed to debate policies on a democratic basis before they are decided, then obey unswervingly the central group's decision. In practice, the Central Committee of the Communist party and the dictator who heads it make all the decisions from the top and impose them on the people as a whole.

Dictatorship of the Proletariat. In Marx's theory, this would be a temporary dictatorship by the workers over society until all classes disappeared and the state "withered away." In Communist practice, the term describes a dictatorship, "in the name of the workers," by the party leadership—and finally one man—over the proletariat and everybody else.

Peaceful Coexistence. Contrary to the implications of the words, this is a technical, Communist-coined phrase used to note a temporary stage in the conflict with capitalism. Marked by increased economic and political conflict, it is still a battle, but one short of general war. The Communists use this term to lull the world into believing that Communism will triumph only when, and if, its superiority is so evident that it will prevail everywhere by acclamation.

National-Liberation Wars. This describes a "just" war approved of by the Communists, as opposed to an "unjust" war. It relies on guerrilla warfare, usually led by Communists, and is most successful where oppressive governments exist. Then Communists can play on righteous resentments to overthrow one tyranny and install their own.

People's Democracies. This is a term developed to explain the Communist dictatorships which were set up by the Red Army in the eastern European countries it occupied. Actually the result is that the countries have no democracy, and the people no voice in running them.

following September. A huge granite statue of Stalin was in time reared atop Prague's tallest hill, symbolizing the end of democracy.

Free Elections, Communist Style. All this showed the West that Communists gave their own meanings to the "democracy" and "free elections" they had pledged at Yalta. To them a free election was one in which only Communists could win. To them the Communist dictatorships they set up in Europe were "people's democracies," although there was no democracy and the people had no voice.

The West now got another harsh lesson as relations with the Russians in Germany worsened. In talks on Berlin the Communists had conceded that access to the city through 110 miles of Soviet-occupied territory was implicitly guaranteed in the arrangements for joint occupation of the country. By 1948, relations among the Allies were getting progressively worse. Stalin had looted the Eastern zone of Germany and commandeered almost the entire agricultural output for shipment eastward. The Allies responded by merging their zones for economic purposes and later undertaking a major currency reform. In June, as a reprisal, Stalin suddenly blockaded Berlin and forbade access to the Allies. There was no longer any question that the cold war was in full force.

A COMMUNIST'S OWN VIEW OF STALIN

Milovan Djilas, a top Yugoslavian Communist, visited with Stalin in 1945 and wrote in his book *Conversations with Stalin* that Stalin was convinced that another war would come. "At one point [Stalin] cried out . . . 'The war shall soon be over. We shall recover in 15 or 20 years, and then we'll have another go at it.'"

On another occasion Stalin asked about Albanian relations with Yugoslavia. Djilas began to explain. "I had not even finished when, to my surprise, Stalin said: 'We have no special interest in Albania. We agree to Yugoslavia swallowing Albania!' . . . At this he gathered together the fingers of his right hand and, bringing them to his mouth, he made a motion as if to swallow them. I was astonished, almost struck dumb. . . . Again I explained: 'It is not a matter of swallowing, but unification.'

"At this Molotov interjected: 'But that is swallowing.' And Stalin added, again with that gesture of his: 'Yes, yes. Swallowing! But we agree with you: you ought to swallow Albania—the sooner the better.'"

Preparing for the Cold War

As Stalin began the cold war abroad, he prepared the Soviet Union for it at home. Few countries have been left as ravaged as the Soviet Union was left by Hitler's hordes. The area west of the Urals had been seared. Nearly every family had lost one or more members among the more than 20 million dead. Great power dams, like the Dnieprostroy, had been blown up, along with bridges and railroads. The U.S.S.R. could not have survived, much less won, without the tremendous new industrial complex that Stalin had built in the 1930s to the east beyond the Urals, or without the more than $11 billion worth of United States' tanks, trucks and other wartime aid.

Simply rebuilding this damage would have seemed work enough for the Soviet Union for a decade. Certainly the Russian people thought only of peace. But Stalin's thoughts were of making the U.S.S.R. the most powerful nation in the world.

In a speech in February 1946, he called for "a new mighty upsurge of national economy, which will enable us to increase the level of our production . . . three-fold as compared with the prewar level. . . . we must [produce] 50 million tons of pig iron per year, 60 million tons of steel, 500 million tons of coal and 60 million tons of oil." Ambitious as this seemed at the time, Stalin's 15-year goals were uncannily close to what the U.S.S.R. was actually to achieve.

Ready for a New War. Stalin made it clear, too, that despite the blood they had shed together, he had no faith in the friendship and good intentions of his wartime allies. In the carefully veiled language of Communism, he told his people that they must prepare for "any eventuality," a sure reference to war.

In his speech Stalin set another target which was to be remembered in the days of Soviet H-bombs, Sputniks, and earth-orbiting cosmonauts: "I have no doubt that if we render the necessary assistance to our scientists they will be able . . . to surpass the achievements of science outside . . . our country." Three years after these remarks, the Soviets had exploded an atomic bomb. Later they were to come remarkably close to beating the United States to the creation of the awesome H-bomb.

New Terrors and Tyranny. The Russian people, after all their heroism and sacrifices, had surely proved their right to be trusted. Instead, they got still more repressions and persecutions. The more than five million Soviet citizens who had been prisoners or forced laborers under the Germans were treated as suspected traitors and many were executed. Every soldier who had been west of Warsaw had seen the superiority of the western way of life over the Soviet Union's. They, too, were watched closely, and the slightest sign of nonconformity was ruthlessly punished.

Always intensely suspicious of his associates, Stalin now became more so. The older he grew—he was 67 in 1946—the fewer people he trusted. The party higher-ups began nervously wondering who might eventually succeed him. The three most durable old Bolsheviks, who had managed somehow to survive his purges, were Foreign Minister Molotov, the trade boss Anastas Mikoyan and the heavy-industry boss Lazar Kaganovich.

However, Stalin's most likely successor would come from those men who owed all they had to "Great Stalin." Three stood out as potential rivals for power:

▶ *Andrei Zhdanov,* a Politburo member, was 50 in 1946. He had shot up from a district party-secretary to become boss of Leningrad. As its political leader during the great wartime siege, he was made a national hero. In 1947 he helped organize and then headed the Communist Information Bureau (Cominform), successor to the Communist International (Comintern), which had been abolished in 1943. He was thus in charge of major Communist parties outside the U.S.S.R., giving them the orders to adopt a militant antiwestern stand and to follow strict discipline from Moscow.

▶ *Georgi Malenkov* became a full Politburo member in 1946, while only 44. He had fought in the Soviet army at 17. Later, he caught Stalin's eye as secretary of a school party cell where he bitterly fought all anti-Stalinist opposition. Stalin got him a responsible job with the Central Committee at 23. In 1939 he became a secretary of the powerful Central Committee. During the war he was in charge of procurement and technical equipment for the army and air force.

STALIN AND HIS EAGER DISCIPLE

In 1937, Khrushchev, still in Stalin's shadow, is seen taking part in an official ceremony. The 43-year-old Khrushchev had recently played a vital role in the rush job of building Moscow's grandiose subway. He had shot up to be party chief of Moscow, from which post he denounced Stalin's purge victims as agents of Adolf Hitler. And the purge profited Khrushchev: he got the Ukraine leadership formerly held by one of the men killed at Stalin's orders.

IN TOKEN OF THE ALLIES' DETERMINATION TO KEEP BERLIN FREE, AN AMERICAN

In 1943 he was put in charge of rehabilitating territory formerly occupied by Germans, and in 1946 became a deputy premier.

▶ *Nikita Sergeyevich Khrushchev* was 52 in 1946. A miner's son and onetime shepherd boy from Kursk province close to the Ukraine, he had worked as a mine mechanic in the Donets Basin, risen through party work in the Ukraine to be boss of the building of Moscow's famed subway. In 1938, as Communist chief in the Ukraine, he ruthlessly purged party ranks. During the war he helped take over and reorganize the captured districts of Poland. After the war Stalin sent him back to the Ukraine to restore its all-important agriculture. He was a self-made "rough diamond" compared to the highly cultured Malenkov and Zhdanov, and he was far less frequently mentioned for the top position.

Zhdanov versus Malenkov. In the first postwar years, Zhdanov, although he was locked in a struggle for power with Malenkov, seemed to be Stalin's favorite. Malenkov was moving captured German factories to Russia. Zhdanov campaigned to leave the factories in place and make East Germany a key Soviet industrial base instead of stripping it. The top Soviet economic planner, N. A. Voznesenski, supported Zhdanov. An investigating commission headed by Mikoyan recommended that the dismantling be stopped. Zhdanov won and Malenkov slipped into obscurity.

That was in 1946. In August of that year Zhdanov emerged as the

CARGO PLANE BREAKS THE 1948 BLOCKADE ESTABLISHED BY THE COMMUNISTS

cultural dictator of Communists. He upbraided the Soviet cultural community for various faults. He singled out world-famous Russian intellectuals for harsh criticism and ordered writers, artists and composers to create works marked by a genuine "Socialist realism."

In less than two years, however, Malenkov had made a sudden comeback and resumed his post in the powerful Secretariat. Just as suddenly, on August 31, 1948 Zhdanov died—under still mysterious circumstances. Immediately thereafter, a ruthless purge of his followers began. Stalin executed Voznesenski, who had proposed some mild reforms, for "trying to restore capitalism in Russia."

A New United States Policy

Even before the Berlin blockade, the Free World had begun to marshal its defenses against further Communist expansion. Winston Churchill, speaking at Fulton, Missouri, in 1946, summed up the situation by saying, "From Stettin in the Baltic to Trieste in the Adriatic, an iron curtain has descended across the Continent." He called for closer Anglo-American co-operation to check any "temptations" to ambition or adventure.

In the United Nations, the United States and Britain insisted that the U.S.S.R. honor its earlier agreement to remove its troops from Iran at the end of the war. The Soviet delegate, Andrei Gromyko, in protest at such mistrust, staged the first of many subsequent "walkouts." But Stalin did withdraw his troops, leaving behind a short-lived puppet regime in the border province of Azerbaijan.

The United States began shifting from a policy of "patience and firmness" to a definite "containment" policy in order to block Communist expansion. In September 1946, after the Soviets rebuffed an American offer for a 25-year treaty against renewed German aggression, Secretary of State James Byrnes made an important speech at Stuttgart, Germany. This address signaled a changed American attitude toward defeated Germany, which now was to be regarded a potentially powerful ally. Byrnes ended all talk of destroying Germany's industrial power by pledging the United States to support the rebuilding of the factories and mills shattered in the war. In March 1947, President Truman announced his plan, which became known as the Truman Doctrine, to support free countries threatened by "armed minorities or by outside pressure," and he sent military and economic aid to back Greece and Turkey against Soviet threats.

U.S. AID TO WAR-TORN NATIONS

Food (like this sugar at a London dock), materials and funds provided by the U.S. Marshall Plan helped Europe recover from World War II. The program has advanced over $30 billion in economic aid. The London *Times* said in 1954: ". . . no nation has ever come into the possession of such powers for good or ill . . . and no nation in history has used those powers . . . with greater vision, restraint, responsibility and courage."

The Marshall Plan. At Harvard, in June 1947, the new Secretary of State George Marshall, chief of staff in World War II, proposed a plan whereby the United States would provide loans if European nations would coordinate efforts to rebuild their war-damaged economies. This proposal was to become famous as the Marshall Plan. The Soviets came to a conference in Paris, called to work out plans for this gigantic undertaking, but Molotov bluntly rejected the proposals Britain and France put forward. He walked out of this meeting and forbade all eight satellites—still nominally independent—from joining a larger western European conference, as some of them wished to do. The U.S.S.R. also launched the Cominform to coordinate worldwide Communist action, to lead the Communist parties of France and Italy in fighting the Marshall Plan, and to tighten Communist control over eastern Europe. But within three years, more than $11 billion in American aid was to help Europe's devastated nations restore their economic health in a joint recovery program.

The Communist seizure of Czechoslovakia followed swiftly after President Beneš had indicated his interest in the Marshall Plan. A few weeks after that seizure, in March 1948, Britain, France and the Benelux nations—Belgium, The Netherlands, Luxembourg—signed the Brussels Treaty of mutual assistance against any new aggression. In April, the same five nations and 11 others joined to form the Organization for European Economic Cooperation (OEEC) to coordinate the Marshall Plan. Then in June came the Berlin blockade.

A Victory for Firmness. Had the West allowed the blockade to stand, West Berlin would have quickly starved to death without food, fuel and other materials from outside. President Truman met the challenge with a massive airlift which for 11 months performed incredible feats. The airlift fed free Berlin, clothed it, heated it. Above

Communist Europe

Communist countries

Free World alliances

THE COMMUNIST BLOC, shown in red, has some real cracks. Yugoslavia is Communist, but has not been a consistent follower of Moscow. Albania, though allied with the Soviet Union, sides with Red China and has earned the Kremlin's enmity. The free nations (white) guard the West against aggression.

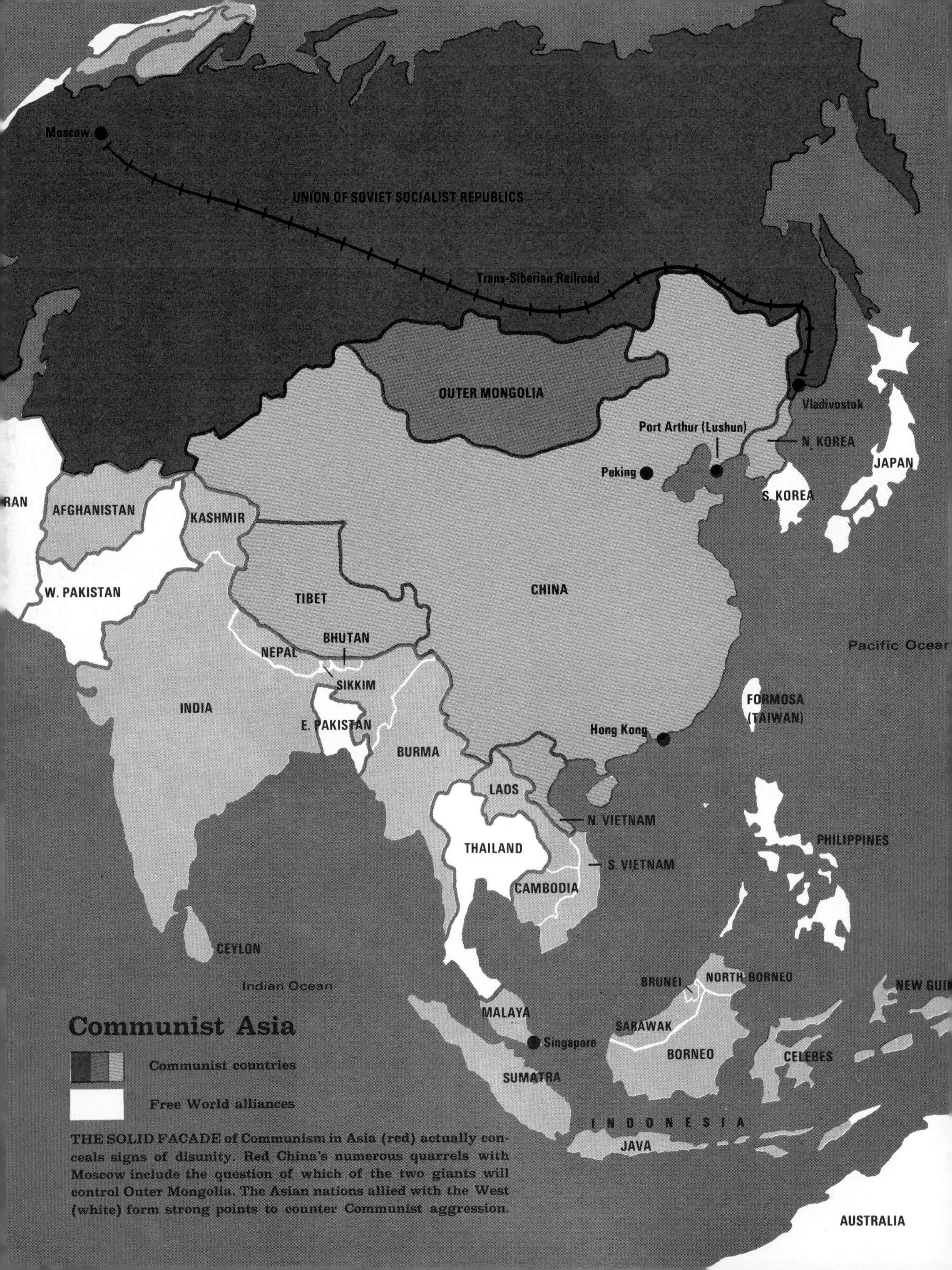

Communist Asia

Communist countries

Free World alliances

THE SOLID FACADE of Communism in Asia (red) actually conceals signs of disunity. Red China's numerous quarrels with Moscow include the question of which of the two giants will control Outer Mongolia. The Asian nations allied with the West (white) form strong points to counter Communist aggression.

all it gave Berlin the spirit to defy Stalin. In May 1949, the Soviets suddenly agreed to lift the blockade. Courage and firmness had won.

By then, the Free World had taken additional steps against aggression. In April 1949, the United States along with Canada, Denmark, Norway, Iceland, Italy and Portugal joined the five Brussels Treaty powers to form the North Atlantic Treaty Alliance and the North Atlantic Treaty Organization (NATO). NATO organized the first international peacetime army, designed to prevent new wars by having a force in being, ready to defend free Europe.

The Cold War Grows Hot

Following the end of the war with Japan, the United States had occupied Korea south of the 38th parallel, and Soviet forces occupied the northern section. It had also been agreed that Korea would be unified under "free elections." The Soviets withdrew their troops, formed a well-armed Communist puppet state in industrialized North Korea and refused to allow the United Nations to supervise the pledged free elections. The United Nations did hold such elections for South Korea, and a republic was formed. The United States withdrew its own armed forces in 1949.

While this was going on, the situation was deteriorating throughout Asia. During World War II, the United States had sent arms and advisers to the Chinese Communists. The Communists were then fighting Japan from their stronghold of Yenan in northwestern China, where they had fled from Chiang Kai-shek's Nationalists. The United States also encouraged Generalissimo Chiang to work with the Communists against Japan. In the territory they captured, the Chinese Communists undertook only mild changes, leading some western reporters to describe their policy as long-overdue agrarian reform in the ownership of land, the assessment of taxes and so on.

With the Japanese surrender in 1945, the Communists dropped all pretenses. They renewed the civil war with Nationalist forces and by the end of 1949 had driven the last of them from the mainland. Chiang fled to the island of Formosa, 100 miles offshore, where he re-formed an army of 500,000 men and continued to be recognized by the United States as the head of the legitimate government of China. But the Communists held the Chinese mainland itself—a major factor encouraging Communist aggression in Asia.

Attack in Korea. At dawn on Sunday, June 25, 1950, the well-armed, well-trained North Korean army slashed across the 38th parallel against Republic of Korea forces. President Truman immediately asked for an emergency session of the U.N. Security Council. By chance, the Soviet delegate had been absent since January in protest over the seating of Chiang's delegate to speak for China. With the Soviet not present to veto action, the Security Council that

CHINA FALLS TO MAO'S COMMUNISTS

Men of Chiang Kai-shek's forces *(above)* reached a haven in Formosa after the fall of China in 1949, Communism's greatest victory since the Russian Revolution. Chiang had begun fighting Communists in 1927. Later he drove them into long exile in Yenan Province in China's northwest. After the Japanese surrendered in 1945, the Red Chinese, with Soviet help, secured enough material to equip the armies that would drive the Nationalists from the mainland. On Formosa, Chiang's army maintains the island as a possible base for liberation of the homeland.

same day called the North Korean attack a "breach of the peace" and urged members to "render every assistance to the United Nations."

This was an historic milestone: it was the first attempt by the United Nations to punish and defeat aggression. President Truman immediately committed United States land forces to defend South Korea as a "police action." This, too, was a significant break with the past, for under the Constitution only Congress can declare war.

The undeclared war in Korea took 33,600 American lives before its indecisive end. But the aggressors were forced back to their prewar lines and were served notice that the Free World was ready to fight.

The Free World did gain some victories in Asia. In the Philippines, the Communist guerrillas were crushed by a great democratic leader, Ramon Magsaysay, who won his people to his side through reforms. In Malaya, the British fought a fierce, nine-year jungle war against the Communist-led Malayan and Chinese guerrillas, and they finally re-established control.

FATEFUL DECISION TO DEFEND KOREA

President Truman *(above)* developed a policy to restrain Communism from further expansion. His "Truman Doctrine" in 1947 sent U.S. aid to fend off imminent Communist aggression in Greece and Turkey. One of Truman's toughest decisions came in 1950, when Communist North Korean troops suddenly invaded South Korea. Even as the U.N. Security Council branded the invasion as "an act of aggression," Truman sent U.S. troops to Korea to halt the Communists. Later the U.S. was joined by other U.N. forces to stop this Communist aggression.

The Terror of Stalin's Last Days

In January 1953, Stalin showed signs of starting a new purge, this time of some of his closest associates. A story on the very last page of *Pravda*—subsequently branded as one of Stalin's fabrications—revealed that the mysterious death of Andrei Zhdanov in 1948 had at last been "solved." He had been poisoned, the story revealed, by the same doctors looking after the leaders of the Kremlin. The doctors had been undermining the health of the Kremlin's leaders by false diagnoses, and they were planning more murders. All this was startling enough. But so were additional phrases implicating Lavrenti Beria, head of the secret police, for failing to discover the plot.

The denunciation of Beria could only mean that Stalin was preparing to purge him and anybody else connected with Beria he wished. But abruptly everything was changed. On March 4, 1953, the party leaders announced that Stalin, then 73, had suffered a cerebral hemorrhage two days earlier that caused him to lose "consciousness and the power of speech." (Doctors later would point out that loss of speech could scarcely be determined while a man was unconscious.) On March 6, an announcement that Stalin had died the previous night was coupled with an appeal for "the greatest unity of leadership and the prevention of any kind of disorder and panic."

Who Would Follow Stalin? Two big questions loomed: Could Stalin's total power, built on total terror which made millions of Russians hate and fear him, possibly survive the man?

Could the survivors, even if they could keep power, find some way of using it which would not set all of them at each other's throats?

There were no legal guides for the surviving leaders' future actions. Their party, having seized power initially from the people's own

FIGHTING IN KOREA, U.S. Marines withdraw under heavy attack from Chinese Communists who had joined the North Koreans. Although U.N. forces were driven back from the Chinese border, they succeeded in repulsing the Communist invasion of the Republic of Korea. More than 250,000 American troops saw action in Korea.

duly elected assembly, had no legal right to power. How could a dictator be named to succeed Stalin when the Constitution authorized no dictator in the first place? Moreover, the Russian people, knowing that the leaders had been nothing more than Stalin's vassals, would not fear them as they had feared Stalin.

Fascinated, the world watched the merciless struggle for power among Stalin's survivors.

A New Struggle for Power. The most likely winner seemed to be Malenkov. As the top member of the Secretariat next to Stalin, he controlled the party machine. As deputy premier he had vast influence over the whole industrial and governmental bureaucracy.

The next most likely surely seemed Beria, who as head of internal security controlled the secret police, and as minister of the interior controlled a substantial part of the national economy—including the development of atomic energy.

The speculation outside the U.S.S.R. did not mention Khrushchev, whose rise in recent years had gone unnoticed.

The day after their announcement of Stalin's death, the chieftains

A DEAD DICTATOR AND HIS HEIRS make their last appearance together as Communism's elite pays its final respects to Stalin, who lies in state in March of 1953. Stalin's coffin is flanked by two guards and party stalwarts *(left to right)* Molotov, Voroshilov, Beria, Malenkov, Bulganin, Khrushchev, Kaganovich and Mikoyan. Of

agreed that Malenkov should take one of Stalin's posts as chairman of the Council of Ministers or Premier. Since Malenkov already headed the party secretariat, this gave him both of Stalin's old jobs—and too much power in his colleagues' eyes. A few days later Malenkov resigned the party post, and Khrushchev became the leader of those who remained on the Secretariat.

Somewhat earlier, doubtless to placate the powerful Soviet army, Marshal Georgi Zhukov, the hero of Stalingrad, had been brought back to become deputy minister of defense from the obscure outpost where, jealous of his wartime popularity, Stalin had exiled him.

One thing Malenkov, Khrushchev and the others apparently could agree on was that Beria, as boss of the secret police, was dangerous to them all. They acted quickly. On July 10, 1953, *Pravda* announced without any warning that Beria had been stripped of all power and positions. Not until the following December did it reveal that he had been tried and executed for, among other charges, having been a "British agent" in Lenin's day.

The Showdown. The battle for supremacy now narrowed to a fight between Malenkov against the comparatively unknown Khrushchev. It was waged over a basic question of policy: Should priority be given to the needs of the consumer or to heavy industry?

The people, as always happens when a tyrant dies, were expecting a relaxation of pressures—not only in the U.S.S.R., but in all the satellite countries as well. And in the fall of 1953, Premier Malenkov did signal a turn toward more freedom and more comforts for the average Russian. Reversing Zhdanov's earlier statements on culture, he encouraged debates on varying approaches to literature, art,

this group, only Mikoyan still survives in a major position now that Khrushchev has supreme power. Even Stalin, whose corpse was placed on exhibit alongside Lenin's, has since been discredited by Khrushchev. On November 1, 1961, Stalin's body was removed from its Red Square place of honor and buried in a simple grave.

the drama. He promised more shirts, shoes, dresses and motor cars. He granted amnesty to many prisoners.

Now head of the party, Khrushchev could give increasing attention to the woeful state of Soviet agriculture. In Stalin's last years, managers of the farm program, fearful of purges, had simply created rosy statistics that concealed the great lag in agricultural production. Now Khrushchev proposed solving the U.S.S.R.'s chronic shortage of food by instituting a vast program of plowing and planting millions of acres of "virgin lands" in Siberia and other semiarid regions. To this end, he demanded and got most of the Soviet Union's farm machinery production for the next year assigned to his program.

But carrying out this program would make it harder for Malenkov to live up to his promises on consumer goods. Khrushchev was active in other ways against Malenkov. On a visit to Communist China, Khrushchev promised its chief, Mao Tse-tung, vast amounts of industrial aid. This would place even heavier strains on Russian heavy industry, and Malenkov was put on the defensive. Khrushchev pressed harder: he linked Malenkov with the hated Beria as instigator of the purges which followed Zhdanov's death.

Khrushchev to Power. At a meeting of the Supreme Soviet on February 8, 1955, a functionary astounded the audience by rising to read a written request by Malenkov that he be allowed to resign and be replaced by "another comrade with greater administrative experience." The statement made the sort of confession and self-accusation that used to be familiar at Stalin's purge trials. Those confessions in Stalin's time used to be followed by executions, but Malenkov remained briefly as a deputy premier and as a member of the

Presidium. Khrushchev then nominated as Malenkov's successor that "faithful son of the Communist Party" Comrade Bulganin, who, since 1948, had been a full member of the Presidium (as the politburo was renamed in 1952). Into his job as defense minister went Marshal Zhukov.

KHRUSHCHEV PLAYS PRINCE BOUNTIFUL

Khrushchev congratulates Mao Tse-tung at the 1954 celebration in Peking of the Chinese Communists' fifth year in power. Georgi Malenkov, then Soviet premier, was trying to provide added consumer goods for the Russian people. Khrushchev promised to send Mao lavish shipments of heavy Soviet tools and machinery to help Red China industrialize. Such commitments made it hard for Malenkov to carry out his domestic policies and heightened his political warfare with Khrushchev. The next year Khrushchev forced Malenkov to resign.

Since he had put Bulganin in the job, Khrushchev, as had Stalin, now really controlled both government and party. Technically, Khrushchev could still be outvoted by other members of the Presidium, but he had achieved the necessary strategic springboard for total power.

Khrushchev and the Satellites. Having consolidated his position at home, Khrushchev now turned to protect the Soviet position in the increasingly restive Communist satellites. In East Berlin, the people had staged riots in June 1953, which came so close to revolution Soviet tanks had to put them down. Tito's Yugoslavia, which had broken free of Stalin in 1948 to pursue Communist goals in its own national way, was still independent of Moscow, and was an embarrassment to Soviet leaders. The $2 billion in aid from the United States had helped Tito make his country more prosperous than most of the satellites. And his "Workers' Councils," which had given the people considerable autonomy in determining their own production plans, wages and so forth, had set off demands in Hungary, Poland —even in the Soviet Union—for similar privileges. Stalin had executed many satellite leaders suspected of sympathy with Yugoslavia, but he had been unable to touch Tito. In May 1955, in an attempt to patch up relations with Yugoslavia, Khrushchev flew to Belgrade with Premier Bulganin and Mikoyan and talked with Tito.

Khrushchev was now ready to thrust himself upon the world stage. Churchill had long been calling for a "meeting at the summit" in the hope that the world's leaders could find some way for Communism and the Free World to reconcile their differences. But Eisenhower had called for Soviet deeds, not words, to prove a desire for reconciliation. The Russians provided such a "deed" by suddenly agreeing in late spring 1955 to sign a long-sought treaty with Austria, which would withdraw the occupying Soviet army from that country and allow it to take up the free life of a neutral. Eisenhower came to the summit at Geneva in July 1955, to meet Bulganin and Khrushchev and his old wartime friend Marshal Zhukov.

Undoubtedly, Khrushchev wanted to gain the propaganda effect of a peaceful "spirit of Geneva," reflected in the photos of Eisenhower and Bulganin in smiling camaraderie. Such photos were circulated by the U.S.S.R. all through the satellites in an attempt to bolster its claim that, regardless of Eisenhower's repeated demand for "liberation" of captive nations, the United States was on good terms with the U.S.S.R. and would not go to war to free the satellites. At the Geneva meeting, the Soviet delegates also agreed in principle to "reunification" through "free elections" for Germany, but Khrushchev and Bulganin hurried off right after the summit conference to assure the East German puppets that no such actions would take place.

Amidst these foreign maneuvers, Khrushchev sought to make himself popular at home as a man who, unlike Stalin, went around the country to meet and talk with ordinary people.

Policies of the 20th Congress. The Communist party's 20th Congress, which was held in February 1956, rocked the Communist world to its foundations, and rocks it still. Khrushchev's need for a clean break with Stalinism was urgent in order to gain more flexibility in his policies. The farm problems demanded a massive revision of Stalin's policies. So did the red tape of overcentralized industry and the need to revise accepted dogma to accommodate Yugoslav and other "deviations" without a bitter party battle.

The 20th Congress laid down these important policies:

▶ *War Is Not Inevitable.* Despite Lenin's preachment that "wars are inevitable as long as imperialism exists," Khrushchev declared that "the world camp of socialism" has now become strong enough to make capitalists fear to launch new wars; it possesses "not only the moral but also the material means [that is, armies and weapons] to prevent aggression." This new fact makes possible something else:

▶ *Peaceful Coexistence.* Peaceful coexistence seeks ultimate Communist victory in a sharpened competition with capitalism at every level—ideological, political, economic and scientific. In this competition Communism is to so demonstrate its superiority that all peoples, everywhere, will want to adopt it voluntarily. Victory might even come about through the ballot, if Communists could capture a majority in democratic parliaments and then transform them "into a genuine instrument of the people's will"—in other words, a Communist dictatorship. But all this is not quite so peaceful as it sounds. Where democracies fail to surrender voluntarily—or, as Khrushchev put it, "where capitalism is still strong and has a huge military and police apparatus"—the final victory would still require "a sharp class, revolutionary struggle," or civil war.

▶ *Alliance with Neutralists.* As a companion to this concept, Khrushchev described "a vast zone of peace" containing a majority of the world's uncommitted peoples who could join forces against the West. This was made possible "by the emergence in the world arena of a group of peace-loving . . . Asian and African states" which refused to be drawn into military blocs. Part of "peaceful coexistence" with the West was a race to win the support of these emerging nations. To win it, Communism could soft-pedal its slogans about violence and co-operate with the "bourgeois nationalist leaders" whose nations would inevitably be drawn toward socialism.

Many Roads to Socialism. Khrushchev quoted Lenin's 1917 remark: "All nations will arrive at socialism—this is inevitable—but not all will do so in exactly the same way." "People's democracy" in

KHRUSHCHEV EATS SOME HUMBLE PIE

Khrushchev arrives in Yugoslavia in 1955 to give Marshal Tito a friendly handshake. Stalin had called Tito the vilest names imaginable and had sought to have him murdered or overthrown. This visit could have been a very humiliating experience for Khrushchev, but he put all of the blame on Beria and other "despicable agents of imperialism." While the explanation did help ease relations with Yugoslavia, it also was an important factor in encouraging the satellites to seek relaxation of Moscow's strong rule.

the satellites was cited as a new form of socialism. The deviations of Chinese Communists he called "creative Marxism in action. . . ." Using this approach, he could accept Tito's differing forms of "economic management and organization of the state apparatus" as merely another variation of "socialist construction."

FRUITLESS MEETING AT THE SUMMIT

Premier Bulganin *(left)* was the titular leader of the Soviet Union when President Eisenhower met him "at the summit" in Geneva in 1955. Bulganin, who was taking his orders from Nikita Khrushchev, ostensibly reached agreement on disarmament and elections in Germany. When the meeting was over, Khrushchev and Bulganin went to Germany to assure their puppets that they had nothing to fear. And far from disarming, the U.S.S.R. permitted the Czechs to ship arms to Egypt, which helped stir up the Suez Canal crisis within a year.

Unmasking Stalin Himself. Having made these major departures from Stalinism, Khrushchev was now ready to downgrade the dead dictator himself and to disown any personal guilt for Stalin's crimes. With detailed documentation, Khrushchev tore into the "cult of the person of Stalin." He unfolded the horrifying story of the hundreds and thousands of men—most of them prominent Communists—who had been murdered at Stalin's orders for things they had never done. He neither mentioned nor deplored the murder of millions of Russian peasants during the forced collectivization of the 1930s.

Actually, Khrushchev himself had applauded the murders, whether of Communists or peasants, at the time they happened. In 1936, for example, when Stalin was using the Kirov murder to eliminate Kamenev and Zinoviev, among many others, *Pravda* quoted Khrushchev as calling them "fascist degenerates" and "miserable dwarfs" who "lifted their hands against the greatest of all men, our friend, our wise leader, Comrade Stalin." In 1937, when 13 more old Bolsheviks were doomed, Khrushchev turned out 200,000 Muscovites to demonstrate their "full approval" of the fate of these "traitors," and he praised Stalin as "the beacon that guides all progressive mankind."

Now, in 1956, Khrushchev could report that the term "enemy of the people" was used by Stalin to justify "the most cruel repression . . . against anyone who in any way disagreed with Stalin . . . the only proof of guilt used . . . was the 'confession' of the accused himself. . . secured through physical pressures [torture.]"

The extent of the terror was indicated by Khrushchev's report that of 139 Central Committee members and candidates elected at the 17th Party Congress in 1934, 70 per cent were later killed. Of 1,966 delegates to that Congress, 1,108 persons were arrested for revolutionary crimes. Stalin even suspected President Voroshilov of being a British agent and put recording devices in his apartment.

Khrushchev exposed Stalin's insane vanity and self-glorification.

▶On September 4, 1951, Stalin "issued an order making 33 tons of copper available for the construction of . . . an impressive monument to Stalin" on the Volga-Don Canal.

▶He loved to see the movie, "The Unforgettable Year 1919," showing him "on the steps of an armored train . . . where he was practically vanquishing the foe with his own saber."

▶In rewriting history, Stalin "marked the very places where he thought that the praise of his services was insufficient," often adding some of this "loathsome adulation" in his own hand.

Khrushchev ended with a solemn pledge: "Comrades! We must

abolish the cult of the individual decisively, once and for all." But he cautioned the delegates to keep the revelation secret.

The Oppressed Peoples Rise. But how could such a revelation of incredible deeds be kept secret? Khrushchev had to let the seven million rank-and-file members of the party know that Stalin had been desanctified. So summaries of his speech were rushed all over the country to be reported, again "secretly," to various party organizations. Thousands of meetings assembled more than 40 million people who learned that Stalin had done evil things beyond imagining.

The news spread like wildfire through the satellites. The Hungarians had been getting more and more restive ever since the ouster of their premier, Imre Nagy, who had followed Malenkov's line. In his place was a vicious Stalinist, Matyas Rakosi. The Poles, always a fiery and rebellious people, also had been chafing.

Khrushchev's speech set off tremendous pressure for more freedom in both Hungary and Poland. In response, the authorities permitted a discussion club for intellectuals to open in Budapest during the summer of 1956. It was named for Sandor Petöfi, a Hungarian revolutionary poet of 1848. A good deal of the talk at the Petöfi Club centered on Rakosi's hanging of the high party official Laszlo Rajk. Rajk, whose hands were far from clean, had been hanged and unceremoniously buried in a ditch by his fellow Communists, but Khrushchev had recently ordered him posthumously "rehabilitated." At one of the meetings, on June 19, Rajk's widow, who had been jailed with him, rose to tell a chilling tale of "cruel years in jail."

Turning to the white-faced party officials, she cried: "You not only killed my husband but you killed all decency in our country. . . . Murderers cannot be rehabilitated: they must be punished!"

The audience of 2,000 people, a third of them army officers, arose to give her an ovation. News of the speech spread all over Budapest. On June 27, crowds formed as early as 4:30 p.m. for the next Petöfi Club meeting, scheduled for 7 p.m. Its purpose was to restore the good name of several hundred newspapermen who had lost their jobs under various Stalinist decrees. For nine solid hours—with no smoking, drinking, eating and without anyone leaving the room—Hungarians said what they really thought for the first time in years.

Events were now exploding all over the Communist empire. Tito had arrived in Moscow on June 1 for his first visit since the break with Stalin. On June 20, the day after Mrs. Rajk's speech, Khrushchev and Tito issued a joint declaration recognizing that "the path of socialist development differs in various countries and conditions."

"Bread! Freedom!" Within a week, serious troubles erupted in the satellites. In Poland, in the industrial city of Poznan, an international fair was under way to show off the "fruits" of Communism. But overworked, underfed workers took advantage of the presence of western visitors to shout: "Bread! Freedom!" Police rushed in and

A WIDOW'S TALE OF MONSTROUS CRIMES

The speech Laszlo Rajk's widow gave at the Petöfi Club on June 19, 1956, shocked Budapest. Her husband had shown no mercy when he had power, but Mrs. Rajk's account of his hanging and her own jailing somehow made all of Communism's crimes seem even more monstrous.

She told how she was in a nearby cell and could hear the jailers when they came for her husband. She could hear the sounds of the hanging. "In the silence of the dawn I heard the doctor announce that he was dead." But the guards told her nothing. "For five years I had no word of my baby."

"Comrades," she said, "there are no words with which to tell you what I feel facing you after cruel years in jail, without a word, a crumb of food . . . or a sign of life reaching me from the outside, living in despair and hopelessness."

Her demand for a party house cleaning led to tremendous crowds at the next Petöfi Club meeting. A group of people shouted, "Down with the regime." From that cry came the demonstrations that soon led to revolt.

IN THE EAST BERLIN UPRISING, two youths stage a futile fight with stones against Russian tanks. This spontaneous demonstration, begun by building workers on June 16, 1953, was followed by strikes and riots all over East Germany. The Communists declared martial law to regain control, but trouble continued for months.

the angry workers attacked them. In the end, 53 lay dead, hundreds of other workers were in jail.

In April, Wladyslaw Gomulka, the Polish Communist leader whom Stalin had imprisoned for deviationism, had been released. After the Poznan uprising the demand for his leadership rose all over Poland. On October 19, 1956, yielding to this demand, the Polish Central Committee readmitted Gomulka to its ranks. At the same time, the Politburo was dissolved, thereby dismissing Marshal Konstantin Rokossovsky. Gomulka immediately announced wide reforms of Stalin's worst repressions.

The dismissal of Rokossovsky had wide repercussions. Rokossovsky, though a Pole by birth, actually was a high officer in Stalin's Soviet army, and the Poles regarded him as an alien carpetbagger. This dismissal was too much for Khrushchev and he flew to Warsaw. In two lengthy sessions, he insisted that Gomulka reinstate Rokossovsky and the other deposed Stalinists in a newly formed Politburo. Gomulka's supporters, who knew the ways of the Russians, had prepared for the meeting by having rifles and pistols issued to the workers in the important Warsaw factories. When Khrushchev threatened to order the Soviet army to move on Warsaw, Gomulka told

IN THE POLISH REVOLT Poznan workers, seeking higher wages and freedom from Russian control, march toward secret police headquarters in June 1956. Some 30,000 workers staged a general strike, but tanks and troops were rushed in to suppress the revolt. Casualties were officially reported as 53 dead, 300 wounded.

him that the workers of Warsaw were ready to fight if need be.

Khrushchev gave in. Gomulka was now named First Secretary with power to implement reforms, including Rokossovsky's ouster. Soon Gomulka would even turn the lands of the hated collective farms back to the peasants. A Communist satellite leader had successfully defied the Kremlin—at least on internal policy—and won.

The Hungarian Tragedy. In Hungary, the people's demand for justice swelled irresistibly. Dictator Rakosi was dismissed, only to be replaced by another Stalinist, Ernö Gerö. Hundreds were released from jails, and a Danube steamer excursion was allowed to take 300 Hungarian intellectuals on a holiday trip to Vienna.

This glimpse of what life could be like in a free country, in a bustling Vienna now free from the Soviet occupation, was "a complete and total shock to the visitors," wrote a foreign correspondent. "After they came back many writers couldn't work; their whole life had been changed." There was talk all over Budapest of "free elections."

On October 6, the new Gerö regime tried to placate some of the rebellious spirit by holding a ceremonial reburial of Laszlo Rajk's body. Thousands marched in the funeral procession in a silent demonstration. The silent people of Budapest were remembering the

Widow Rajk's anguished cry: "Murderers cannot be rehabilitated. They must be punished!"

Within hours, the news from Warsaw of Gomulka's successful defiance of the Kremlin raced through Budapest. On October 22, over 4,000 students of the Building Industry Technological University met as a "parliament" in the main hall. They voted a list of "Sixteen Demands," three of which especially stung the Gerö government: that Rakosi be tried for his crimes, that Russian troops get out of Hungary, and that free and secret elections be held. When the state radio refused to broadcast those particular demands, students all over the university typed copies of them. Soon, batches were in every factory, pinned up on walls, tied to trees.

RECONCILIATION IN POLAND

Khrushchev greets Polish leader Wladyslaw Gomulka in 1959 on the 15th anniversary of the Communist capture of Poland. Gomulka, who had been arrested in 1949 for disagreeing with his Moscow bosses, in 1956 was reinstated as Communist party secretary and as ruler of the country after the riots in Poznan. With amazing audacity, Gomulka then stood up to Moscow and instituted an internal policy relatively independent of the Kremlin. But in the years that have followed, Gomulka has gradually restricted the early promises of liberalization.

The next day, October 23, thousands of students and workers gathered in the square outside the parliament building, calling for Imre Nagy, who had been readmitted to the Communist party only the week before. Nagy appeared briefly. Some of the students moved on to the radio building, once again seeking air time for their demands—including one that Nagy become premier. Some of the hated "AVH" (secret police) guarding the building became rattled and fired into the crowd. The crowd, peaceful until then, ran wild. They attacked the AVH and seized weapons. The regular police, who shared the hatred for the AVH, opened their arsenals to rebel workers. Now armed, the people stormed the radio building and began shooting down the secret police as they fled. Political prisoners were released. In Budapest's factories, and all over Hungary, workers met and elected "revolutionary" and "workers" councils.

Soviet Tanks in Budapest. At dawn on October 24, the Hungarian Central Committee named Imre Nagy prime minister. But he was kept under guard and could do nothing. The Politburo members asked Nagy to sign an appeal for Soviet troops. When he refused, they issued it anyway. That same night, Soviet tanks crunched into Budapest. Hungary's own army began fighting the Russian forces, using tanks which the Russians had supplied. Even children fought the Soviet tanks—with crude bombs made of gasoline-filled bottles.

On October 27, Nagy emerged free to form a genuine people's government, including Béla Kovács, leader of the Independent Smallholders' party which had won the last free election in 1945. Cardinal Mindszenty, imprisoned since 1948, was released and gave his blessings to the Nagy regime.

A national hero emerged, Colonel Pal Maleter, a 36-year-old army officer, commander of the Kilian Barracks. Wave after wave of Soviet assaults pounded the barracks, but Maleter and his brave men held firm. After the battered Soviet forces finally withdrew from Budapest on October 30, Nagy made Maleter his defense minister. Moscow said that Soviet forces would be withdrawn from Budapest.

Treachery in Budapest. On November 2 and 3, the U.N. Security

Council in New York was considering Premier Nagy's request that the U.N. protect Hungary's neutrality. It adjourned until Monday on the Soviet delegate's assurance that negotiations for withdrawal were in progress. On the evening of November 3, Maleter, now promoted to general, went to Soviet military headquarters to complete these negotiations. After a banquet in their honor, Maleter and his aides were seized and whisked away.

At dawn on Sunday, November 4, new waves of Soviet tanks smashed through Budapest. Hungary's brief days of self-won independence now ended in blood and agony. Premier Nagy took refuge in the Yugoslav Embassy. When he left it, under the Soviet pledge of safe-conduct to his home, he was grabbed by waiting men. In some undisclosed dungeon, he and Maleter were subsequently executed.

So much for the pledged "word" of Communists.

The murder of Hungary created the greatest revulsion among the Communists and their sympathizers abroad since Lenin had downed the Kronstadt sailors in 1921. Thousands of Soviet students asked why Communist soldiers had shot down fellow Communists. Furthermore, Khrushchev's position became shaky. Despite his previous demotions of die-hard Stalinists like Molotov and Kaganovich, they were both still on the Presidium. Given a good issue, they might well be able to throw him out.

A Plot against Khrushchev. Khrushchev's opponents bided their time, since any sudden disturbance in the U.S.S.R. immediately following the Hungarian upheaval might endanger them, too. But by April 1957, Khrushchev was getting too powerful. He awarded himself a second Order of Lenin for his "brilliant performance" in developing the virgin lands. He had the papers run a full-page picture of himself. He began attacking the authority his rivals still possessed. Molotov, Kaganovich and Malenkov decided the time had come to act. Premier Bulganin, though fearful of openly opposing Khrushchev, let the plotters meet in his office and agreed to sanction a new government if they could succeed in overturning Khrushchev.

Voroshilov was willing to join. So were M. G. Pervukhin and Maxim Saburov, two economic-planning experts who were first deputy premiers along with Mikoyan. All told they had at least as many supporters on the 11-man Presidium as did Khrushchev. They were ready.

Political Arithmetic. A Presidium meeting was called for June 18 to discuss a relatively trivial matter. Khrushchev's followers have since given this report of what happened there. From the moment the meeting opened, a majority began voting against Khrushchev on issue after issue, made sweeping attacks on all phases of his policies and accused him of starting his own "cult of personality." Finally, his resignation as first secretary of the party was demanded. The vote was seven to four. Only one thing went wrong. Khrushchev would not accept their decision.

A CRIME KHRUSHCHEV FAILED TO MENTION

One of Stalin's crimes that Khrushchev neglected to mention concerned Stalin's old friend Abel Enukidze. In the days when Stalin was planning bank robberies in Tiflis, Enukidze was helping run the first Bolshevik underground printing press in Baku. Later he was one of four men chosen to make up a symposium honoring Stalin on his 50th birthday in 1929.

In 1935, Beria began to rewrite the party's early history to make it appear that Stalin had run everything in the Caucasus. However, Beria's history contradicted Enukidze's earlier article in the *Great Soviet Encyclopedia,* which gave Stalin no credit for the Baku press activities. Enukidze wrote a special article for *Pravda* to "correct [his] errors" and to give all credit to Stalin.

But soon Beria charged that Enukidze had "falsified the history of the Bolshevik organizations." Then, a rising young Communist attacked Enukidze as "a mortal enemy of the people" and the old Bolshevik was soon executed. The young man who attacked him was Nikita Khrushchev.

A SOVIET TANK COMMANDER EXECUTES HIS ORDERS TO CRUSH OUT HUNGARY'S MOMENTARY FREEDOM

Bulganin is supposed to have reproached him, in a somewhat hangdog manner since he was knifing the man who made him premier, by saying: "Well, we are seven and you are four."

Khrushchev told them: "In mathematics, two and two are indeed four, but that does not apply to politics. There, things are different."

And then Khrushchev proceeded to prove that they were. Under formal party rules, one fourth of the Presidium could demand a full session of the Central Committee. Khrushchev insisted that only such a full session could take so important a decision as the deposing of the first secretary. Through his control of the party machinery, Khrushchev knew that he could find his strongest support in the full session. He called it.

All day and all night, June 21 and 22, members of the Central Committee came by plane and train. Marshal Zhukov, himself recently elevated by Khrushchev, sent military planes to fetch those who could not make connections. In all, some 300 top Communists gathered for the historic confrontation.

At the full meeting Malenkov, Molotov and Kaganovich restated all their accusations against Khrushchev. They accused him of glorifying himself in a new cult of personality. They accused him of talking like a demagogue about his role in "solving" the farm problem. But they got little support in their attack, and they lost two of their Presidium "majority," Pervukhin and Saburov. Marshal Zhukov, the pre-eminent hero of the nation, made a ringing speech in support of Khrushchev. When the vote came, Khrushchev won.

The Antiparty Group. Khrushchev did not waste a second in moving to clean out his enemies. All of them, despite sharp variations on particular policies, had been opposed to Khrushchev, so he simply lumped them together as "the antiparty group." He accused them of every conceivable crime in the Communist lexicon. He had Molotov, Malenkov and his former mentor Kaganovich ousted from the Presidium and the Central Committee. Saburov was fired from the Presidium only, and Pervukhin reduced to a provisional or "candidate" member. Just as swiftly Khrushchev moved his own supporters, including Marshal Zhukov, into the vacant places. At the same stroke Khrushchev got four new openings added to the Presidium and filled them with his own men. Where a few days before he had seven enemies out of 11 members, he now had 15 members and had chosen nine of them himself.

Khrushchev let the now humiliated Bulganin stay on as premier, possibly in order to avoid giving the outside world the spectacle of a complete upheaval of the leadership. All this left only one possible major rival: Marshal Zhukov, commander of the powerful armed forces and the only professional soldier ever to rise to full membership in the Presidium. In October 1957, while Zhukov was touring Yugoslavia and Albania, Khrushchev simply dropped him from the

A NATION RISES TO FIGHT FOR FREEDOM

A freedom fighter lurks in a Budapest doorway during the wild days of October 1956. The world cheered as tiny Hungary rose against the might of the Soviet Union and its brave people clawed their way to freedom. When the U.S.S.R. violated its vow to withdraw and subjugated Budapest with fresh armor, thousands of Communists all over the world quit the party in revulsion. For a "workers' state" had coldly murdered workers rising against an intolerable tyranny.

Presidium, removed him as defense minister and, just as Stalin had done, sent him back to some obscure new assignment.

In March 1958, nine months after Khrushchev had won his victory, he removed Bulganin and became both premier and first secretary—combining the two top jobs Stalin had held.

Thus Nikita Khrushchev reached the pinnacle of Soviet power. At first, some westerners, encouraged by Khrushchev's merciless denunciations of Stalin, dared hope for some lessening of Communism's implacable hostility to the West, some retreat from its aggressive, expansionist aims. Instead, Khrushchev has proved himself an even bolder antagonist than Stalin, willing to take far bigger chances. For all of Stalin's stubborn toughness, he was careful not to use crude blackmailing tactics such as Khrushchev's threats to hurl nuclear rockets. Where cautious Stalin confined his probes to the Soviet Union's own borders, Khrushchev has not hesitated to barge into Egypt, to make a stab at the distant Congo and even to penetrate the Western Hemisphere in Cuba.

Time and again Khrushchev has proved himself the master of the "rolling crisis" technique, through which he turns tension on or off at will as with a faucet. Using this technique, he has managed to keep the Free World vacillating between excessive peaks of optimism and excessive anxiety. Thus Khrushchev's water-faucet techniques saw him running a warming bath of "spirit of Geneva" optimism in 1955, followed by the cold shower of rocket threats during the Suez Canal crisis of 1956. He raised war fever with menacing moves at Quemoy and Matsu Islands off China in 1958—then lowered it with the cordial "spirit of Camp David" in his meetings with Eisenhower in 1959. At Vienna in 1961, Khrushchev told President Kennedy that he would force the West out of Berlin. This threat evaporated in the face of American firmness. But in 1962 Khrushchev set up missile bases in Cuba, and the world came to the edge of a nuclear war before a strong stand by the United States forced him to back off.

All these actions had one thing in common—an unchanging, unrelenting determination to keep the Free World off balance, constantly on the defensive, constantly yielding ground to his advances. To restore its sense of perspective, the West must stop being surprised or alarmed by such off-again, on-again tactics and begin taking them for granted as part of the continuing battle for the world, in which there are no cheap, quick victories. The faster the West comprehends these important points, the sooner it can evolve a positive and advancing strategy of its own.

PAVLOV'S DOG AND SOVIET STRATEGY

Communism's technique of raising expectations only to dash them resembles the "conditioned reflex" experiments of Dr. Ivan Pavlov. This famous Russian scientist discovered that after a dog has been trained to associate the sound of a bell with his feeding time, the ringing alone is sufficient to start the flow of digestive juices in anticipation of the food.

If this pattern, once it has been learned, is deliberately broken, the confused animal may have a mental breakdown. If applied to humans, the technique is called "brainwashing."

Using such brainwashing techniques, Communist interrogators subjected U.S. soldiers taken prisoner during the Korean War to tortures to break their wills. Then, to avoid further torture, they would confess to the most fantastic crimes.

The Soviet Union has long used the Pavlov "conditioned reflex" to train children to unquestioning obedience. It appears that Russian scientists believe that an entire nation's will to resist can be undermined by subtle variations of the brainwashing method.

5 The Reality:
Life under Communism

RUSSIAN WORKER

5 The Reality:

Life under Communism

Wherever Communism has set its hobnailed boots, bleak and dreary grayness has overwhelmed the peoples whose lives, somehow, must go on. But the extent of the dreariness can vary enormously depending on where the individual lives. As the place in which most of the patterns of Communist life were originated, the Soviet Union is considered first in this chapter. This discussion is followed by a review of conditions in Red China and finally in the European Communist states.

Living in the U.S.S.R. Today

The Soviet Union's population of 220 million inhabits a "nation of nations." There are 15 republics in the Union, some 180 ethnically distinct peoples, speaking more than 120 different tongues. The tremendous stage on which Communism has unfolded (8,650,000 square miles) is almost as large as the United States, China and India *combined.*

It is a northern land: 50 of its major cities lie farther to the north than Edmonton in Canada; Moscow is at the same latitude as Labrador, Leningrad at the latitude of the southern tip of Greenland. Eleven time zones span this vastness, and in some northern sections the sun never sets during the "white nights" of summer. Then one can read a newspaper at midnight in the streets of Leningrad. And when clocks strike midnight there, it is 10 the next morning at the easternmost reach of the Soviet Union. The U.S.S.R. boasts the world's longest train ride—about 6,000 miles from Leningrad to Vladivostok on the Trans-Siberian Railroad, or roughly twice the distance of a transatlantic crossing.

Once the Ural mountains are left behind, most of this tremendous distance across the U.S.S.R. is a flat, unrelieved saucer circled by a rim of rocks, a vast plain stretching unhindered for thousands of miles across Eurasia. Through it flow a hundred thousand rivers.

The Domination of Winter. More than any other single thing, the winter dominates the lives of the Russians. "Winter is the great waster and consumer," observes Wright Miller in his book, *Russians as People,* "wearying body and soul for more than half the year. . . . The winter eats up armies of labor to keep city roads usable. In the most important avenues bulldozers attack the snow at once, pushing it into great heaps to slip down the sewer manholes which are left open and unguarded. . . . If no more snow falls for a long time, drab bands of sweepers attack the city ice with pick and shovel and pneumatic drill. The [switches] at tram and railway junctions must be kept clear day and night, and this work, like so much unskilled work in Russia, is done by women. . . .

"In the worst weather it is so cold that it seems to burn. You launch yourself out of double doors into the street and you gasp. You narrow your shrinking nostrils to give your lungs a chance to get acclimatized, but you gasp again and go on gasping. Ears are well covered against frostbite, but eyebrows and mustache grow icicles in bunches, and sweat runs from under your fur cap and freezes on your temples. . . ."

The Eternal Repressions. Colder than the Russian winters is the climate of freedom. No matter how much the Soviet Union achieves in industry or in science, in human terms its policies of repressing the individual seem to remain eternal. Among Lenin's first acts was the suppression of all opposition newspapers. The U.S.S.R. still has only a one-party press, and no point of view opposing the government is allowed expression. Radio and television, too, are state-controlled and blare forth only what the party dictates. Hundreds of millions of dollars are spent each year to "jam" reception of distasteful foreign broadcasts by creating artificial static. Education, though it sets rigorous and exacting standards of excellence which the West might respect, is saturated through and through with propaganda and brainwashing. Unions have no power to strike. Until recently

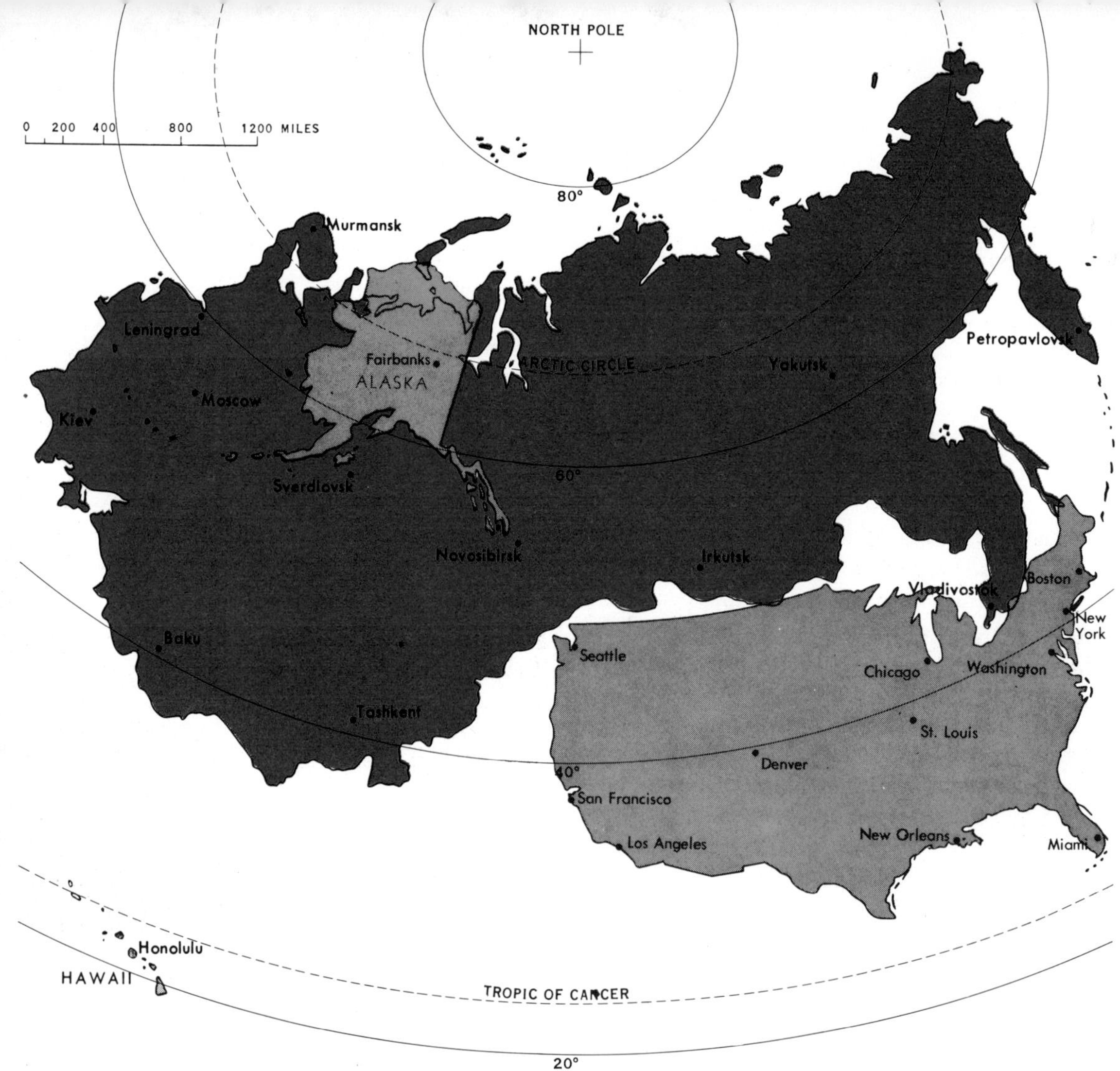

WORLD'S LARGEST NATION, the Soviet Union *(red)* is over twice the size of the U.S. (The map shows both countries in their proper latitudes.) The U.S.S.R. is some 8,650,000 square miles in area, and over 6,000 miles in width from Leningrad to Vladivostok on the Pacific. To cross this immense land by train takes almost 10 days.

workers were not even allowed to change their jobs without permission, and though they may now do so in theory, regulations make it extremely difficult in practice. Religion is tolerated in the Soviet Union, but no youth who wants to rise in the Soviet hierarchy of management, science or any other field dares openly to proclaim his faith. Elections are held, but there is only one slate of candidates, from only one party.

A Thirst for Truth. Since Joseph Stalin's tyranny ended in March 1953, the cruder kinds of terror have gone. To the 120 million Russians who are under 29 today and who make up 55 per cent of the Soviet Union's entire population, Stalinism is little more than a bad childhood memory. The young have not been broken by the fear that haunts their fathers or been infected with the blind faith that guided some of their Bolshevik grandfathers.

The word this generation seems to use more than any other is "truth." They want to know, first and above all, what is really "true" about what is going on in the world. Somehow, they can sense when official stories distort the truth. For example, university students simply refused to believe the official charges that the Hungarian revolution was started by "fascists" and "reactionaries." When lecturers gave them this explanation, they shuffled their feet or rustled papers to show their disbelief.

Bluejeans, Jazz and Dancing. Young Russians are extravagant followers of western fads and customs. They were fascinated by the 1957 World Youth Festival, which brought 30,000 young foreigners into Moscow for a propaganda jamboree. The festival was aimed at impressing non-Communists with life under Communism. Instead, after mingling for the first time with their contemporaries from five continents, many young Russians seemed to be profoundly impressed by the free, privileged life that is the lot of youth outside Russia.

The Kremlin periodically has backed away from its stubborn resistance to "bourgeois" western tastes in clothes, jazz and dancing. The regime has yielded to the young people's demands for their own distinctive styles, and even bluejeans are now being manufactured in the U.S.S.R.

At Moscow's swimming pools, old-fashioned swim suits have yielded to two-piece costumes for girls. Moscow University's youths call their girls "Janes" after Tarzan's sweetheart, whose acquaintance they have made in old movies which did not reach Russia until after World War II. These coeds are using eye shadow, painting their nails and sporting stylish hairdos.

More and more, Soviet youths listen to official propaganda and slogans with cynicism. But the young people are loyal to Communism as the only political system they know. They startle westerners by criticizing the regime in one breath, then announcing in the next that under Communism the U.S.S.R. will "outproduce" America.

The greatest single affliction of youth is simple boredom. Endless bitter jokes denounce the drabness of life in the Soviet Union today. Asks one: "Is there life on Mars?" Answer: "No, there isn't any there, *either*." Another joke has a Russian saying, "In ten years we will pass America." Answers the other: "Let me know when we do. I want to get off."

The Heavily Burdened Student. All education in the Soviet Union is centrally controlled by the state and education is free. Most of those who are bright enough to go on to college or higher technical training receive scholarships paid for by the state. These average about 25 rubles a month ($27). Out of this the students pay a nomi-

A PASSION FOR CULTURE

Learning at leisure, this young Soviet girl is typical of many Russians who devote themselves with the utmost seriousness to the pursuit of knowledge. The younger Soviet generation seems to possess an almost obsessive desire for "truth" —as opposed to the lies it now attributes to the era of Stalin.

nal sum for room rent, food and clothing, and they still have a little left for pocket money.

At whatever level, Soviet students have to work hard, so hard that for years prominent Soviet medical authorities have feared that the health of the youth might be endangered by their being overburdened. But in recent years even heavier burdens have been put on them. In the eighth to 10th grades, for example, a student has to study 10 and frequently 12 hours a day. He spends five to six hours daily in the classroom and three-and-a-half to four hours on homework. Two days a week he must devote two to three more hours a day to industrial training, frequently in a factory. On other days he may have to give two or more hours to "politico-social" duties such as meetings of the Young Communist League (the Komsomols) or the Pioneers, another youth group that discovers and trains potential Communist leaders.

A PIONEERING SPACE PROGRAM

A broad smile wreathes the face of Soviet cosmonaut Pavel Popovich, who made a historic 48-orbit trip around the earth. This was one of the high points of the Soviet space program that started with the launching of the first Sputnik in 1957 and achieved a spectacular success in August 1962 by having two men in orbit at the same time.

The subject matter the Soviet student studies is exacting. All Russian students who graduate from high school have studied physics for six years, chemistry for five years, biology for five years and astronomy for one year.

These days Soviet students are feeling the brunt of a major educational "reform" that Premier Khrushchev instituted in 1958. What provoked it was the fact that the low birth rate of the wartime years —during which more than 20 million Russians were killed—was giving the Soviet Union a manpower shortage at the time the country was launching major expansions of its industry. The biggest shortage is presently in the 16- to 18-year-old age group.

The effect of the new Soviet education laws is as follows: Most students will leave school at age 15 to spend the rest of their lives working in factories or on farms, although some of them will continue their education on a part-time or spare-time basis. Those youngsters who remain in school must at some point work in factories or on farms for two years before they can be eligible for higher education. However, this work prerequisite is waived for students entering high-priority fields such as mathematics, science and engineering. The majority of boys will also have to do two years of military service, so they may well be 26 by the time they graduate from college.

Soviet Science. The world's scientists have great respect for the high place that the U.S.S.R. has given to science. Pre-Communist Russia had many first-rank achievements—in physics, in geology, in soil science and in other fields. The periodic Communist claims—which have become subjects for satiric cartoons in the West—that Russians first invented the telephone, the radio, the automobile and so forth, have at least a little basis in fact. Even if they did not actually get there first, Russian scientists did make certain discoveries in all these fields.

Under Communism, the Russians have given preference to the teaching of science. A career in science has also attracted many of the brightest youngsters in the country, since they were less apt to encounter political difficulties in that field than in the social sciences where Stalin demanded total conformity to Communist ideas. Science was a sort of refuge for inquiring minds.

Soviet scientists and technicians have proved themselves extremely capable in the area of applied research. When they tackled the problem of the atomic bomb, they solved it very quickly. And some American scientists now believe that the Soviet Union's Igor Kurchatov solved some of the major problems of the hydrogen bomb even before the United States did.

Furthermore, the sudden Soviet ascendance in space rocketry in 1957 gave proof of the occasional superiority of a completely state-dominated system when it decides to apply huge resources and priority to a given problem.

Nevertheless, Communism does not seem to stimulate new ideas in pure—as opposed to applied—research among scientists. Since 1917 only four Russians have won the Nobel Prize in science. During the same time, 56 scientists in the United States have won Nobel Prizes in science.

AN EXPANDING NUCLEAR INDUSTRY

A Russian technician performs one safety check on equipment for handling radioactive substances. To further their atomic programs, Soviet leaders have appropriated large sums of money for advanced research. Six large-scale nuclear power plants are now scheduled for completion by 1965.

Biased Studies and "Communist Morality." In Soviet schools, political bias permeates every subject taught. For example, here is a problem in second-grade arithmetic: "Before the Great October Revolution workers used to work 12 hours per day; now they work only 8 hours per day. By how many hours has the working day been reduced since the . . . Revolution?"

As part of its indoctrination effort, Soviet education seeks to ground students in "Communist morality." Since Communism rejects religion, it also rejects the western moral values based primarily on religion. Therefore, Soviet children are taught to distinguish right from wrong not on the basis of fundamental moral values, as we understand them, but rather on the basis of Soviet doctrine. Thus, killing another is wrong, but it was "morally right" for Stalin to kill millions of people during the forced collectivization of the farms. A child should respect his father and his mother, say the Communists, but a statue stands in Moscow in honor of 11-year-old Pavlik Morosov, whose father was executed after young Pavlik denounced him as a hoarder of grain. The child should obey and respect his teacher, say the Communists, but should inform upon her if she is tolerant toward an expression of religious views.

The nature of these Communist standards understandably leads to confusion. Soviet educators have occasionally complained that "pupils were growing up to be 'totally dishonest,' that violations of 'elementary honor' and of 'common honesty and truthfulness' were widespread." One Soviet educational journal openly admitted that the following student delinquencies were commonplace: "Total disrespect for socialist labor, desire to sponge on everyone, disrespect toward adults, continuous lying, excessive profanity, outright acts of debauchery, petty crimes, and distrust of everyone."

THE PERSECUTION OF A TRUE PATRIOT

Boris Pasternak won the Nobel Prize in 1958 for his gripping novel *Doctor Zhivago.* Although Soviet editors had rejected the book, it was printed abroad, earning world praise but Kremlin denunciation. Actually, the novel spoke Pasternak's love for his country, a love so strong that he refused to leave even when Khrushchev asked him to go. Pasternak died in 1960, a true patriot whose glory will far outlast official Moscow's displeasure.

The Teaching of Atheism. Schools indoctrinate students in atheism. Teachers-in-training and students of philosophy and history must complete specific studies in the historical background and theories of atheism.

Nevertheless, there is a growing interest in religion. In the past decade, the Baptists claim to have increased membership in the Soviet Union from 500,000 to around one million. Writing in the Moscow *Literary Gazette* in 1962, Alexander Osipov, a former professor of theology and one of the editors of the last Russian Bible, said that in many areas of the Soviet Union over 50 per cent of the children are still christened. Osipov explained that "although not all the parents are religious, they still baptize their children because they say, 'It is the custom. . . .'" There is an active participation in religion in the rural areas. Curiously enough, youths who are attracted to religion do not seem attracted to the Orthodox Church because they regard it as a branch of the government.

Party Membership. In the country of the "dictatorship of the proletariat," the road to full membership in the Communist party—which effectively wields the dictatorship—is long and rocky. It is not enough merely to be a member of the proletariat, for by now this presumably includes all 220 million citizens of the Soviet Union. But only some 8.8 million are permitted to be full members of the party. (Usually they work up by way of the Pioneers and then the Komsomols—youth groups.) Add to this, nearly 850,000 candidate members, and the number of citizens eligible for government positions is restricted to only 4.4 per cent of the total population. These favored few have successfully passed the most rigorous scrutiny by party members charged with determining who will enter and who will be denied the privilege of party membership.

Tolya's Summer "Vacation." As an example of how the state —and party—impose upon the "free" time of Russian youths, here is a recent experience of a high-school graduate named Tolya. He went off to spend the summer with his grandparents in the countryside west of Moscow, looking forward to swimming and fishing. Toward the end of July an uninvited visitor, a youth about two years older than himself, came to see him. What he had to tell Tolya sounded like *Komsomolskaya Pravda,* the youth newspaper: "It is the duty of every patriotic Soviet citizen and Komsomol member to do his part in the effort to boost food production. Will you join our volunteer brigade to help neighboring collective farms with the harvest?"

Tolya said he had worked hard all year and had only a few vacation weeks left before facing up to tougher studies in college. "Besides," he said, "I keep hearing farmers say the brigades are more of a hindrance than a help."

THE NEW GENERATION includes swaggering teenagers who try to mimic western styles. Russian youth is skeptical of the heroism and self-sacrifice that the state expects of its citizens. Khrushchev has criticized as "unhealthy attitudes" young people's interest in modern art, jazz and American authors like J. D. Salinger.

The other youth furrowed his brow. "Of course, it's all up to you, comrade. Think it over and let us know at the District Komsomol Committee. We got your name from a list sent us by the Moscow Committee."

Tolya's peace of mind was shattered. That night, instead of sleeping, he turned over and over in his mind the possible consequences of his refusal. Perhaps a letter describing his uncooperative attitude had already been sent off that afternoon to the Moscow Committee. Once something derogatory of that sort was put in writing and became a part of one's dossier, or "characteristic," as it is called, it could become a kind of curse, turning up at intervals throughout the years to work its victim's repeated undoing.

Early in the morning, Tolya made his way to the nearby village where the local party and Komsomol organizations had their offices. The front of the one-story frame building was bedecked with red bunting inscribed with slogans telling how much wheat, how much fodder, how many potatoes this district was going to deliver to the state. Inside, Tolya's visitor of the previous day gave him a form to sign and shook his hand. "I felt sure of your decision so I'd already included your name on the list," he said. "Report back here at nine a.m. tomorrow with your gear."

And that was the end of Tolya's summer holiday.

Industrial Growth. At great deprivation to its people the Soviet Union has managed to achieve an impressively swift rate of industrial growth, particularly in heavy industry.

Soviet figures on what has been accomplished are exaggerated and confusing. Even so, American economists are convinced that great strides have been made. One reliable United States study shows that the Soviet Union in a decade (1950-1960) has managed to more than double industrial production and triple electric power production.

The managers of Communism's large industries, who long had to live in fear of Stalin's capricious purges, now enjoy a good deal of power and independence. Under Stalin, great waste and inefficiency grew up through the rivalry and lack of coordination among the various bureaucracies charged with responsibility. Two steamer fleets were operated on the same river by two different ministries, one sailing empty in one direction while the other sailed empty in the opposite. One large quarry was being worked by eight small enterprises, each representing a different ministry.

Khrushchev, however, has been trying to increase efficiency by decentralizing authority. No longer do all economic decisions have to be made in the Kremlin. Regional Economic Councils have been established in 105 different regions to handle the decisions formerly made by officials in the Kremlin. These councils are familiar with local situations and are able to study the available resources and

U.S. and Soviet Production Compared: U.S.S.R. Output (Red) Is Shown as

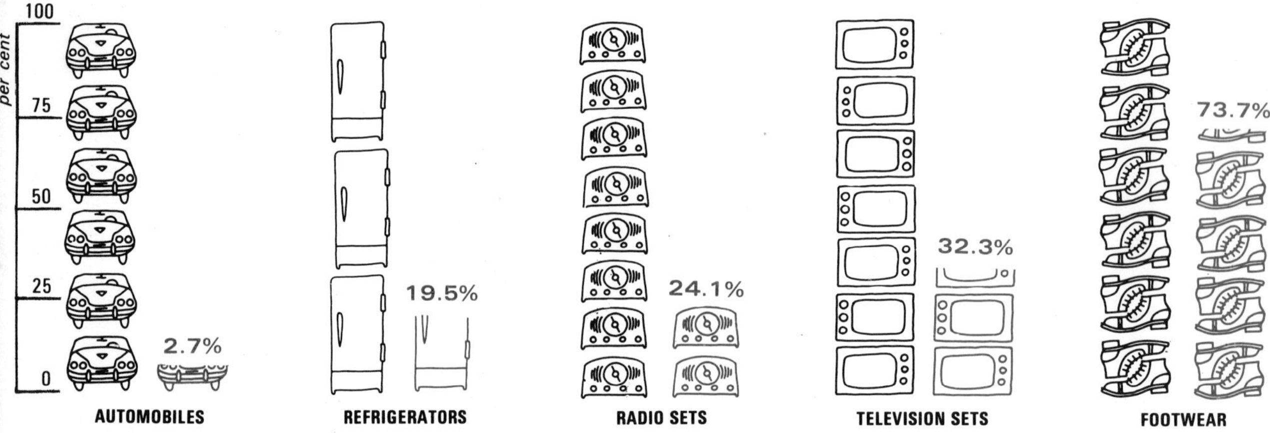

IN CONSUMER GOODS, as this chart of 1961 production shows, the U.S. ranks far ahead of the Soviet Union. The Russians concentrate on turning out military equipment or machinery for heavy industry rather than autos, radios and TV sets. And even Russians complain about the poor quality of consumer goods that are available.

allocate them in a more efficient manner. The system also makes it possible for one industry to utilize the "by-products" of another without the incredible red tape that used to exist.

Nevertheless, the famous system of "blat" still survives. The word means roughly "pull" or "influence." The saying used to go, Blat is higher than Stalin, meaning that any law or regulation can be circumvented. When an industrial manager is worried that promised materials will not arrive on time or in the right quantity, he turns to a specialist known as a *tolkach*, or "pusher." The *tolkach* is a lively, energetic man who knows how to establish a working friendship with the proper officials in factories and ministries. He has as his "accounts" many factories around the country who pay him to be their "representative." Since the pusher's activities are illegal, he gets extremely high pay, often concealed as handsome presents from grateful plant managers. The use of "blat" arose out of fear of failure to meet the production quotas which Stalin set at an unrealistically high level. To avoid imprisonment or death, many managers faked their statistics to make it seem that quotas had been met. One state farm, Khrushchev has revealed, even went out and bought butter in the free market, at high prices, in order to fulfill the "norm," or quota. Sometimes "blat" veers over into what the state punishes severely as economic crimes.

Economic Crimes. The terrible shortage of basic creature comforts during most of Communism's history has given rise to what the Soviets called economic crimes. The crimes may be as minor as a worker's theft of tools. A more spectacular incident involved a man

a Percentage of U.S. Output (Black)

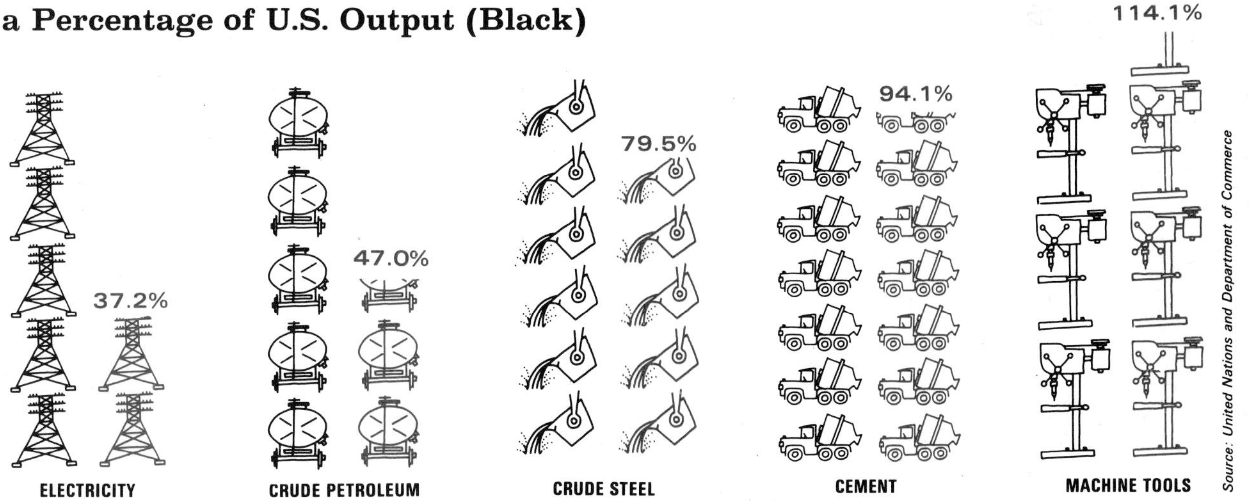

37.2% 47.0% 79.5% 94.1% 114.1%

ELECTRICITY CRUDE PETROLEUM CRUDE STEEL CEMENT MACHINE TOOLS

Source: United Nations and Department of Commerce

IN PRODUCER GOODS, the Soviet Union is emphasizing electric power (now expanding at a rate of 11.5 per cent a year) and heavy industry. This is reflected in the speed with which the Russians are approaching U.S. levels in petroleum, steel and cement. In the production of machine tools, the U.S.S.R. has already surpassed the U.S.

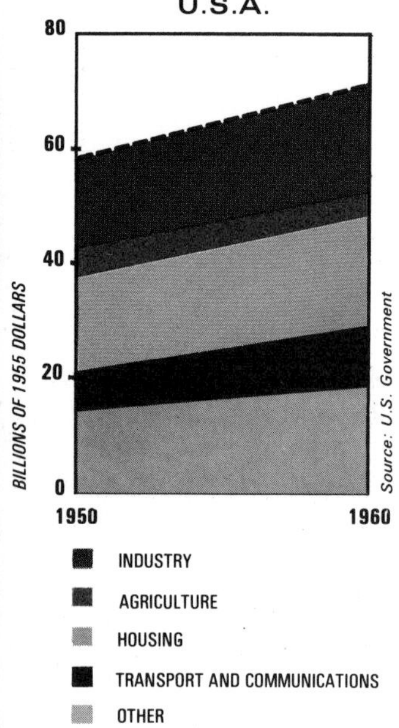

CAPITAL SPENDING IN THE U.S.

The dotted line on this chart shows the growth of capital investment in the U.S. from 1950 to 1960. The major purposes for which the money was invested are shown in the various colored sections below. For example, the amount spent for new industrial plants and equipment *(dark red)* is somewhat less than the amount spent for new housing *(pink)*. The comparative data for the U.S.S.R. appear on the opposite page.

who built a $27,000 house over a period of five years, although he had earned only $15,000 during that time. He tried to explain it away by saying it "took a lot of scrimping," but the house was confiscated. The death sentence is apparently being imposed with more and more frequency for economic crimes.

In the very early days Communists used to preach that capital punishment was simply another evil growing out of capitalism and its alleged insistence that property rights are superior to human rights. Now Communism has reached the point where Boris Nikiforov, head of the Criminal Law Department of the U.S.S.R. Institute of Jurisprudence, went out of his way to defend executions for economic crimes in a letter to *The New York Times:*

> Whoever appropriates state or public property encroaches on the basic principle of life of Soviet society, hence on the basic principle of life of every Soviet man. That is why the Constitution of the U.S.S.R. says that Socialist property is sacred and inviolable.

What Mr. Nikiforov was really saying is that under Communism the state places a higher value on property than on human life.

The Life of an Auto Worker. In the Soviet Union, everyone works for the state. It is illegal for any private citizen to employ anyone to produce a commodity for sale. Whether he works in a factory or on a collective farm, the state—in other words, the Communist party—is the worker's boss. What this means is illustrated by the life of a factory worker named Vasily, who works for the Likhachev Automobile Works outside Moscow.

Likhachev is an immense industrial complex that employs 20,000 workers (20 per cent of them women) at an average wage of about $105 a month, which is higher than that paid by the average Russian factory. Likhachev makes not only trucks and buses, but bicycles and electric refrigerators as well.

The plant is almost a self-contained city. Around it rise blocks of tall new apartment houses for the workers. The factory has its own schools. A worker born in Likhachev could go from kindergarten all the way through an engineering institute without leaving. The factory also provides theater, music, motion pictures, lectures, sports and dances. There are 20 restaurants, with meals priced at only a fourth to a third of the cost elsewhere. There are medical and dental clinics that provide free services for workers and their families. The housing shortage is acute, but new apartments equipped with gas and electricity are being built constantly. The apartments range from one to three rooms, and rents amount to 5 to 6 per cent of a worker's wages. Workers have to make their own minor household repairs and do their own painting.

The factory has a 3,000-acre farm that produces most of the meat, dairy foods and vegetables consumed by the workers. Likhachev operates a resort on the Baltic Sea for its workers and a resthouse in the village of Vaskino in Moscow Province. But so few workers own automobiles that the auto factory has no need for a parking lot.

The Autoless Auto Workers. Though the wages are considered good, very few men can support a family on their pay alone, so wives have to work as well as husbands. Nurseries and kindergartens are maintained to make it easier for mothers to work.

Vasily has toiled here a quarter century. Although he is intelligent and conscientious, he has from the beginning deliberately shunned advancement, including a chance to enter an engineering school and qualify for a degree. The more important one's job, he has learned, the greater the risk. In the purges of the 1930s the casualty rate was greatest for those at the highest levels.

However, Vasily's proficiency on the job had carried him ahead at a steady rate. During the war, when the Nazis threatened Moscow, he was evacuated beyond the Urals, along with most of the equipment and personnel of the plant. In a few months the workers were producing scout cars and other vehicles in a new plant deep in the hinterland.

His wife followed with their two children, but Vasily's mother stayed on in their one-room flat in Moscow. It was lucky she did, for she kept the room and its contents intact; others who had left their rooms locked but unattended came back to find the locks broken and the contents plundered, and occasionally strangers were occupying the premises. Vasily's family had living quarters to come back to after the war.

Vasily sometimes earns, with bonuses and overtime, as much as 250 rubles a month (about $275), a very high figure for most skilled workers. He bought a combination television, radio and record-player console at GUM, the big Moscow department store, though his family of five were still living in two small rooms.

Housing was the only major source of annoyance for Vasily and his wife. She urged him to enter their name for one of the new blocks of apartments which had been going up since the 1950s. He did so, and although they had to wait a year and a half to get in, one day they were notified that they could move into a new three-room apartment—a rare luxury in Moscow.

The Most Persistent Shortage. Thousands of others are not so lucky as Vasily. Of all the shortages which the Soviet people have endured in 45-odd years of Communism, the most persistent—and the most annoying—is that of housing. When Yuri Gagarin became the first human to orbit the globe in 1961, he was awarded the privilege of moving out of a two-room apartment into a four-room one. "Gagarin had to go around the world to get another room," sighed his envious admirers.

A tremendous number of new apartments are being built in the

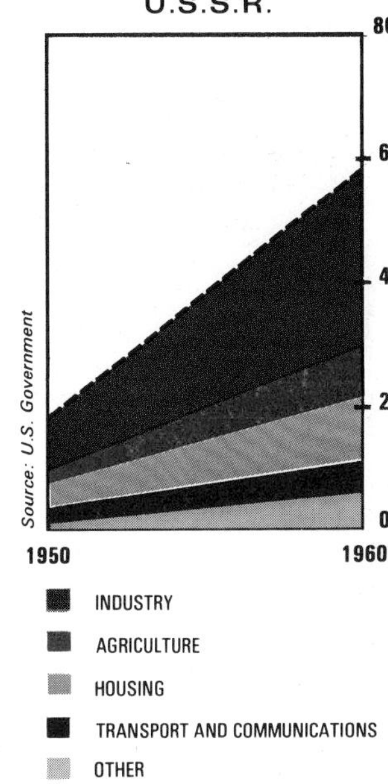

CAPITAL SPENDING IN THE U.S.S.R.

The dotted line on the chart above shows a much sharper rate of increase in Soviet capital investment as compared with the U.S., though the total invested is still some $12 billion less than in the U.S. This increase is due mostly to large expenditures on heavy industry investment *(dark red)*, with less spent in areas more directly benefiting the average Russian. In these areas, the U.S. is far ahead.

Soviet Union, but the quality of the construction often leaves much to be desired. Only a few years after they were occupied, many of the new Moscow apartments began to crack and crumble. Khrushchev has conceded this: "Sometimes as a result of haste new buildings are put into use with many defects. The working people, naturally, are highly annoyed at this, and rightly so! Those responsible for such defects in newly built houses should be rapped over the knuckles."

Strangers in One Room. Joseph Novak, as a young intellectual from one of the satellite nations, was able to see Soviet housing close up, and he describes it in his book *The Future Is Ours, Comrade:* "Soviet rules governing the number of people who are supposed to occupy a certain living area are [rigid]. According to my observations, the basis for assigning the population to an apartment is not the number of rooms or the family bonds of the people in the apartment, but solely the size of the living area.

"If . . . the rule is that one person can live in an area of six or seven square meters, then an apartment of 40 square meters [about 20 x 21 feet] should accommodate from four to six persons. This applies even if the apartment has only one room and if these persons are of different sexes and ages, and total strangers to each other.

"In each apartment the group of tenants is closely bound together by the limited area and by the common use of certain facilities—corridor, kitchen and bathroom . . . each tenant has a strictly defined area of his own . . . I have seen all kinds of screens, partitions, barriers and curtains made of linen, cardboard or paper used for this purpose. Sometimes a piece of furniture such as a wardrobe is used as a divider."

The Upper Class. Communism was supposed to create a "classless society" but it has not. The prominent figures of Soviet society are not the party heads, who live apart from the rest of the people, but cultural and professional people: actors, writers, musicians, dancers, journalists, artists, architects, professors, scientists, engineers and doctors.

A small number of extremely successful artists may earn $2,200 in a very exceptional month. Scientists may regularly make as much as $1,500 a month or more. Next come professors and managers earning from $440 to $1,100 a month.

How well can they live on these incomes? Judging Soviet living standards by income is difficult because of the tricky Soviet tax system. This is based on a turnover tax, a type of sales tax that is levied primarily on consumer goods. The tax rate fluctuates widely from item to item, depending on the needs and programs of the government at the time.

The government raises about 50 per cent of its revenue—and 65 per cent of all taxes—by the turnover tax. This kind of tax tends to hit hardest at those with the lowest incomes. In many instances,

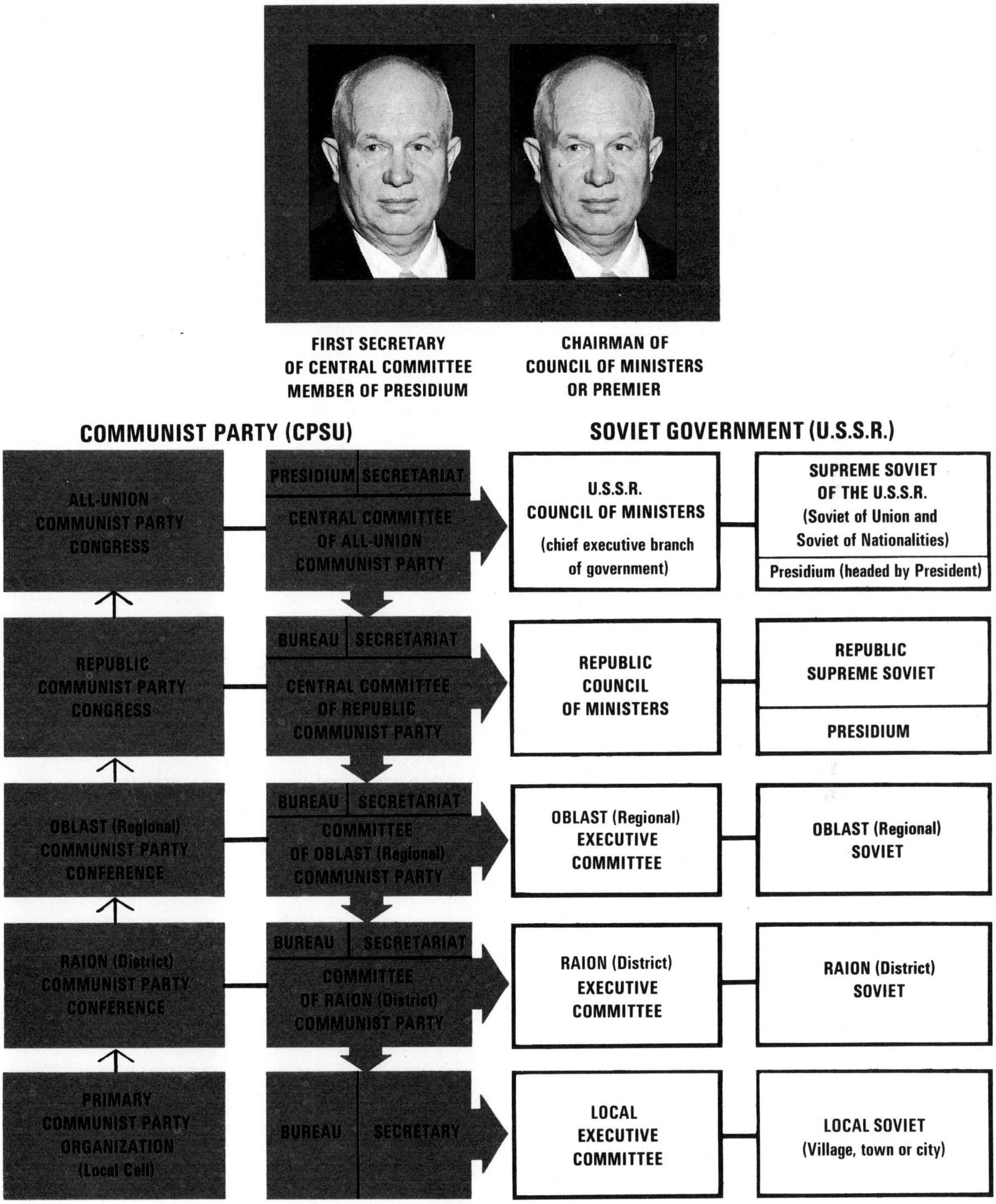

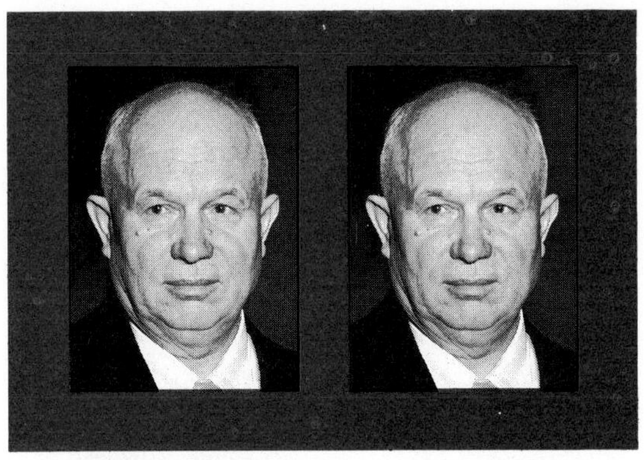

FIRST SECRETARY
OF CENTRAL COMMITTEE
MEMBER OF PRESIDIUM

CHAIRMAN OF
COUNCIL OF MINISTERS
OR PREMIER

COMMUNIST PARTY (CPSU)

SOVIET GOVERNMENT (U.S.S.R.)

ALL-UNION COMMUNIST PARTY CONGRESS	PRESIDIUM / SECRETARIAT; CENTRAL COMMITTEE OF ALL-UNION COMMUNIST PARTY	U.S.S.R. COUNCIL OF MINISTERS (chief executive branch of government)	SUPREME SOVIET OF THE U.S.S.R. (Soviet of Union and Soviet of Nationalities); Presidium (headed by President)
REPUBLIC COMMUNIST PARTY CONGRESS	BUREAU / SECRETARIAT; CENTRAL COMMITTEE OF REPUBLIC COMMUNIST PARTY	REPUBLIC COUNCIL OF MINISTERS	REPUBLIC SUPREME SOVIET; PRESIDIUM
OBLAST (Regional) COMMUNIST PARTY CONFERENCE	BUREAU / SECRETARIAT; COMMITTEE OF OBLAST (Regional) COMMUNIST PARTY	OBLAST (Regional) EXECUTIVE COMMITTEE	OBLAST (Regional) SOVIET
RAION (District) COMMUNIST PARTY CONFERENCE	BUREAU / SECRETARIAT; COMMITTEE OF RAION (District) COMMUNIST PARTY	RAION (District) EXECUTIVE COMMITTEE	RAION (District) SOVIET
PRIMARY COMMUNIST PARTY ORGANIZATION (Local Cell)	BUREAU / SECRETARY	LOCAL EXECUTIVE COMMITTEE	LOCAL SOVIET (Village, town or city)

THE COMMUNIST PARTY'S IRON RULE of the U.S.S.R. is shown in this schematic chart. Red arrows indicate how the party organization dominates Soviet organs of government at every level. In theory the party chooses its leader, as indicated by black arrows. Actually both the party and the government are controlled from the top.

the tax raises the price by roughly 100 per cent over and above the cost of the article. It acts as a powerful brake on consumption. The amount of the tax is kept secret from the citizens, who know only the total price they must pay.

The Soviet Union's leaders do not claim to have achieved "true Communism" yet. The 22nd Party Congress in 1961 adopted a new program, which offered the promise that Russia would move out of its present phase of "socialism" into "true Communism." When that happens, Khrushchev promised, every Russian will enjoy free subway rides, free utility services, free meals in collective cafeterias and many other benefits. Khrushchev did make one reservation: The U.S.S.R. will deliver all this, he said, only if world peace can be preserved. But the biggest threat to world peace is precisely Communism's determination to conquer the world.

The Chronic Farm Crisis. Communism's greatest single failure has been a chronic inability to meet the goals set for its farm programs. In 1957 Khrushchev boasted that within three years the Soviet Union would pass the United States in meat production. Early in 1962 he conceded that the effort had failed, that meat production was the Soviets' biggest headache. He raised meat prices 30 per cent to give collective farmers an incentive to produce more.

Through all the years of collectivization and farm failures, one telltale fact has stood out: The peasants who were allowed to maintain small private plots and to keep a cow and a few other animals pro-

The Work of One Farmer Feeds This Many People:

COMPARATIVE OUTPUT of Soviet and American farmers is shown above. In the U.S.S.R. 22 per cent of the population is engaged in agriculture, compared to less than 4 per cent in the U.S. The Soviet lag in production is explained in part by poor climate, but also by the lack of incentive for people who work on collective farms.

duced twice as much per acre on their private plots as the collective farms did. Instead of drawing from this the obvious lesson that private production could solve his food problems, Khrushchev insisted that private production made the crisis worse: "The little worm of individual property," he once charged, "still sits in the mind of the *kolkhoznik* [collective farm worker]."

By 1962 Khrushchev had sunk some five billion dollars into a desperate experiment to cultivate the "virgin lands," 100 million acres of dry prairie land in Siberia and Kazakhstan that had never before produced a crop. He began replacing grass crops with grain, overlooking the fact that nearly all of the U.S.S.R. is too far north for consistently successful grain crops. Many feel that the newly planted lands will simply turn into a great dust bowl. Although the experiment has increased the quantity of foodstuffs to some extent, it has been a serious disappointment because it has not solved the problem of food shortage.

Communism's leaders have traditionally been at odds with the peasants. Boris Pilnyak, the novelist, recalled how Lenin discussed the farm problem and illustrated his talk by grabbing at his own throat, saying: "Either we choke the peasants or they choke us." A system which called for the rule of the proletariat, or factory workers, when the vast majority of Russians were peasants had to oppress the peasants or be overthrown by them. Stalin himself told Winston Churchill, in one of their wartime conversations, that the

One Day's Wages for a Factory Worker Will Buy:

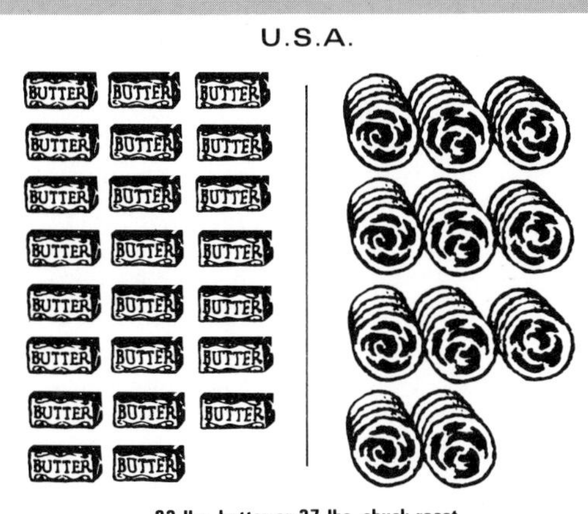

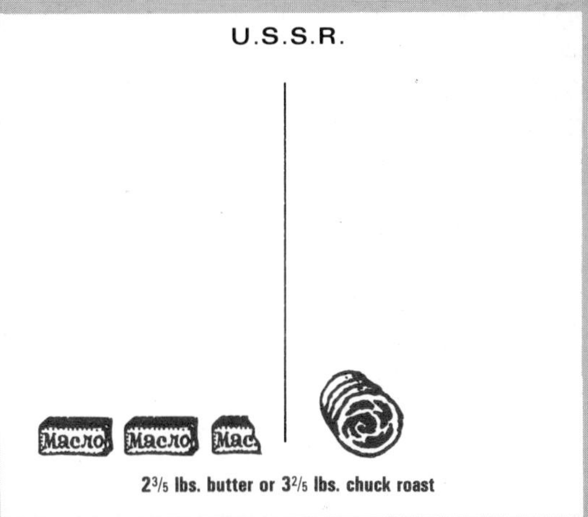

RELATIVE PURCHASING POWER of Russians and Americans shows a vast difference in what a day's pay will buy. The difference arises partly because the Russian worker earns less than his American counterpart, but also because food costs are higher in the U.S.S.R. and will remain so until farms become more efficient.

forcible collectivizing of the farms was a harsher test for him than the war itself. "It was fearful," said Stalin. "Four years it lasted. . . . It was all very bad and difficult—but necessary."

Khrushchev has blamed Russia's present farm problems largely on Stalin's "wrong notions" about agriculture. "I recall his once asking me," he told an American in 1962, "when I was working in the Ukraine, 'What's the situation?' I said there was not enough grain for animal husbandry. 'What do you need grain for?' he asked. I answered: 'To feed the pigs, to feed poultry.' 'What do you want to feed the pigs for? Let them scrounge around for their food.' "

Soviet Exploitation of Workers. What Communism has achieved in the Soviet Union has best been summed up by philosopher Sidney Hook in these words: "Almost from the very beginning, the Communist rulers had absolute power to deny any peasant or worker access to farm or factory, to decide what should be spent and saved—and how—and to determine the conditions and rewards of work. . . . Under such a setup, workers can be and have been exploited more intensively, i.e., more 'surplus value' has been sweated out of them, than under other forms of legal ownership since the early days of the industrial revolution."

The Communist rulers have never hesitated to weep crocodile tears over the "plight" of workingmen in capitalist countries. But it is safe to say that no capitalist employer in a western nation would dare to impose any of the restrictions on labor that in the Soviet Union—the "workers' state"—are accepted as a matter of course.

Study, Work and Play under Communism

Students in a physiology laboratory *(right)* at the Tadzhik Academy of Science testify to the Soviet Union's concentration on universal education, and its special emphasis on the training of scientists. In the 16 pages that follow are other close-ups in color of life among the people—now numbering one third of the world's population—who live under Communism. The photographs tell a story of intense competition with the West at every level. Under the constantly reiterated slogan of overtaking and surpassing America, the U.S.S.R. is utilizing huge hydroelectric plants, pouring out fiery rivers of molten steel, breaking the soil of the "virgin lands" across the Urals and toughening the muscles of whole populations through mass sports.

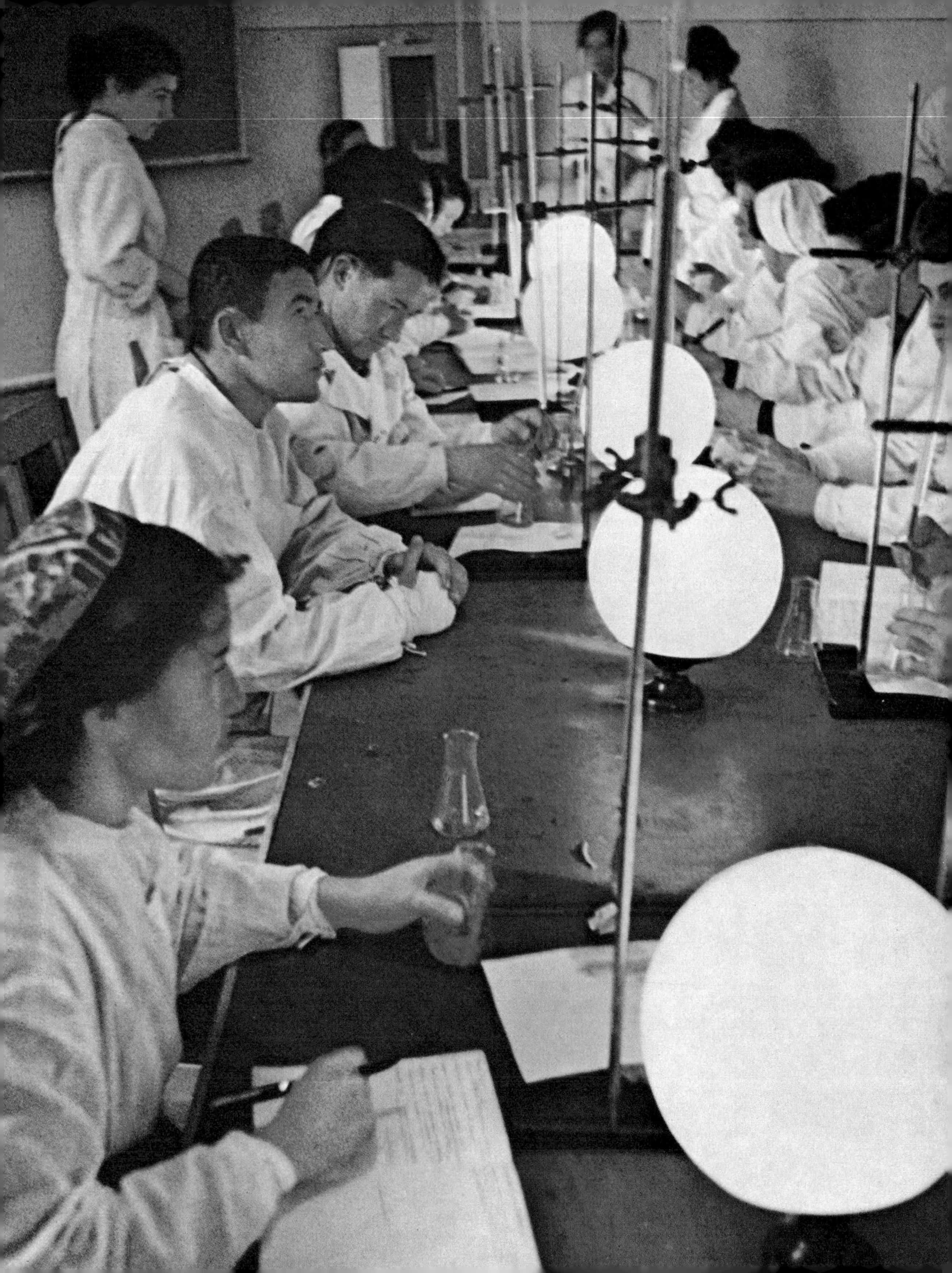

Electricity and Steel—Twin Supports of the Soviet Economy

A MIGHTY POWER SOURCE, the impressive building enclosing the turbines of the Kuibyshev hydroelectric station, one of the world's largest, dwarfs a throng at the dedication ceremony in 1958. The Soviet Union gives priority to power generation, and in 1961 succeeded in raising its production of power to a total of 327 billion kilowatt-hours. The United States' power production for the same year came to 878.5 billion kilowatt-hours.

A GOLDEN SHOWER of liquefied steel *(right)* illuminates a mill in Georgia. In 1961 the U.S.S.R. produced 71, the United States 89 million metric tons of steel.

The Vexing Problem of Food for a Multiplying Population

HARVESTING GRAIN, a woman uses old-fashioned methods on a farm near Alma-Ata. It takes nearly 22 per cent of the population to raise enough food for Russians, compared with less than 4 per cent in the U.S.

SHOPPING FOR MEAT, housewives wait patiently outside a butcher shop in Tashkent. Meat is short in the U.S.S.R. and has always been expensive. To make things worse, prices were raised 30 per cent in 1962.

GATHERING FIREWOOD, a farmer drives a wagon over a snow-covered collective farm in the Ukraine. Geography adds to the U.S.S.R.'s agricultural dilemma. Much of the land lies north of the 50th parallel, where summers are short and the growing season so brief that only crops that mature rapidly can be grown successfully.

A Hard and Laborious Life in the Distant Lands of Vast Siberia

SCHOOLGIRLS do required farm labor *(left)* in remote Khabarovsk, near Red China. Students work for fixed times in farms or factories.

HOUSEWIVES dressed for warmth *(opposite)* tramp the sidewalks of Yakutsk. Some Siberian areas have permafrost only three feet down.

A FARM BOY drives a wagon *(below)* across a stream on a state farm near Irkutsk, Siberia. His village of 7,000 has five schools.

РЕМОНТ
ЧАСОВ
всех систем
ГАРАНТИЯ ОДИН ГОД

Modern Homes for the Favored Few at the Top of the Heap

A NEW APARTMENT HOUSE boasts bright balconies. Two rooms are considered very luxurious for four people and the apartments go first to the Soviet elite —intellectuals, artists, scientists and political leaders.

CONSTRUCTING A WALL, women masons work on a building *(left)* in Irkutsk. Russia's housing shortage is so acute that emphasis is on quantity rather than quality. As a result, many new buildings quickly deteriorate.

The Amazing Variety of Performing Arts in the U.S.S.R.

SOVIET FILMS range from adventure movies, like the one being made above, to fine drama. Russian directors, such as the great Sergei Eisenstein, pioneered in the development of documentary movies in the early 1920s.

THE BOLSHOI THEATER, Moscow's famed opera and ballet house *(opposite)*, maintains a high level of performance and is regularly sold out. But in the "workers' state," visitors and Soviet elite get the best seats.

Center of World Communism

Fireworks and searchlights silhouette the star-tipped towers of the Kremlin during a jubilant Moscow celebration. Ancient fortress of the Tsars, this is now the capital of world Communism. Gleaming in the distance are the onion-shaped domes of St. Basil's Cathedral, an ancient structure looking out on Red Square.

Entire Nations Regimented for Totalitarian Displays

A SNAPPY PARADE enters a Leipzig stadium *(opposite)* in East Germany. The country has boasted it has 1.3 million men, women and children organized for sport.

A MASS DEMONSTRATION by platoons of girl athletes *(above)* fills a vast Prague stadium. At this eight-day sports spectacle more than 700,000 athletes performed.

A Future of Hunger

Drably dressed Chinese jam a street in Shanghai. Communist China now has a population approaching 700 million and will face the problem of feeding one billion within 20 years or less. But even now, millions are underfed.

Life in the Other Communist States

For all the grimness of life in the Soviet Union, it is a paradise compared with Communist China. The vast millions of Chinese are the unluckiest of all of Communism's subjects. Never in the last century of foreign intervention and civil wars that have ravaged the country have China's people been so near total ruin and starvation. One fact alone tells the grim story: In 1962 the average Chinese was getting less than 1,000 calories in his daily diet, though a minimum of 2,300 calories is required to maintain health and productive energy. What this means is that millions on millions of Chinese are slowly starving to death.

AUTHOR OF A DISASTROUS PLAN

Chinese leader Mao Tse-tung developed a grandiose scheme which he called the "Great Leap Forward." Intended to short-cut China's economic development and bring it to full Communism within a few years, the plan has been a disastrous failure.

Mao's "Great Leap." For a brief period in 1956 and 1957 Mao Tse-tung, the top Chinese Communist, seemed to go through a "liberal" Communist phase. He announced that in Communist China there was room for "a hundred flowers to bloom" and invited everyone to throw his ideas into the collective pot, no matter how unusual they might seem. Hundreds of intellectuals who had been chafing under the rigors of the dictatorship obliged; many ideas did indeed bloom. But Mao suddenly reversed himself and arrested all those whose ideas seemed dangerous. Although this may not have been the original intention, the net result was that potential enemies of the regime trapped themselves by revealing their true thoughts and identities.

Then in 1958, Mao announced a "Great Leap Forward." Instead of passing through a "bourgeois" phase of capitalist development, Red China was to make the transition into ideal and complete Communism in one jump. It would become overnight a modern industrialized nation.

To this end, Mao organized the entire population into a new enterprise based on "the communes." These were like nothing so much as ant hills, in which thousands of worker ants would toil endlessly, under the prodding of soldier ants, with no letup and with scant reward. Millions of peasants were crowded into hopelessly inadequate quarters and fed in communal kitchens. They were driven to the factories or roads or fields before dawn to work like convicts under the watchful eye of the "people's militia."

With one stroke of the pen Mao launched the "tractorizing" of China's farms, apparently deliberately ignoring the fact that almost all Chinese farms are terraced hillsides or rice paddies where tractors cannot be used. He tried to "collectivize" a nation whose farmers have always been engaged principally in raising their own food on small family-held plots.

To speed up China's new "iron age," Mao asked millions of families to build small, "beehive" blast furnaces in their own back yards and melt down metal scrap for "village steel." The result was a sudden increase in China's production of pig iron—but the "back yard"

CHINESE FARMERS WORK A COMMUNE FIELD. STARTED BY MAO IN 1958 AND NOW ALMOST ABANDONED AS

product was of such dubious quality that most of it proved useless.

The nation was called to attain other goals: to exterminate flies, mosquitoes and sparrows. Large posters appeared in every village: "Swat the fly!" was their message. They showed young heroes of Chinese Communism doing just that. Red China solemnly listed in its annual "production" achievements the weight of all flies, mosquitoes and sparrows killed.

A Strained Friendship. The missionary spirit of the "Great Leap" was encouraged by the sight of thousands of Soviet technicians who came in to help China build and run the new industrial plants Khrushchev had promised to help finance for Mao. But the friendship between the two great Communist powers had already been strained by Khrushchev's attack on Stalin—i.e., on the deification of a single leader. After all, Mao was China's own Stalin, using the same forced-draft methods Stalin had used to build Communism in a short time. To show his disapproval, Mao gave Stalin's pictures greater prominence in Red China at the very moment Khrushchev was tearing them down in the U.S.S.R.

"Lunatics and Maniacs." In 1959 Khrushchev paid a personal visit to President Eisenhower and toured the United States preaching a line of "peaceful coexistence" between Communism and capitalism. Like United States leaders, he was familiar enough with the terrible power of thermonuclear weapons to wish to avoid war. Mao, who had no nuclear weapons, but had two and one half million men in active service and millions more in the local militia, denounced such "soft" talk. He regarded it as a betrayal of Lenin's prophecies that Communism must "destroy" capitalism or be destroyed by it. Many Americans do not recognize the intense hatred of capitalism—

A FAILURE, THE COMMUNE SYSTEM HAS INCREASED RATHER THAN LESSENED FOOD SHORTAGES IN CHINA

and of American capitalism in particular—that Mao's propagandists are instilling in the Chinese people. Even little children are taught to hate the "American imperialists."

Mao took the extreme position that if nuclear war came, Red China could lose half its people and still have over 300 million left—enough to rule what remained of the world. Before long, Khrushchev was talking of "lunatics and maniacs who want war." Clearly he meant to include Mao in this category. Furthermore, Khrushchev sharply curtailed his technical aid to China and many Soviet technicians in China went back home.

The result of Mao's "Great Leap Forward" was catastrophic. The blow came, moreover, as China underwent three successive years of drought, whose terrible effects were compounded by the man-made disasters of the communes and other disruptions of Chinese life. It is impossible to grasp the enormity of this catastrophe in terms of multitudes of people. Some idea of the tragedy involved can be gathered from the story of one woman, who finally managed to reach freedom in Hong Kong with her five children. They had lived in Wuchang, 300 miles west of Shanghai.

"Pale, Rubbery Faces." "Just before we left," she told an American in Hong Kong, "our monthly rice ration was barely enough to last for three days per month. We had to supplement it by adding grass picked from the river embankment. We ate all sorts of things which even cattle wouldn't touch, such as tree bark. Whenever women got together the talk turned to 'location,' that is, the location of a place where edible grass could be found. My children often went out of Wuchang when too hungry and brought back some grass and asked me to boil it into gruel.

AN OASIS OF FREE TRADE

These Rumanian farm women are selling vegetables they have grown. After fulfilling the quota demanded by the state, they are free to peddle any surplus at open-air stands. Communist states wink at the existence of free markets where people can buy—at exorbitant prices—the goods which the state stores somehow never have in sufficient quantity.

"I saw many people with pale, rubbery faces. There were others whose legs seemed inflated like long toy balloons. Many suffered a particular pain in the back. No need to ask a doctor the reason. It was simply malnutrition.

"We got meat or fish only four times a year, on national holidays. Many fishermen were hauling lots of fish down the Yangtze at Wuchang. Once I asked one of them why we were unable to get fish. He saw nobody else was in earshot and said, 'The fish all go to big brothers.' By big brothers he meant the top Communist officials.

"People walked about in rags. How else could they dress? Cotton cloth ration for the first half this year [1961] was a tiny piece only two and a half feet square. Out of this bit you're supposed to make underwear, shirts, socks in addition to outer garments. It's simply impossible. People smelled, naturally, because there's no ration of soap."

While she and her children slept one April night her husband slipped out and hanged himself from a willow tree. "I don't blame him," she said. "Death is the easiest way out. It's worse than a pig's life in China."

Life in Communist Europe. A correspondent reported after a visit in 1962 that Albania "is with Communist China, the most oppressive police state in the world, even more depressing because of its tiny size." Its dictator, Enver Hoxha, has executed thousands of people, including a woman who was a national hero of Albania's resistance movement during World War II.

Poland, on the other hand, thanks to having won the right to its own brand of Communism, is perhaps in its domestic policy the freest of all satellites. Its capital, Warsaw, is a city of laughter compared to the unrelieved misery of East Berlin. Moreover, Poland, having broken up its collective farms, is the only satellite which has been able to fulfill its planned production in agriculture.

Even in Poland, however, the government has been persistently clamping down on the greater freedom of expression that was permitted after the 1956 showdown with Khrushchev. The Polish people, realizing that Gomulka must walk a tightrope to prevent the Russians from completely taking over again, endure these new repressions. They live relatively well, partly through the help of millions of dollars worth of money orders and packages sent by American relatives.

Rumanians were once Europe's gayest and most uninhibited people. Their fertile plains gave them a bountiful food supply. But under Communism, the Rumanians are going hungry, and few even dare tell political jokes.

Thanks to American aid, Yugoslavia has been in relatively good condition in recent years and, because it pursued an "independent" Communist course, the government permitted greater contact with the West than might have been expected. However, dictator Tito's domain has recently begun to encounter economic difficulties. Tito has called on his high officials to be more austere in their personal lives, a sure sign that austerity had already become the way of life for the average Yugoslavian.

In Hungary the people are trying to make the best that they can out of life under Communism. Dictator Janos Kadar, after coming to power behind the Soviet tanks which crushed the 1956 revolt, has been easing the pressure. Frankly conceding that the great majority of Hungarians are anti-Communist, Kadar has even allowed non-Communists to hold some of the top jobs in the economy.

In Bulgaria a major problem for the regime is presented by the "nylon intelligentsia," young people who admire the West and prefer western music and books to those of the Communist world. The regime had placed its highest hopes on these educated and privileged members of the Communist society. Their disaffection is a severe blow.

The Most Exploited Nation. Of all the Communist countries Czechoslovakia, which had the most to yield, has been the most systematically exploited. Consider the following:

▶ A Czech worker cannot buy a suit for himself or a coat for his wife from the high quality woolens of his country's own factories—unless he has dollars or other sound foreign currency with which to shop at the state-owned shops. But when a shipment of the finest Czech woolens comes to Moscow's GUM department store, any Soviet citizen can buy all the yardage he needs, for rubles.

▶ Czechoslovakia manufactures splendid modern buses and some of the finest automobiles in Europe. But the taxis of Prague are dilapidated. Old-fashioned streetcars still meander through its streets, though Moscow and Leningrad both have the latest thing in Czech-produced buses.

▶ Czechs love good food and were accustomed to getting it cheaply from their proficient farmers. They still eat better than other Communist subjects. But under the iron pattern of collectivization forced upon them, farm production has barely attained the prewar levels of 1938. Communism managed to turn abundance into deprivation.

▶ Czechoslovakia was the epitome of a prosperous middle-class nation. Its skilled workers, executives, teachers, tradesmen, doctors, engineers, lawyers were the core of its democratic thought and pro-American sentiment. They have been ruthlessly uprooted as "reactionaries." Doctors were forced to sell their equipment to the state and become "state employees." Lawyers were ordered to switch to "productive jobs," and many had to become factory workers, coal miners or construction workers.

A former lawyer told an American correspondent: "It has become a major problem to make a bare living. After 10 hours of work in our factory, I'm so exhausted that all I want is to go home and lie down and see no one. I no longer worry about next year—I worry whether I'll be able to work next week. I'm sure Communism won't last for-

PRIVATE BUSINESS DESPITE COMMUNISM

A Warsaw shopper takes a closer look at a garment offered for sale in the Szembek Square open market or *ciuchy.* Although almost anything from shoestrings to hot cabbage soup is on sale at the *ciuchy,* the real attraction is American clothing sent to Poland in gift packages. Recipients of clothes that do not fit can easily dispose of them at prices high enough to get other needed items, also in short supply.

ever—tyranny never does. But it's here to stay for a while. So all of us try to make life easier for ourselves."

Does this mean that the country's famous industry has been wrecked? To the contrary, Czechoslovakia's production has been more than trebled since the Communists seized power. But it no longer makes enough of the consumer goods which gave the people such a high standard of living. Instead, the Czechs turn out the heavy goods demanded by their Russian exploiters. This sturdy nation, with less than half of 1 per cent of the world's population (13.5 million), turns out 7 per cent of the world's machine tools and 5 per cent of its locomotives.

Czech goods go to build new factories in Moscow, or wherever else the new imperialists direct them, and the only monetary return Czechs get is in the form of rubles or other "soft" currencies. When Moscow decided to "give aid" to Egypt and Iraq it was Czech rifles, Czech buses, Czech locomotives which the Kremlin sent. And in Czechoslovakia railroads are falling apart.

The Country of the Wall. The systematic destruction of democracy in Czechoslovakia was a tragedy. But the situation in East Germany is perhaps the most dangerous single threat to the peace—and the very existence—of the entire world.

After the bloody suppression of the 1953 revolt in East Germany, the people apparently gave up trying to fight back. But at least they could flee. In the next eight years, close to two million people escaped to the West—331,000 in 1953—most of them through free Berlin. But on August 13, 1961, the Communists erected the Berlin wall to halt this mass exodus, and police guarded its accesses with machine guns. After that, only those ready to risk their lives could make

These Sad, Fear-Haunted People Come from Different Backgrounds, but They Have One

EAST GERMANY

HUNGARY

the break for free Berlin. Yet day in and day out, a few managed to do so. More than 12,000 successfully broke through to freedom within the first year after the wall was built.

The wall began as a symbol of Communism's callous power, but soon it became a symbol of weakness, of Communism's inability to gain its way. It was a daily affront to its own people—even to the people of Moscow, where students openly expressed their distaste for the wall. The wall began to have a worse effect: it penned in people's thoughts and set hatred fanning and mushrooming, "like too many people living in too small a house," as one refugee put it.

On top of the almost total demoralization of the country, the food shortage created by collectivization grew worse in 1962. Foreign Trade Minister Anastas Mikoyan came to East Germany with a substantial loan and trade agreement to keep bankrupt East Germany operating until the next harvest.

In 1962 the people of East Germany were telling this revealing joke:

> In an East German jail, three men are in a cell. One asks another: "Why are you here?" He replies: "Sabotage. I came to work 10 minutes late." "And you?" he asks the second. "Espionage," says the second. "I came to work 10 minutes early." "Why are you here?" "I came to work exactly on time," says the first man. "Then they noticed I had a watch from the West."

"The present situation," correspondent James Bell reported recently, "is much uglier than that of the 1953 East German uprising. At that time, people, as groups, had general political objectives they hoped to achieve. Now, any hope of reforms, of political or economic change, has disappeared. And, while no one talks much because there

Thing in Common: All Are Fugitives from Communism

CUBA

RED CHINA

are 20 Russian army divisions nearby, each man is brooding on his personal wrongs, and scheming to get those he hates when and if he can.

"The recent killing of a *Grepo* [a border policeman] along the wall brought confused accounts, ranging from claims it was done by a West Berliner leading a group of women and children to an escape tunnel, to a story that he was shot down by his own comrades. The latter could be true, so nasty is the situation between even officials of the regime. Some sources feel that if the lid were lifted for only a short time, there would be a number of plain outright murders in East Berlin. The wall has penned in too much hatred, and by itself closed off the last safety valve.

"The possibility now is one of mass breakouts. They may come in groups of up to several hundred, or thousands at once. They probably would be armed, self-contained groups which would shoot their way out, catching the relatively thin line of *Grepos* by surprise."

This was the powder keg, dangerous to all concerned, that the wall had created.

COMMUNIST GUARDS BAR AN ELDERLY COUPLE FROM THE FREEDOM THEY SEEK IN WEST BERLIN

6 The Challenge: What We Can Do

U.S. PEACE CORPSMAN

6 The Challenge: What We Can Do

What are the wisest policies and plans to which prudent Americans should dedicate themselves in the global struggle with Communist imperialism? Intelligent answers to these questions require a clear-eyed appraisal of some of the major forces at work in today's world, and a determined effort to bend these forces in a direction favorable to the Free World.

Free World Strongholds. It is now clear that the chief threat of Communism does not lie in the industrially developed countries, where Marx thought it would take over, but in the less developed rural areas of the world. In the highly industrialized areas, the Free World has held and improved its position, despite the shrewd Russian policy that seeks to fragment the joint effort of the democracies by trying to aggravate the honest differences that will always crop up among friends.

The steady improvement of the Free World's position is evident, for example, in an amazingly prosperous Japan, risen from the ashes of total defeat in World War II and now advancing toward greater freedom and democracy. It is most abundantly evident in the growing prosperity of a free Europe finding political as well as economic unity in the Common Market.

The union of France, West Germany, Italy, Belgium, the Netherlands and Luxembourg is a logical outgrowth of the Marshall Plan. The pooling of ideas for economic reconstruction which that plan set in motion helped lead to the European Coal and Steel Community, formed in 1951. The members of this organization exercise joint control of their coal and steel industries for the benefit of all.

The success of this enterprise led to ratification of the Treaty of Rome in 1957, which created the Common Market. This treaty provided a step-by-step expansion of free trade among the members through gradually lowering tariffs. It also recognized the possibility of eventual political as well as economic union. The Common Market has created larger prospects of trade for all the participating nations and has expanded their total markets beyond the dreams of its fondest advocates. A few figures comparing the economic life of these nations in 1957 and in 1961 speak volumes:

- Industrial production . . . . up 32 per cent
- Gross national product . . . up 29 per cent
- Per capita consumption . . up 15 per cent
- Imports . . . . up 15 per cent
- Exports . . . . up 33 per cent

All this points to an event of enormous significance. When the six nations making up the Common Market and the other nations of western Europe are viewed individually, they look outweighed, outgunned and outmanned in contrast to the gigantic Soviet Union. But once all these nations join together, their combined resources will outweigh those of the U.S.S.R. in population and in industrial production, as well as in the number of advanced scientists and well-trained specialists.

A united Europe will be a powerful force which will continue to have common interests with the United States, as indeed the United States has with it. Recognizing this, the U.S. Congress in 1962 took unprecedented steps to match Europe's free trade policy with lower American tariff schedules. In 1962 Britain was moving in the direction of joining the Common Market and most of free Europe was expected to do so in time.

The growing strength of a united Europe will enable the continent to take on a greater share of the burden previously borne by the United States in manning Europe's own defenses. It will also enable western Europe, as its prosperity increases, to assume a larger share of the Free World's biggest economic problem—helping the underdeveloped nations to enter the age of modern technology without losing their freedom in the process. For, as the history of Communism demonstrates, Communist successes have generally been achieved in nations where industrialization is in its earliest phase.

The Threat of Undeclared Wars. It is now clear that, barring a major war begun by accident, one of the greatest challenges the Free World is likely to face lies in what Premier Khrushchev calls "national-liberation wars." This is simply a roundabout term for what might better be called "indirect aggression," or the waging of undeclared war by Communist guerrillas. In this type of war, small groups of highly trained men infiltrate remote areas. They live among, sometimes marry into, the peasantry. Wearing no uniforms, they are undistinguishable from these poor people. They can make swift, damaging raids on government convoys and strong points, and then melt into the protective coloration of village life. An outstanding example of this type of war is the conflict which began in 1954 between the Communist forces called the Viet Cong and the government of South Vietnam in Southeast Asia.

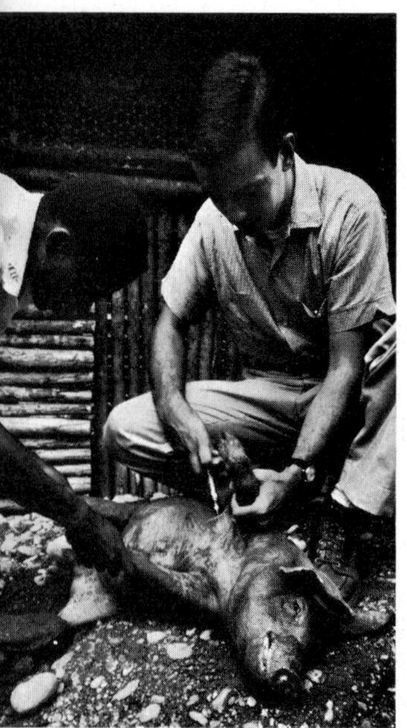

HELPING HAND OF THE PEACE CORPS

In Colombia one of the U.S. Peace Corps' volunteers shows a farmer how to inoculate his pigs against cholera. Through this program and other projects, the U.S. is helping underdeveloped nations improve living standards, thus fortifying them against Communism's subversion.

In November 1960, at a meeting of 81 Communist parties in Moscow, the delegates resolved that the tempo of undeclared wars should be stepped up. Two months later Premier Khrushchev gave a talk on the subject which President Kennedy later made required reading for all top leaders of the United States government:

> "Can such wars recur?" said Khrushchev. "Yes, they can. Can such uprisings recur? Yes, they can. But they are wars in the nature of popular uprisings. Can conditions in other countries come to a point where the people take up arms? Yes, they can. What should our attitude be in regard to such uprisings? It should be most favorable. . . . Communists support such just wars fully and without reservations, and march in the van of the peoples fighting for liberation."

Learning Guerrilla Tactics. President Kennedy interpreted this declaration as being a thinly veiled instruction to all Communists everywhere to launch guerrilla wars, wherever possible. His interpretation of Communist plans was supported by the torment of another country, Laos, a neighbor of South Vietnam, which was in the throes of Communist guerrilla activity. At the same time obvious efforts were being launched by Ho Chi Minh, the Communist leader of North Vietnam, to increase guerrilla infiltration of South Vietnam in an effort to overthrow the legitimate government.

President Kennedy's response was to order a large increase in United States preparations for man-to-man combat—particularly in the training of anti-guerrilla forces. During the period that followed World War II, most of our military thinking had concentrated on the problems of worldwide nuclear warfare. But from 1961 on, hundreds of specialists trained in jungle fighting tactics were sent to instruct Vietnamese regular soldiers and to ferry them by helicopter into the swamps and mountains where the Communist guerrillas hide.

As a part of this preparation, President Kennedy also required all

DEFENDING A FREE NATION against Communist assault, a U.S. Military Assistance Advisory Group captain and a Vietnamese officer supervise the loading of troop helicopters for an attack on Viet Cong guerrillas. Undeclared wars like that in South Vietnam are one of Communism's greatest challenges to the Free World today.

top commanders to familiarize themselves with a handbook on guerrilla warfare. It was prepared by the Chinese Communist leader Mao Tse-tung in 1937 and was his guide during his eventual takeover of China. This victory made him Communism's recognized world leader in guerrilla warfare. His tactics were widely copied, for example, by the Algerian rebels in their successful war (November 1954-March 1962) against the French. They were used by Cuba's Ernesto (Che) Guevara to help Fidel Castro turn an original band of 12 rebels into a guerrilla force which finally captured the country.

Sympathy and Terror. Guerrilla warfare is a technique in which Communists have no monopoly. It was practiced by American frontier fighters—notably "Swamp Fox" Francis Marion—against the British redcoats, long before Karl Marx was born. However, United States anti-guerrilla forces in a region like Vietnam face a serious handicap. The Communists in many of their own operations have been able to win—sometimes through sympathy, sometimes through terror—the support of the village people, who help them to hide. Communist guerrillas cultivate support in two ways:

1) The technique of friendship: Guerrillas are dependent for their survival on the good will of the people of the countryside in which they are fighting. Therefore, the guerrillas strive to convince the poorer sections of the population that only Communism is concerned with the interests of the people; that the officials of the legitimate government have no sincere interest in improving conditions for the underprivileged.

2) The tactics of terror: When persuasion fails to win the support of the villagers, Communist guerrillas threaten, and carry out, terrible reprisals on those who refuse to cooperate with them.

To defeat the Communists' sympathetic approach, America must encourage local governments to effect genuine reforms. To counter terror, the United States must continue to provide specialized military assistance to oust the Communist guerrillas. In proper proportions, these two approaches can preserve the freedom of nations threatened by the Communists.

The Problem of Subversion

To some observers, Communism presents an equal challenge here at home. To what extent is internal subversion by members of the United States Communist party and their sympathizers a threat to the United States in this global struggle?

The largest vote that United States Communists have ever been able to muster for their own presidential candidate on their own ticket was 102,785 in 1932, at the depth of depression. The Communist vote dropped to 80,159 in 1936, even though the Soviet Union's opposition to Hitler's Germany aroused considerable popular support in the United States. It was also the period when Communist organizers had achieved substantial influence—now dwindled to insignificant proportions—in the labor movement. In 1940, after the Hitler-Stalin pact of 1939, the Communist vote fell to 46,251.

As the hostility of the Soviet Union toward the United States grew in the years after World War II, membership in the United States Communist party gradually sank to less than 10,000. Under the Smith Act of 1940, most of the top leaders of the United States Communist party were tried in 1949 and sentenced to prison as members of a conspiracy to overthrow the government by force and violence. The Communist party, though still legal, could no longer be regarded as a political party alone, but as a vehicle for subversion and espionage under the control of a foreign power. Once this was determined, the party's illegal activities became the proper subject for surveillance by the Federal Bureau of Investigation, and all its movements and decisions became quickly known.

Subversion in High Places. In 1948 the famous Alger Hiss case set off a wave of national concern over Communist penetration of the government itself. Hiss had been an influential member of the State Department, had accompanied Roosevelt to the Yalta Conference and had acted as organizing secretary of the United Nations. Microfilms produced by Whittaker Chambers, a onetime courier for a Communist spy apparatus, revealed that Hiss had been supplying secret government documents to the ring. The Hiss investigation brought out evidence that this small ring had penetrated to high places and exercised an influence far beyond its size.

This led to a wave of congressional investigations which sometimes flagrantly violated individuals' legal safeguards and groundlessly damaged many individual reputations. Fortunately, these near-hysterical excesses soon subsided, with the result that the nation could give proper, and not exaggerated, concern to Communist penetration. The Smith Act has been reinforced by the Internal Security Act of 1950. And official agencies, such as the FBI, have always been charged with the responsibility of keeping the constant but quiet watch that the actual danger required—and their effectiveness is a part of the public record.

The Arms Race and Arms Control

The two great giants—the United States and the Soviet Union—which are locked in the battle for the world are also engaged in an open contest as to which will prove stronger, the way of Communism or the way of freedom. At the beginning of his first Five-Year Plan, Stalin set the goal of some day "overtaking and surpassing" the United States. Nikita Khrushchev, too, often refers to this goal.

This struggle has found its chief expression in an astronomically expensive arms race. The Soviet Union threw immense national treasure and effort into developing its own atomic bomb. And Russian scientists also proved capable of solving the far more difficult problem of making the hydrogen bomb. Furthermore, because they began their development of powerful booster rockets several years before the United States did, the Russian scientists gained a lead in the race for space which they were able to maintain in 1962 by orbiting two cosmonauts simultaneously.

Deterrence and Disarmament. The United States now spends close to $50 billion a year on defense, or 10 times President Coolidge's entire annual federal budget in the 1920s. The Soviet Union spends at least this much—and possibly more, according to current estimates. These sums represent an enormous burden on both countries.

The United States has no aggressive designs on the Soviet Union or any other country, but it is determined to maintain a "deterrent" so strong that any nation which risked a surprise attack upon the United States would itself be certain of destruction. Great progress has been made toward achieving this goal through the development of Polaris-firing submarines which provide a constantly moving and concealed platform for launching thermonuclear weapons. Progress is also being made through building "hardened" missile sites on land with concrete silos that could withstand anything but a direct hit.

ALLIANCE OF COMMUNIST STATES

In its swift rise to world power, Communism has become a system involving military and political alliance as well as political doctrine. The Warsaw Pact of 1955—so called because the meeting was held in the Polish capital—formalized a military alliance under which the Soviet Union and its European satellites mutually pledged to come to the defense of one another in the case of "aggression." It was the Russian answer to the inclusion of West Germany in the North Atlantic Treaty Organization. When the Soviet Union decided to invade Hungary in 1956, it used the existence of the pact as a pretext, claiming that Hungary's "legal government"—i.e., the puppet regime—had "asked for troops."

At the same time, the United States has sought to persuade the U.S.S.R. that it is in the long-term interest of both countries to limit the arms race. The United States, for example, has proposed the gradual destruction of nuclear stockpiles and delivery systems, provided each country agrees to adequate inspection and control. In the past the Soviets have refused to agree to any effective system of inspection on their own territory. They have similarly thwarted all efforts to obtain agreement to end nuclear tests. But the United States will persist in seeking a workable system for arms control.

Our Long-Range Attitude toward the Soviet Union

The United States has no quarrel with the Russian people. It sympathized with their 1917 Revolution and was the first great power to recognize the Provisional Government. While the Communist system is repellent to the American people, the United States of course recognizes the right of the Russian people, or any people, to live under any form of government they prefer. The United States' only quarrel arises from the persistent attempt by the U.S.S.R. to force its system on other peoples against their will, by subversion and by direct and indirect aggression. This attempt must be and will be resisted.

As to the long-range outcome of the struggle, some thoughtful Americans take great hope from the fact that the Soviet Union is endeavoring to give a first-class—though doctrinaire—education to so many millions of its young people. The existence of an educated group like this, dedicated to the quest for truth in the sciences, raises the hope that such people will begin to question untruths which they are told about events and government activities which affect their daily lives. Moreover, as Soviet industry expands its capacity, the Russian people are likely to grumble unless Communism finally shows some material results for all the sacrifices it has long exacted. As the desire for truth, freedom and a better life increases, Russian public opinion may slowly push its rulers in the direction of freedom and away from tyranny. This is an optimistic view for the long term, to be sure, but it is held by a thoughtful realist like Allen Dulles, former head of the Central Intelligence Agency.

Tarnished by Terror. Furthermore, the disparity between the promises of Communism and its persistent failures of performance become more glaring as the years go by. The chronic failures of agriculture—still severe in Russia and close to a disaster in China—have brought consternation to the Communist leadership and terrible punishments to scapegoat officialdom. "I believe the Communist position is becoming more and more vulnerable . . . ," said Allen Dulles in 1962. "Some of the steam has gone out of the early, evangelical, fanatical drive of Communism, and it is a tarnished thing. It can never really live down Stalin's record of terror."

Transforming Capitalism. While Communism has responded to its internal crises by repressing individuals and hobbling the economy, capitalism has been transforming itself to meet the challenges of an ever more complex world. As a result of capitalism's own last and worst depression, in the 1930s, the United States has moved to provide "built-in cushions" against a recurrence of such bad times.

▶ These include governmental systems of unemployment insurance, providing up to 39 weeks' compensation in some states, which guarantee that a worker who becomes unemployed during a recession will continue to receive an income. Furthermore, his continued purchasing power prevents the recession from deepening.

▶ They also include corporate pension funds, now totaling more than $30 billion and growing at the rate of $3 billion a year, which provide a constant source of new strength to the economy by increasing the purchasing power of retired people.

▶ They include social security for the aged, and privately financed medical and hospital insurance for the ill. And they include high-wage union contracts which prevent the "going wage" from tending toward what the hungriest worker would be willing to accept.

Equally significant has been the development of regulatory agencies, such as the Securities and Exchange Commission (SEC) which protects the interests of the investing public; of conservation and power districts, like the Columbia Basin Project, which have exercised a salutary effect on the preservation and intelligent utilization of national resources; of joint government and private enterprises such as those which launched the Telstar satellite and made possible the application of atomic power in private industry.

The "class war" which Communism preaches—the idea of irreconcilable hostility between owners and workers—has become ridiculous in America's fluid society. In the United States, this year's factory worker may be next year's employer. In any case, the worker's sons and daughters are almost certain to have the opportunity for college educations and be free to become doctors, engineers, teachers or other specialists. And when nearly one out of every six adult Americans owns some shares of stock in capitalist enterprises, workers also have become owners in a very real sense.

The Task of Democracy. It now becomes America's task to continue its generous program of helping the less developed nations of

AWESOME DETERRENT TO ATTACK

A submarine-launched Polaris missile streaks for the target from under water. Missile-firing submarines are among the most effective weapons in the U.S. defensive arsenal. Always on the move, they are prepared to let fly nuclear missiles at any nation that launches a surprise attack.

Asia and Africa to take the road to abundance. The recently established Peace Corps is an excellent example of American assistance to underdeveloped areas. This kind of help is, of course, called for by the injunction of the world's great religions that men should live as brothers and help their neighbors. It is also called for by common prudence and enlightened self-interest, since the whole world today is explosive with revolutionary ferments.

▶ The miracles of modern medicine have reduced the incidence of many diseases that formerly afflicted backward regions. Now populations are growing far faster than the productive capacity of primitive forms of agriculture and industry. Consequently a serious crisis is in store for many emerging nations.

▶ The revolution of communications—with not only supersonic transport, but very soon universal television by way of space satellite platforms—will shrink all national boundaries to insignificance. In the process, even the least advanced peoples will be stripped of their ignorance about the good life which others already have and which they can dream of achieving.

▶ With the unlimited power of atomic energy looming on the horizon, it is possible to foresee a time when there will no longer be "have-not" nations. Then the abolition of poverty from the world—the greatest revolution in all history—may become possible.

In a revolutionary age, our own Declaration of Independence still proclaims the truest and most enduring revolution in man's history. "The Declaration of Independence," Lincoln said in 1861, ". . . gave liberty, not alone to the people of this country, but, I hope, to the world for all future time. It was that which gave promise that in due time the weight would be lifted from the shoulders of all men."

A Positive Program. Since the Russian people themselves are not and cannot be our enemy, it is possible to hope that "victory" in the cold war will come not through military action, but through a change in the conditions which caused the conflict.

Until signs of such a transformation emerge, the Free World must assume that Communism will continue to seek to conquer the world by dividing and undermining it. We must fight back by supporting the use of our nation's resources in helping others. In addition, as individuals, each of us has the duty to do everything in his power to defeat the Communist threat by making our own democracy stronger in every possible way.

How, then, can we best do that? By extending, perfecting and defending the rights and freedoms which Communism denies.

▶ *We must ensure free speech.* Communism flatly denies the right to free speech. We must never suppress the honest views of others, no matter how much we disagree with them. Let us take as our own the famous credo attributed to Voltaire: "I disapprove of what you say, but I will defend to the death your right to say it."

▶ *We must maintain a free press.* We must take care not to join in the suppression or intimidation of newspapers or magazines whose views may not agree with our own. We should voice our protests loudly and clearly but fight clean and fair.

▶ *We must preserve free elections.* We must do everything in our power to strengthen our own electoral procedures. Every citizen who is qualified to vote has a duty to do so. He will help strengthen democracy by making financial contributions, no matter how small, to the party of his choice. By taking a personal role in that party's activities at the local level, he will help improve the caliber of candidates, increase the willingness of able men to participate in government and prevent the party from being dominated by special or selfish interests. He will also do everything in his power to see that the right to vote is not denied to any of his fellow citizens. The Constitution gives that right to every adult citizen, and that guarantee must be made real if we are not to seem hypocritical in criticizing Communism's denial of free elections.

▶ *We must uphold our laws.* During Stalin's reign, every Soviet citizen lived in dread of a knock at the door by the secret police in the middle of the night; thousands upon thousands so aroused were dragged away never to be seen again. In the reaction against Stalin's brutal excesses, the Soviet people have hoped for and are getting more protection against arbitrary arrest and imprisonment by the secret police. But what made these excesses possible in the first place was that the Soviet citizen does not enjoy that bedrock of our own liberties—*habeas corpus*—which assures that any citizen who has been arrested will be released unless he is publicly charged with some offense, and if charged he must be given a fair and prompt trial by a judge or by a jury of fellow citizens. So long as we maintain vigilance over these basic rights, the Russian experience can never be duplicated here. But we will all be in greatest danger of losing these rights if we ever acquiesce in their being denied to any individual—however we may loathe or hate what he stands for. By the same token, criticism of our courts or their decisions, if it becomes so abusive as to question the loyalty or patriotism of the judges and juries, endangers our safeguards of the law.

▶ *We must defend the right to dissent.* Communism has room for only one point of view—the party line; once this is handed down, not even Communist leaders can challenge it. There is no "other side" to any argument. Throughout its history, American democracy has produced hundreds of extraordinary, sometimes extremist and fanatical spokesmen and movements. Some of these odd groups even nominate their own candidates for President. They preach everything from vegetarianism and anti-vivisection to the imminent end of the world. They range from the far Right to the far Left of the political spectrum. They are living, healthy symbols of the pluralistic

SMILING, CONFIDENT AMERICANS HEARING A PRESIDENTIAL CANDIDATE ARE

nature of our society, which tolerates any point of view so long as it is not clearly treasonable or obscene. While it is our right to dispute any particular opinion, we must beware of joining in any hue or cry to silence or persecute any person or group.

▶ *We must raise our educational sights.* Communism provides an example of educational opportunities that Americans cannot afford to ignore. Despite its heavy content of Communist propaganda, education in the U.S.S.R. is of a generally high quality. Moreover, the

PROUD OF THEIR POWER TO CHOOSE THEIR OWN LEADERS IN FREE ELECTIONS

Communist leadership does not balk at spending a large portion of the national income for education, with the very sound expectation that this investment will pay for itself many times over. Educational standards in the United States have undergone rigorous re-examination since the launching of the first Soviet Sputnik woke us up to our deficiencies. But we still face a tremendous challenge and a great opportunity to lift our system of education to the high level that our prosperous country can afford and must have.

What all of these things add up to, of course, is making American democracy stronger by understanding its essential strengths and being prepared to assert them. At the same time, we must be willing to work to improve this remarkable institution by removing imperfections as they appear, by making sure that practice lives up to principles, and by ensuring that our government continues to work for the greater good of the greatest number while preserving the right of each individual to his individuality.

A Lifetime Project. This is no short-term project. If the world is spared the cataclysmic destruction of nuclear war, it is likely that the contest between the Free World and Communism will remain a part of our daily lives for many years to come. There are those, at home as well as abroad, who mourn that in such a contest democracy is at a disadvantage and that we had better use some of our opponents' "efficient" methods if we hope to prevail.

A little more than 20 years ago, this same argument was presented under somewhat similar circumstances. Then it was Adolf Hitler who promised to wipe out "decadent" democracy and create a "thousand-year Reich." A good number of prominent Americans seriously believed that Hitler would do just that, and proposed that instead of fighting we should learn to cooperate with the irresistible force of Nazism. Speaking out of professional knowledge, these military and political experts explained that Hitler's airplanes were far and away the best in the world and his pilots superior to any airmen ever seen. Finally, they warned, Hitler's totalitarian state was better able to concentrate on its goals since there was no necessity to consult the people before taking action.

Substitute Vostok space capsules for airplanes and Soviet cosmonauts for Nazi pilots, and it is possible to see a certain unmistakable resemblance between the world situation then and now. But the history of World War II demonstrates that the democracies, despite the "handicaps" of representative government and a decent respect for the rights of individuals and the opinion of mankind, were able to assemble mighty armies, build the weapons of war and mount the offensives that ended the vainglorious dreams of the sawdust Caesars in Berlin, Rome and Tokyo.

The lesson is clear. We can never defeat Communism by fear or trembling or by attacking our own political institutions. But we can defeat it by demonstrating our faith and confidence in our way of life, and by proving to the world that the American pledge of "liberty and justice for all" can become a reality for all mankind.

Appendix

Chronology
Glossary
Bibliography
Index

CHRONOLOGY

Before February 1918, the Russians used a calendar which was some days behind that used in western Europe. Consequently there is confusion as to the dates which precede the adoption, in 1918, of the new style, or Gregorian, calendar. The dates used throughout this book are based upon the modern calendar.

1818, May 5: Karl Heinrich Marx born in the German Rhineland
1848: Revolt in Europe
1848, Feb.: *Communist Manifesto*
1849: Marx emigrates to England
1855: Alexander II becomes Tsar
1861: Serfs liberated in Russia
1867: *Capital,* Volume I published
1870: Lenin born
1871: Paris Commune uprising
1879: Trotsky and Stalin born
1881: Alexander II assassinated
1883: Marx dies; Plekhanov founds League for Emancipation of Labor
1887: "Sasha" Ulyanov executed
1894: Nicholas II becomes Tsar
1895: Lenin arrested for revolutionary activities; later exiled
1898: First Party Congress in Minsk proclaims the establishment of the Russian Social Democratic Labor party (RSDLP)
1900: Lenin returns from Siberia; goes abroad to publish *Iskra*
1902: Socialist Revolutionary party formed out of Populist movement
1903: Second Party Congress at Brussels and London; open split between Mensheviks and Bolsheviks
1904-1905: Russo-Japanese War
1905: General strikes and uprising; Trotsky organizes first Soviet
1905, Jan.: Bloody Sunday massacre
1905, Oct.: Constitutional Democratic party (Cadets) formed; Tsar's "October Manifesto" promises reforms
1905, Nov.: Lenin returns home
1906: First Duma convenes; Lenin flees Russia
1906-1911: Peter A. Stolypin serves as Tsar's prime minister
1907: Second Duma called and dissolved after three months
1907-1912: Third Duma
1912-1917: Fourth Duma
1914: World War I begins; St. Petersburg renamed Petrograd
1916: Lenin publishes *Imperialism, the Highest Stage of Capitalism*
1916, Dec.: Rasputin murdered
1917, March: February (by old calendar) Revolution starts; Duma ignores Tsar's order to disband
1917, March 12: Duma and Soviets both set up governing groups
1917, March 15: Tsar Nicholas II signs abdication
1917, April 16: Lenin back from Switzerland; issues "April Theses"
1917, July: Kerensky attacks Germans; riots in Petrograd; Lenin flees the country
1917, Aug.: Kerensky named as the prime minister of the Provisional Government
1917, Nov. 7: October (by old calendar) Revolution; the Bolshevik forces take over government
1917, Nov. 8: Bolshevik decrees on peace and land. Lenin chairman of Soviet of People's Commissars; country called Russian Soviet Federated Socialist Republic
1917, Nov. 25: Elections for constituent assembly
1917, Dec.: Cheka established and the Red Terror begins
1918, Jan. 18-19: Constituent assembly meets and is dispersed
1918-1921: Civil war and period of "war Communism"; free states established in Poland, Finland, Latvia, Lithuania and Estonia
1918, March: Seventh Party Congress adopts name "All-Russian Communist (Bolshevik) Party"
1918, March 3: Brest-Litovsk treaty
1918, July 16: Tsar executed
1918, Nov. 11: Armistice ends the first World War
1919: Comintern established
1921, March: New Economic Policy (NEP) adopted
1921, March 1-18: Kronstadt revolt
1922: Stalin now party secretary
1922, April 16: Treaty of Rapallo
1922, Dec.: Establishment of the Union of Soviet Socialist Republics (U.S.S.R.) including the R.S.F.R. in an expanded federation
1923: Stalin, Zinoviev and Kamenev form ruling triumvirate
1924, Jan. 21: Death of Lenin
1925, Jan.: Triumvirate removes Trotsky as commissar of war
1927: Stalin seizes greater power; Trotsky and Zinoviev ousted
1928-1932: First Five-Year Plan
1929, end of year: Stalin undisputed head of U.S.S.R.; beginning of forced collectivization of peasants
1933: U.S. recognizes U.S.S.R.
1933-1937: Second Five-Year Plan
1934, Dec. 1: Kirov murdered
1935-1938: Stalin's purges
1936-1939: Spanish Civil War
1936, Aug.: Trial of Zinoviev, Kamenev and other leaders
1936, Dec. 5: The new "Stalin" constitution adopted
1938-1942: Third Five-Year Plan
1938, March: Trial of Rykov, Bukharin and other top leaders
1938, Sept.: Munich Pact
1939, March: Germans occupy Czechoslovakian territory
1939, Aug. 23: Nazi-Soviet nonaggression pact with secret protocol
1939, Sept. 1: Nazis invade Poland; beginning of World War II
1939, Sept. 17: Soviet intervention in Poland
1939, Nov. 30: The Soviet Union attacks Finland
1940, June-July: U.S.S.R. annexes Latvia, Lithuania and Estonia; seizes territory from Rumania
1940, June 22: Fall of France
1940, Aug.: Trotsky assassinated
1941, June 22: Nazis invade U.S.S.R.
1941, Dec.: Pearl Harbor and entry of U.S. into World War II
1943: Comintern dissolved
1943, Nov. 28-Dec. 1: Teheran Conference meets
1944, June 6: Allies land in France
1944, Aug.: Warsaw uprising
1945, Feb. 4-11: Yalta Conference
1945, March: Communist takeover in Rumania
1945, May 8: End of war in Europe

1945, July 17-Aug. 2: Potsdam Conference
1945, Aug. 14: V-J day
1946-1950: Fourth Five-Year Plan
1947, Sept.: Cominform established
1948: Stalin splits with Tito
1948, Feb.: Communist take over in Czechoslovakia
1948, June: Berlin blockade
1950 to 1953: Korean War
1951-1955: Fifth Five-Year Plan
1952, Oct.: 19th Party Congress
1953, Jan. 13: "Doctors' Plot" announced in *Pravda*
1953, March 5: Stalin dies; Malenkov becomes new premier and first secretary; within a few days Khrushchev in effect replaces Malenkov as first secretary
1953, July: Beria ousted as head of secret police and later shot
1955, Feb.: Bulganin replaces Malenkov as premier
1955, May: Austrian peace treaty
1955, May-June: Khrushchev and Bulganin go to Yugoslavia to make peace with Tito
1955, May 14: Warsaw Pact
1955, July: Geneva summit meeting
1956, Feb. 14-25: 20th Party Congress; downgrading of Stalin
1956, April: Cominform dissolved
1956, Oct.: Gomulka reinstated in Poland after June riots in Poznan
1956, Nov.: Soviet troops end briefly successful Hungarian revolt
1957, Feb. 27: Mao Tse-tung's "Let a Hundred Flowers Bloom" talk
1957, June: Khrushchev defeats antiparty group to clinch power
1957, Oct. 4: U.S.S.R. puts first Sputnik into orbit
1958, March: Khrushchev replaces Bulganin as premier; now holds both of the top jobs
1959: Khrushchev visits the U.S.
1959, Jan.-Feb.: 21st Party Congress
1960, May: U-2 incident; Paris summit conference breaks up
1960, Sept.: Khrushchev at U.N. General Assembly meeting
1961, June: Khrushchev meets Kennedy in Vienna, threatens separate treaty with East Germany
1961, Aug.: Berlin wall erected
1961, Aug. 31: Russians announce intention to resume nuclear tests
1961, Oct.: 22nd Party Congress
1962, Aug.: Russians orbit twin cosmonauts
1962, Oct.: U.S.S.R. intensifies arms build-up in Cuba; U.S. imposes arms quarantine

GLOSSARY

This is a directory and brief description of important people, places and terms mentioned in the book. The reader may wish to turn to these for quick reference.

Antiparty group. Khrushchev's name for the members of the Presidium who tried to overthrow him in 1957 and whom he then succeeded in ousting from power.

"April Theses." The insurrectionary program published by Lenin after Russia's first 1917 Revolution.

Beria (byā´ryĭ•yȧ), Lavrenti (1899-1953). Secret police chief under Stalin. Removed from Presidium in 1953, arrested, and reportedly shot by his fellow Presidium members.

Bolshevik. See box, page 10.

Bourgeoisie. The merchant middle class that rose with the growth of the cities. With the coming of industrialization, this group became the enterprisers who built and owned factories, employed wage earners. Used as a term of opprobrium by Marx.

Brest-Litovsk. City in western Russia where the Bolsheviks signed a costly and humiliating peace treaty with Germany on March 3, 1918.

Bukharin (bŏŏk•hä´rēn), Nikolai (1888-1938). Economist who became the party's chief theorist and editor of *Pravda* from 1918 to 1929. Executed in Stalin's purges.

Bulganin (bool•gȧ´nyin), Nikolai (1895-). Soviet premier from 1955 until Khrushchev dismissed him in 1958 and took the job himself.

Capitalism. An economic system in which the land, resources and means for production and distribution of goods are essentially kept in private hands and subject to competition.

Central Committee. The governing group of the Russian Communist party, now about 130 strong, which theoretically makes policy decisions for the party and thus for the Soviet government. See chart, page 141.

Cheka. The secret police established shortly after the Revolution in 1917 and replaced in 1922 by the GPU. Its sinister work has continued under various names including OGPU, NKVD, and MVD. The MVD was replaced in 1962 by the Ministry of Public Law and Order.

Chernishevsky (chĭr•nĭ•shāf´skĭ), Nikolai (1828-1889). 19th Century Russian writer whose utopian novel *What Is to Be Done?* greatly influenced Lenin's generation.

Chernov (chĕr•nôf´), Victor (1873-1952). Socialist Revolutionary minister in Kerensky's provisional government and chairman of the ill-fated constituent assembly of 1918.

Cominform. Communist Information Bureau founded in 1947 to coordinate Communist party action in France, Italy and particularly the satellites. Dissolved in 1956.

Comintern. The Communist International, formed in Moscow in March 1919 to work openly for the establishment of Communism throughout the world. Dissolved in 1943.

Communism. See page 10.

Constitutional Democratic party. Known as the Cadets, this moderate reform party held the largest number of seats in the first Duma and was an important political force until the 1917 Revolution.

Democratic centralism. See page 102.

Duma. Tsarist parliament established as a result of the 1905 revolts.

Dzerzhinsky (dyĭr•zhēn´skĭ), Felix (1877-1926). Organizer and first commissar of the feared Cheka (secret police).

Engels, Friedrich (1820-1895). German socialist; co-founder with Karl Marx of modern revolutionary Communism.

February Revolution. Russian term for the first Revolution of 1917. According to the western calendar, it actually took place in March.

Five-Year Plan. Ambitious program launched by Stalin in 1928 to industrialize the Soviet Union in the shortest possible time and, in the process, to convert its countryside into collective farms. Succeeded by other plans of varying durations.

Gomulka (gŏŏ•mŏŏl´kä), Wladyslaw (1905-). Communist leader of Poland who was ousted from his party post by Stalin in 1948 for "nationalism" and later imprisoned. Gomulka was reinstated, however, in 1956 when pressure within the party and rioting among the Polish people forced his recall.

Great Leap Forward. Mao Tse-tung's program announced in 1958 to industrialize Communist China overnight.

Hegel, Georg W.F. (1770-1831). The German philosopher whose concept of the "dialectic" was used by Marx in formulating his own theories.

"Izvestia." Official government newspaper. See also *Pravda.*

Kadar (kä´där), Janos (1912-). Communist boss of Hungary, put in office by Russian armed forces after the Budapest rising of 1956.

Kaganovich (kȧ•gŭ•nô´vyich), Lazar (1893-). Stalin's heavy-industry boss. It was as Kaganovich's energetic assistant that Khrushchev caught Stalin's attention. In 1957 Khrushchev deposed Kaganovich as a first deputy premier for his membership in the antiparty group.

Kamenev (kä´myĭ•nyĕf), Lev (1883-1936). One of Lenin's chief lieutenants, Moscow party boss and member of the triumvirate who succeeded Lenin. Purged by Stalin.

Kerensky (kĭ•ryān´skĭ), Alexander (1881-). Socialist Revolutionary party member; and dominating figure in the Provisional Government which held office from March 1917 until Lenin's coup in November.

Khrushchev (Krŏŏsh•chôf´), Nikita (1894-). Number one leader of the Soviet Union. First secretary of the Central Committee of the Communist party since 1953, and since 1958 the country's premier (Chairman of the Council of Ministers) as well. See chart, page 141.

Kirov (kē´rŭf), Sergei (1888-1934). Stalin's party chief in Leningrad whose mysterious assassination in December 1934 touched off the great purges of the 1930s.

Kornilov (kŭr•nyē´lŭf), Lavr (1870-1918). General named military commander in chief by Kerensky after the February Revolution, but who later opposed the Provisional Government in a political incident that contributed to Kerensky's downfall.

Krupskaya (krŏŏp´skȧ•yȧ), Nadezhda (1869-1939). Lenin's wife and Russian revolutionist.

Kulaks. Relatively well-to-do peasants, a class liquidated by Stalin in his farm collectivization drive which reached a climax in the early 1930s.

Lenin (lyä´nyĭn), N. (born Vladimir Ilyich Ulyanov), (1870-1924). The founder of Bolshevism and of the Communist state in Russia.

Leningrad. Second largest city in the U.S.S.R. and capital until 1918. Known as St. Petersburg until 1914 and Petrograd until 1924.

Malenkov (mŭ•lyĕn•kôf´), Georgi (1902-). Soviet premier from Stalin's death in 1953 until 1955. A member of the antiparty group, he was ousted from the Presidium by Khrushchev in 1957.

Maleter (mal•ā´tĕr), Pal (1920-1958). Hungarian army tank officer who led troops in the bitter fighting during the 1956 Budapest rising against the Russian forces.

Mao Tse-tung (mä´ō dzŭ´dŏŏng´) (1893-). One of the founders in 1921 of the Chinese Communist party and now the supreme leader of Red China.

Marx, Karl (1818-1883). Father of revolutionary Communism; author of *Capital* and co-author with Engels of the *Communist Manifesto.*

Mensheviks. See box, page 10.

Mikoyan (myĭ•kŭ•yȧn´), Anastas (1895-). Stalin's trade expert, one of Khrushchev's senior collaborators and a Soviet first deputy premier since 1958.

Molotov (mô´lŭ•tŭf), Vyacheslav (1890-). Leading Bolshevik; Soviet premier (1930-1941) and foreign minister (1939-1949), (1953-1956); a member of the antiparty group; since 1957 in relative obscurity.

Nagy (nŏdzh), Imre (1896-1958). Communist premier of Hungary 1953-1955, recalled to office for 12 days just before the Budapest rising of 1956. He was executed by the Communists in 1958.

National-Liberation Wars. See box, page 102.

New Economic Policy (NEP). The economic policy ordered by Lenin in 1921, when spreading hunger and unrest made it advisable to restore certain aspects of private enterprise.

October Revolution. Russian term for the second Revolution of 1917. According to the western calendar, it actually took place in November.

Peaceful coexistence. See box, page 102.

People's Democracies. See box, page 102.

Pervukhin (pĕr•vŏŏ•kēn´), Mikhail (1904-). Soviet planner under Stalin and Khrushchev; lowered in rank after joining the move to overthrow Khrushchev in 1957.

Petrograd. See Leningrad.

Plekhanov (plyĕ•Kȧ´nŭf), George (1857-1918). Father of Russian Marxism; founder of the Russian Social Democratic party. He gradually broke with Lenin after 1903.

Politburo. Powerful Political Bureau within the Central Committee of the Communist party. Renamed the "Presidium" in 1952.

"Pravda" (Truth). Founded in 1912

as the official newspaper of the Bolshevik party and later of the Communist party. The official government newspaper is called *Izvestia (News)*. A popular Russian saying is that "There is no news in *Pravda* and no truth in *Izvestia*."

Presidium. See Politburo.

Rajk (roik), Laszlo (1909-1949). A top Communist official in Hungary, arrested and hanged in 1949.

Rakosi (rä´kō•shē), Matyas (1892-). Communist party boss of Hungary from 1945 until a few months before the Budapest uprising in 1956.

Red Square. Main Moscow square flanked by the Kremlin and by Lenin's tomb. It is the scene of parades and open-air meetings.

Saburov (sä•bo͞o´rŭf), Maxim (1900-). A leading Soviet economic planner, ousted from the Presidium after joining the move to overthrow Khrushchev in 1957.

St. Petersburg. See Leningrad.

Smolny Institute. A onetime fashionable girls' school in Petrograd that was the 1917 headquarters of the Bolshevik revolutionists.

Social Democratic party. See box, page 10.

Socialism. See box, page 10.

Socialist Revolutionary party. Party formed in 1900 by the uniting of several Populist groups. Suppressed by Lenin in 1918 after winning largest single block of votes in the election for the constituent assembly.

Soviet. Russian term for council. The first Soviets were revolutionary committees of workers and soldiers organized during the 1905 uprising in St. Petersburg.

Stalin (stá´lyĭn), Joseph (born Djugashvili), (1879-1953). General secretary of the Communist party from 1922 and undisputed dictator of the Soviet Union from 1929 until his death in 1953.

Stolypin (stŭ•lĭ´pyĭn), Peter (1863-1911). As premier from 1906 to 1911, he firmly supported the supremacy of the Tsar. He died at the hand of a revolutionary assassin.

Summit Conference. A Geneva conference in 1955 at which Eisenhower and other Allied chieftains met Khrushchev and Bulganin. It was so called because Churchill had been urging a "meeting at the summit." The term has since been applied to any major meeting of heads of government.

Sun Yat-sen (so͝on´ yät´ sĕn´) (1866-1925). Chinese revolutionist and first president of the Chinese republic established in 1911.

Tauride Palace. Seat of the 1917 Provisional Government in Petrograd. The Soviets also met there. Location of the ill-fated constituent assembly of 1918.

Teheran Conference. First of a series of Allied heads of government conferences of World War II, November 28 to December 1, 1943.

Tito (tē´tō) (born Josip Broz) (1892-). Communist dictator of Yugoslavia since 1945, who in 1948 broke with Stalin and made Yugoslavia an independent Communist state.

Tkachev (tkä•chôf´), Peter. 19th Century Russian revolutionist who inspired terrorist movements such as the "People's Will."

Tomsky (tŏms´kĭ), Mikhail (1880-1936). Early leader of Soviet trade unions, who committed suicide before his scheduled trial during one of Stalin's early purges.

Trotsky (trôts´kĭ), Leon (born Lev Davidovich Bronstein), (1879-1940). A principal figure in the Bolshevik Revolution; organizer of the Red Army. Eventually exiled by Stalin and murdered by a Stalinist agent in Mexico in 1940.

Tukhachevsky (to͝ok•hŭ•chĕf´skē), Mikhail (1893-1937). Red Army marshal who commanded Russian troops in 1920 in the war against Poland. Later became chief of general staff. In 1937 he was executed by Stalin on trumped-up charges of plotting with the Nazis.

Union of Soviet Socialist Republics. The official name of the country, adopted in 1922. The union consists of 15 constituent republics, of which by far the largest is the Russian Soviet Federated Socialist Republic.

Voroshilov (vŭ•rŭ•shĭ´lŭf), Kliment (1881-). A Red Army commander in the civil war; defense commissar under Stalin; "president" of U.S.S.R. from 1953 until 1960.

Voznesenski (vŏz•nĕ•sĕn´skĭ), Nikolai (1903-1950?). Stalin's top economic planner after the second World War. Disappeared in 1949 and was later executed.

Vyshinsky (vĭ•shĭn´skĭ), Andrei (1883-1954). Stalin's prosecutor in the "show" trials of the 1930s and foreign minister (1949-1953). A familiar figure as Soviet U.N. delegate.

War Communism. Term used to describe the period from 1918 to 1921 during which Russia suffered great economic hardships as a result of the Bolsheviks' effort to impose Communism rapidly and in the midst of war.

White Army. The name given to the anti-Communist military forces which fought in the civil war (1918-1920).

Winter Palace. Tsarist palace and seat of government in St. Petersburg (later Petrograd); center of demonstrations and bloodshed in the uprisings of 1905; stormed in Revolution of 1917.

Yalta Conference. Second meeting during World War II of the three top Allied leaders, February 4-11, 1945.

Zhdanov (zhdä´nôf), Andrei (1896-1948). Stalin's wartime boss of Leningrad; later the harsh overseer of Soviet culture and the international Communist movement until his sudden and somewhat mysterious death in 1948.

Zhukov (zho͞o´kôf), Georgi (1896-). Soviet general in the decisive World War II Battle of Stalingrad and leader of Soviet troops in fall of Berlin. Although he helped defeat the antiparty group in 1957, Khrushchev demoted him and relegated him to obscurity later that year.

Zinoviev (zyĭ•nôv´yĕf), Grigory (1883-1936). One of Lenin's top lieutenants; Leningrad party boss; member of the triumvirate who succeeded Lenin. Purged by Stalin in 1936.

FOR FURTHER READING

These works were selected on the grounds of interest, authority and usefulness in the preparation of this volume. An asterisk (*) marks works helpful for those who wish to pursue particular subjects in detail; a square (■) marks paperback books.

*Armstrong, John A., *The Politics of Totalitarianism.* Random House, 1961.

*Barnett, A. Doak, *Communist China and Asia.* Harper & Brothers, 1960. ■ Vintage Books, 1961, $1.85.

*Beloff, Max, *The Foreign Policy of the Soviet Union, 1929-1941* (2 vols.). Oxford University Press, 1947-1949.

Berlin, Isaiah, *Karl Marx.* Oxford University Press, 1948. ■ Galaxy Books, 1959, $1.50.

*Brumberg, Abraham, ed., *Russia under Khrushchev.* Frederick A. Praeger, 1962. ■ $2.50.

*Brzezinski, Z. K., *The Soviet Bloc—Unity and Conflict.* Harvard University Press, 1960. ■ Frederick A. Praeger, 1961, $2.75.

Campbell, Robert W., *Soviet Economic Power.* ■ Houghton Mifflin, 1960, $1.95.

Churchill, Winston S., *The Second World War* (6 vols.). Houghton Mifflin, 1948-1953. ■ Bantam Books, 1962 (6 vols.), $1.25 each.

*Dallin, David J., *Soviet Foreign Policy after Stalin.* J. B. Lippincott, 1961.

Daniels, Robert V., ed., *A Documentary History of Communism.* Random House, 1960. ■ Vintage Books, 1962 (2 vols.), $1.65 each.

*Deutscher, Isaac, *Stalin, a Political Biography.* Oxford University Press, 1949. ■ Vintage Books, 1960, $1.65. **The Prophet Armed (Trotsky: 1879-1921).* Oxford University Press, 1954. **The Prophet Unarmed (Trotsky: 1921-1929).* Oxford University Press, 1959.

*DeWitt, Nicholas, *Education and Professional Employment in the U.S.S.R.* Published in the National Science Foundation, U.S. Government Printing Office, 1961.

Djilas, Milovan, *Conversations with Stalin.* Harcourt, Brace & World, 1962. *The New Class.* Frederick A. Praeger, 1957. ■ $1.45.

*Draper, Theodore, *The Roots of American Communism.* Viking Press, 1957. **American Communism and Soviet Russia.* Viking Press, 1960.

*Fainsod, Merle, *How Russia Is Ruled.* Harvard University Press, 1953.

*Feis, Herbert, *Churchill, Roosevelt, Stalin.* Princeton University Press, 1957.

Florinsky, Michael T., ed., *McGraw-Hill Encyclopedia of Russia and the Soviet Union.* McGraw-Hill, 1961.

*Haimson, Leopold H., *The Russian Marxists and the Origins of Bolshevism.* Harvard University Press, 1955.

*Hazard, John N., *The Soviet System of Government.* University of Chicago Press, 1960.

Hindus, Maurice, *House without a Roof.* Doubleday, 1961.

Hoover, J. Edgar, *Masters of Deceit.* Henry Holt, 1958. ■ Pocket Books, 1959, 50 cents.

Hunt, R. N. Carew, *A Guide to Communist Jargon.* Macmillan, 1957.

*Inkeles, Alex, and Kent Geiger, eds., *Soviet Society: A Book of Readings.* Houghton Mifflin, 1961.

Jacobs, Dan N., ed., *The New Communist Manifesto and Related Documents.* ■ Harper Torchbooks, 1961, $1.95.

Kennan, George F., *Russia and the West under Lenin and Stalin.* Little, Brown, 1961. ■ Mentor Books, 1962, 95 cents.

Koestler, Arthur, *Darkness at Noon.* Modern Library, 1941. ■ Signet Classics, 1961, 50 cents.

*Lenin, V. I., *Selected Works* (12 vols.). International Publishers, 1935-1938.

Leonhard, Wolfgang, *The Kremlin Since Stalin.* Frederick A. Praeger, 1962. ■ $2.95.

Miller, Wright W., *The Russians as People.* E. P. Dutton, 1961. ■ $1.35.

Moorehead, Alan, *The Russian Revolution.* Harper & Brothers, 1958. ■ Bantam Books, 1959, 50 cents.

Mosely, Philip E., *The Kremlin and World Politics.* ■ Vintage Books, $1.65.

Orwell, George, *1984.* New American Library, 1949. ■ Signet Classics, 1961, 60 cents.

Pistrak, Lazar, *The Grand Tactician: Khrushchev's Rise to Power.* Frederick A. Praeger, 1961.

*Salisbury, Harrison E., ed., *Khrushchev's "Mein Kampf."* ■ Belmont Books, 1961, 50 cents.

Schapiro, Leonard, *The Communist Party of the Soviet Union.* Random House, 1959.

Schwartz, Harry, ed., *The Many Faces of Communism.* ■ Berkley, 1962, 50 cents.

*Seton-Watson, Hugh, *From Lenin to Khrushchev: The History of World Communism.* Frederick A. Praeger, 1960. ■ $2.25. **The East European Revolution.* Frederick A. Praeger, 1956. ■ 1962, $2.25.

Shub, David, *Lenin: A Biography.* Doubleday, 1948. ■ Abridged, Mentor Books, 1961, 50 cents.

Treadgold, Donald W., *Twentieth Century Russia.* Rand McNally, 1959.

U.S. Congress: List of publications on Communism that have been issued by the House Committee on Un-American Activities *et al.* U.S. Government Printing Office, 1961.

U.S. Congress, Committee on Un-American Activities, *Facts on Communism* (2 vols.). U.S. Government Printing Office, 1960-1961, $1.70.

U.S. Congress, *Language as a Communist Weapon.* U.S. Government Printing Office, 1959, 20 cents. *Wordsmanship: Semantics as a Communist Weapon.* 1961, 15 cents.

Vernadsky, George, *A History of Russia.* Yale University Press, 1961. ■ 1961, $1.95.

Wolfe, Bertram D., *Khrushchev and Stalin's Ghost* (including text of Khrushchev's 1956 secret speech). Frederick A. Praeger, 1957. **Three Who Made a Revolution.* Dial Press, 1961. ■ Beacon Press, 1962, $2.95.

INDEX

Absolute monarchies, European 19th Century, 16-19; Russia, 32, 37
Agreements, violations of, 10-11; Yalta, 101-104; Geneva Summit, 118; Hungary, 122-123
Aggression: Communist definition, 102; indirect, 172
Agriculture, Chinese, 161, *162-163, 177; starvation, 161, 163-164
Agriculture, Russian: farm collectivization, 82-83, 142, 143; famine, *45, 74, *75, 83-84; persecution of *kulaks,* 83-84; farm problems and food shortages, 115, 117, 142-144, 148, 149, 177; agricultural production compared to U.S., *diagram* 142, 143; farming, *148, *150
Albania, 102-103, 104, 109, 164
Alexander II, Tsar, 32, 33, 35
Alexander III, Tsar, 35, 37
Alexandra, Tsarina, 46, 47, 59
Algeria, 95, 173
American Relief Administration, 71, *75
Anti-Comintern Pact, 95
April Theses, Lenin's, 50
Arms race, 175-176
Asia, free nations *vs.* Communist bloc, *map* 110
Atlantic community, *map* 12-13. *See also* NATO
Austria: Social Democrats, 11; Russian occupation, 101; peace treaty, 116
Austro-Hungarian Empire, 16, 17

Bakunin, Mikhail, 32, 34
Balkans: German-Soviet rivalry, 96; under Soviet control, 102. *See also* separate countries
Baltic states, Soviet invasion, 96
Beneš, Eduard, 103-104, 108
Beria, Lavrenti, 112, 113, *114, 115, 123
Berlin: Soviets allowed capture of, 101; Allied agreements on, 104; crisis, 126, 166, 168. *See also* East Berlin; West Berlin
Berlin airlift, *106-107, 108, 111
Berlin blockade, 104, 108, 111
Berlin wall, *8, 9, 166-167, *168
Bloody Sunday (revolt of 1905), 42, 52, *53
Bolsheviks, 9, 10; faction formed, 41; in 1905 revolt, 43; in 1917 Soviet, 47, 48, 49; in 1917 election, 68-69; change name to Communist party, 72. *See also* Russian Communist party; Russian Revolution
Bolshoi Theater, *155
Brainwashing, 126
Brest-Litovsk, Treaty of, 71, *72
Brussels Treaty, 108, 111
Bukharin, Nikolai, 78, 81, 86
Bulganin, Nikolai, *114, 116-117, *118, 123, 125, 126
Bulgaria, 102, 165
Byrnes, James, 108

Cadets. *See* Russian Constitutional Democratic party
Capital, Marx, 19, 38
Capitalism: Marx's analysis of, 23-25; ability of reform, 28, 177; imperialist phase, 67
Castro, Fidel, 173
Catechism of a Revolutionist, Nechaiev, 34
Chambers, Whittaker, 175
Cheka, 70-71
Chernishevsky, Nikolai, 32, 34, 36, 40
Chernov, Victor, 70
Chiang Kai-shek, *88, 89, 111
China *(for events after 1949, see also* Red China): rise of Communism in, 88-89, 95; war with Japan, 89, 111; civil war, 111
Chinese Communist party, 89, 111
Churchill, Sir Winston, 96, 97, 98, *100, 101, 143; quoted, 97, 101-102, 107
Class struggle, 11, 23, 117, 177
Cold war, 95, 104; roots of, 101-102; "rolling crisis" technique, 126. *See also* Berlin blockade; Cuba; National-liberation wars
Collectivization: of farms, in Russia, 82-83, 142, 143; reversal in Poland, 121, 164; Red China, 161, 163; Czechoslovakia, 165; East Germany, 167
Cominform, 105, 108
Comintern, 88, 105
Common Market, 171
Communal villages, 22
Communards, *26-27, 28
Communism: choice of term, 22; definitions, 10-11; goals of, 9, 10; methods of, 10-11, 31, 174; perversion of Marxism, 11, 27, 28, 67, 103, 140; roots of, 20, 22
Communist bloc, 9, *map* 12-13, *maps* 109-110
Communist China. *See* Red China
Communist conspiracy, worldwide, 31, 88; popular fronts, 31, 90
Communist expansion, 94, 95, 101-104, 172; U.S. policy, 108, 176; and peaceful coexistence, 117
Communist Manifesto, 14-15, 18, 19, 23-24, 28
Communist parties outside U.S.S.R., 31, 88-89, 105, 108
Condorcet, Marquis de, 18
Congo, 95, 126
Conversations with Stalin, Djilas, 104
Cuba, 11, 12, 95, 126, 173
Curzon Line, 73, 98
Czech Corps, *72-73
Czechoslovakia: 1938 crisis, 92; Soviet occupation, 101, 102; Communist, 103-104, 108, 165-166; mass demonstration, *159

Deutscher, Isaac, 81
Dialectic, Hegel's, 22-23
Dialectical materialism, 23
Dictatorship of proletariat: Marxist theory, 25-26; Communist practice, 67, 103
Disarmament, 118, 176
Djilas, Milovan, 104
Doctor Zhivago, Pasternak, 134
Dostoevsky, Feodor, *33, 35
Dulles, Allen, 176, 177
Duma, 42, 43, 44, 46, 47
Dzerzhinsky, Felix, *70

East Berlin, 9, 164, 168; riots (1953), 95, 116, *120. *See also* Berlin wall
East Germany, 104, 166-168; dismantling of industry, 106; economy, 167; refugees, 9, 166-167; 1953 revolt, 120, 166; sports parade, *159; Soviet armed forces in, 167-168
Eastern Europe: Soviets allowed capture of capitals of, 101; Soviet domination, 95, 101-104, 108. *See also* Satellites
Egypt, 126; Communist arms aid, 95, 118, 166
Eisenhower, Dwight D., 101, 116, *118, 126, 162
Engels, Friedrich, 14, 15, 18, *19, 20, 22
Enukidze, Abel, 123
Europe: 1848 revolutions, 16-18; forms of socialism, 11; U.S. economic aid to, 108; cooperation of western, 108, 171; free nations *vs.* Communist bloc, *map* 109; and NATO, 111. *See also* Eastern Europe
European Coal and Steel Community, 171

Fascism, 90, 91-92
Fechter, Peter, *8, *9
Finland, 96
Formosa, 111
Fourier, Charles, 22
France, 92; Social Democrats, 11; 1848 revolt, 17; Communards, *26-27, 28; and Russian civil war, 73; in World War II, 95, 96, 98; Communist party, 108; and European cooperation, 108, 171
Franco, Francisco, *90, 91
Free World alliances, *maps* 12-13, 95, 107, 108, 111, *maps* 109-110, 171

Gagarin, Yuri, 139
Geneva Summit Conference (1955), 116, *118
George V, King of Britain, *37
Germany: Social Democrats, 11; 1848 revolts, 17; Bolshevik peace treaty with, 71, *72; Communist revolt in (1919), 66, *87, 88; Nazi persecution of Communists, 89; Stalin's policy toward, 89-90; aids Franco in Spanish civil war, *90, *91, 92; Anti-Comintern pact, 95; Soviet-German pact, 94, 95, 96; in World War II, 95-98; Allied occupation of, 101; summit negotiations on, 116-117. *See also* East Germany; West Germany
Gerö, Ernö, 121-122
God That Failed, The, 85
Gomulka, Wladyslaw, 120-121, *122, 164
Goods, production and distribution of: Marxist ideal, 11, 26-27; Soviet reality, 11, 27, 140; pre-Marxian discussions, 22
Gorky, Maxim, 76
Gottwald, Klement, 103
Great Britain, 92; Labour party, 11; Industrial Revolution and consequences, 15-16; and Russian civil war, 73; in World War II, 94, 95, 96, 98, 101; wartime aid to Russia, 96, *99; and European cooperation, 108, 171
Greece, U.S. aid to, 108, 112
Gromyko, Andrei, 107
Guerrilla warfare, Communist, 96, 103, 172-174
Guevara, Ernesto (Che), 173

Herzen, Alexander, 32
Hindus, Maurice, 84
Hiss, Alger, 175
History, Marxist view of, *diagrams* 22-23
Hitler, Adolf, 89, *90, 92, 94, 95, 96, 97, 182
Ho Chi Minh, 172

Hook, Sidney, 144
Hoover, Herbert, 71
House without a Roof, Hindus, 84
Hoxha, Enver, 103, 164
Hungary, 8-9, 96, 102; 1848 revolution, 17; 1919 Communist revolt, 66, *86, 88; unrest in, 116, 119, 121; 1956 revolt, 95, 122-123, *124-125, 176; since revolt, 165

I*diot, The*, Dostoevsky, 33
Imperialism, 67, 102; Communist, 94, 95, 117
Industrial Revolution, 15-16
Industrial Workers of the World, 88
Industrialization, Chinese: "Great Leap," 161-162, 163; commune system, 161, 163; backyard iron production, 161-162
Industrialization, Russian: prewar industrialization, 75, 82, 84, 87, 92; economic progress (1921-1928), 81-82; limited capitalism, 82; Five-Year Plan (1928), 82, 87; collectivization, 82-83, 142, 143; forced labor, 84; economic progress in 1930s, 92; industrial production, 1928 *vs.* 1940, *diagram* 92; consumer goods production, *vs.* heavy industry, 114-115, *diagram* 136-137; postwar industrialization, 136, 144; industrial production compared to U.S., *diagram* 136-137, 146, 147; capital investment compared to U.S., *graphs* 138-139; industrial plants, *146-147
Internal Security Act, 175
International Workingmen's Association, 19, 28
Iran, Soviet troops in, 107-108
Iskra (The Spark), 40, 77
Italy: 1848 revolt, 17; aid to Franco, 91, 92; Anti-Comintern pact, 95; Allied invasion, 98; Communist party, 108; and European cooperation, 171

Japan, 170; war with China, 89, 111; in World War II, 94, 96; Anti-Comintern pact, 95
"July Days" crisis (1917), 50-51

Kadar, Janos, 165
Kaganovich, Lazar, 105, *115, 123, 125
Kamenev, Lev, 76, 78, 79, 80, 81, 82, 85, 118
Kaplan, Fanya, 71
Katyn Forest murders, 98
Kennan, George F., 77
Kennedy, John F., 126, 172
Kerensky, Alexander, 46, 47, 49, 50, *51, 52, 68, 69
Kerensky, Feodor, 36
Khrushchev, Nikita, *94, 95, *105, *115; early career, 106; party secretary, 114-115; eliminates rivals, 115-116, 125-126; farm program, 115, 142-143; and Red China, 115, 118, 162-163; foreign policy, 116-117, 126; with foreign leaders, *116, *117, *122; change of Stalinist policies, 117-118, 136; downgrades Stalin, 118-119; showdown with Gomulka, 120-121; plot against, 123, 125; visit to U.S., 126, 162; promises true Communism, 142; quoted, 28, 117-118, 140, 144, 172; mentioned, 85, 89, 97, 113, 132, 134, 135, 172, 175
Kirov, Sergei, 85, 118
Kolchak, Admiral Alexander, 73
Komsomol, 132, 134
Komsomolskaya Pravda, 134
Korea, division of, 8, 111
Korean War, 8, 95, 102, 111-112, *113
Kornilov, Lavr, 51
Kossuth, Louis, 17
Kovács, Béla, 122
Kremlin, *156-157
Kronstadt revolt, 74-75
Krupskaya, Nadezhda, 38, *39, 40
Kuibyshev hydroelectric plant, *146-147
Kulaks, 74, 83-84
Kun, Béla, 86
Kuomintang, 89

Labor theory of value, 24, 25
Labor unions: in Marx's theories, 25; Lenin's view of, 41; U.S., 90-91; Russian, 92, 129
Laos, 95, 172
Lenin, Vladimir Ilyich, *30, 33, *38, *39, *69, *79; characterization, 76; given name, 30; impact on history, 30-31; departure from Marxism, 30, 38, 41, 67; hopes for world revolution, 31, 66, 88; methods of reaching party goals, 31; boyhood, 33-34; family of, *38; as revolutionist, 35-36, 37-39; theory of party organization of professional revolutionists, 38, 40, 41, 67; Siberian exile, 40; in exile abroad, 40, 41, 44; in 1905 revolt, 43; return to Russia (1917), 48-49, *60; April Theses, 50; stand against Mensheviks and Provisional Government, 50-51; in October Revolution, 51-52; peace, land, bread slogan, 50, 67; as head of government, 67-71, 74-75; use of terror, 70-71, 75; attempted assassination, 71; rule against party factions, 79-80; death and funeral, 80; testament of, 80; writings of, 40; quoted, 38, 43-44, 52, 67, 68, 69, 70, 75, 76, 117, 143; mentioned, 10, 66, 77, 78, 82, 89, 129
Lenin: A Biography, Shub, 68
Lenin's Tomb, *6, 30
Leningrad (formerly St. Petersburg and Petrograd), 9, 46, 71, 129; siege of, 97
Lewis, John L., 90
Lincoln, Abraham, 178; Marx's tribute to, 24
London *Times*, 108
Lvov, Prince Georgi, 47

Magsaysay, Ramon, 112
Malaya, 112
Malenkov, Georgi, 105-106, 107, 113, *114, 115-116, 119, 123, 125
Maleter, Pal, 122, 123
Maniu, Iuliu, 102
Mao Tse-tung, *89, 115, *161, 162-163, 173; war talk, 163
Marshall, George, 108
Marshall Plan, 108, 171
Marx, Jenny, 18, 20, *21
Marx, Karl, *14; boyhood and education of, 18; life and work of, 19-20, 22; family of, 19-20, *21; Carl Schurz on, 25; lasting contribution of, 28; influence on Russian revolutionists, 37; quoted, 14, 23-24, 28; mentioned, 10, 11, 15, 30, 36. *See also* Marxist theories
Marxist movement: in Russia, 37-40, 41; cause of split of, 41
Marxist theories, 22-27; view of history, *diagrams* 22-23; dialectical materialism, 23; class struggle, 23; on capitalism, 23-25; labor theory of value, 24, 25; wage-price-profit relationships, 25; expropriation of expropriators, 25; dictatorship of proletariat, 25-26, 103; wealth distribution, 26-27; view of social reform, 28; historical appraisal of, 27-28, 170; Communist departure from, 27, 30, 67, 103, 140
Masaryk, Jan, 103
Masaryk, Tomáš, 103
Materialism, dialectical, 23
Mensheviks, 10, 42, 47, 48, 50, 51, 70; purged, 75-76
Michael, Grand Duke, 47
Michael, King of Rumania, 101
Mikolajczyk, Stanislaw, 102
Mikoyan, Anastas, 105, 106, *115, 116, 123, 167
Miller, Wright, 129
Mindszenty, Cardinal, 122
Molotov, Vyacheslav, 96, 98, 101, 105, 108, *114, 123, 125
Morality, Communist interpretation of, 76, 133
Moscow, 129; Red Square, *6; Kremlin, *156-157
Munich Agreement (1938), 92, 95, 103
Mussolini, Benito, 92

Nagy, Imre, 119, 122, 123
"National-liberation wars," 96, 103, 172
Nationalist China, 111
NATO, 111, 176
Nazism, 89-90, 182
Nechaiev, Sergei, 34, 35
Neutralists. *See* Uncommitted nations
New York Times, The, 138
New York *Tribune*, 22
Nicholas I, Tsar, 17
Nicholas II, Tsar, 33, *37, 42, 43, 44, 46; abdication, 47; execution, *64, 71
Nikolaev, Leonid V., 85
NKVD, 85
Novak, Joseph, 140
Nuclear war threat, 8, 126

October Manifesto (1905), 42-43
Owen, Robert, 22

Paris Commune (1871), *26-27, 28
Pasternak, Boris, *134
Pavlov, Ivan, 126
Peaceful coexistence, 103, 117
"People's democracies," 103, 104, 117-118
"People's Will," 33, 35, 39, 42, 48
Pervukhin, M. G., 123, 125
Petöfi Club, 119
Philippines, 112
Pioneers, 132, 134
Plekhanov, George V., 37, 38, 40, 68
Poland, 164, *165; re-established, 73-74; in World War II, 95, 98; Soviet-German partition of, 96; Allied negotiations on, 98, 101; Stalin violates Allied agreements, 101; under Soviet control, 102; unrest in, 116, 119-120, *121; relaxation of internal policies, 121, 164
Polish exile government, 98
Polish provisional government, 98, 101
Popovich, Pavel, *132
"Popular fronts," 31, 90, 91
Populists, Russian, 32-33, 37
Port Arthur, Japanese attack on, *40, 42
Portsmouth, Treaty of, 41

Possessed, The, Dostoevsky, 35
Poznan riots, 119-120, *121
Pravda, 49, 71, 77, 78, 112, 114, 118, 123
Proletariat, 25. *See also* Dictatorship of proletariat
Property: communal, 11, 22; man's desire for, 22; Marx's concentration of ownership, 25; Soviet valuation of, 138. *See also* Goods, production and distribution of
Purges: Lenin's, 70-71, 75-76; Stalin's, 83-88, 107, 118; since Stalin, 114; Khrushchev's nonbloody, 115-116, 125-126; of satellite leaders, 116; Red China, 161; Albania, 164

Rajk, Laszlo, 119, 121
Rakosi, Matyas, 119, 121, 122
Rapallo pact, 89
Rasputin, 46, *59
Red Army, 78; in civil war, 73, 74, 75, 78; and Trotsky, 81; loyal to Stalin in terror regime, 84; purges, 87-88; in eastern Europe, 96, *97, 98, 102, 103; in Hungarian revolt, 122, 123, *124
Red China (*for events before 1949, see also* China), 109, 111, 113, 118, *160; strained relations with Russia, 110, 162-163; living conditions, 161, 163-164; "liberal" Communist phase, 161; armed forces, 162; anti-U.S. indoctrination, 162-163. *See also* Agriculture; Industrialization
Refugees, *166-167; East German, 9, 166-167
Ribbentrop, Joachim von, 95, *96
Rokossovsky, Konstantin, 120-121
Rome, Treaty of, 171
Roosevelt, Franklin D., 96, 97, 98, *100, 101, 175
Roosevelt, Theodore, *41
Rumania: German-Soviet rivalry, 96; Communist, 101, 102, 164
Russia (*for events since 1922, see also* U.S.S.R.): 19th Century, 16-17, 31-32, 36-37; revolutionist intelligentsia, 32-33; Marxist movement, 37-40; revolution of 1905, 40, 41-43, 48, 52, *53-55, 77; First Soviet (1905), 42, 43; Duma, 42, 43, 44, 46, 47; in World War I, 44, *45, 46, 50, 71; Soviets (1917), 47, 48, *49, 51; Provisional Government (1917), 47-52; Congress of Soviets, 52, 67; under Lenin, 66-76, 79; Soviet of People's Commissars, 67-68; nationalization of industries, 67, 74; 1917 free election, 68-69; constituent assembly (1917), 69-70; press, control of, 68, 129; Bolshevik dictatorship and terror, 70-71, 75-76; peace treaty with Germany (1918), 71, *72; civil war, 66, *72-73, 74; famine, *45, 74, *75; strikes, 74-75; economic breakdown (1918-21), 74; war Communism, 74-75; New Economic Policy, 75. *See also* Russian Revolution
Russia and the West under Lenin and Stalin, Kennan, 77
Russian Communist party, 10, 72; 1921 Party Congress and temporary retreat, 75; opposition and strikes against, 72-73, 74-75, 79; Politburo, 76; interparty rivalries to succeed Lenin, 76, 79, 81; opposition to Stalin, 84; purges of, 84-86, 87, 107, 112, 114; "Congress of the Victors" (1934), 87; interparty rivalries to succeed Stalin, 105-107, 113-116; 20th Congress (1956), 117; leadership upheaval (1957), 125-126; membership, 134; dominates government, *chart* 141; 22nd Congress (1961), 142. *See also* Bolsheviks
Russian Constitutional Democratic party, 44, 69
Russian people: peasants, *82, 142-143; workers, *83, *128, 130; workers' living standards, 138-139, *diagram* 143; woman workers, 129, 139, *152; political indoctrination, 129, 133; youth, 130-132, 133-134, *135; yearning for truth, 130-131, 176; scientists, 133; moral standards, 133-134; atheist indoctrination, 134; Communist party members, 134; elite, 140; exploitation of, 144; U.S. attitude toward, 176, 178
Russian Revolution, 41, 44; March Revolution, 46-47, *48; abdication of Tsar, 47; "July Days" crisis, 50-51; Bolshevik (October) Revolution, 31, 51-52, *62-63, 78
Russian Social Democratic Labor party, 10, 41, 44, 48. *See also* Bolsheviks; Mensheviks
Russian Socialist Revolutionary party, 42, 48, 51, 69, 70, 76
Russian Soviet Federated Socialist Republic, 68
Russians as People, Miller, 129
Russo-Japanese War, *40, 41-42
Rykov, Alexis I., 81, 86

Saburov, Maxim, 123, 125
Saint-Simon, Comte de, 22
Salinger, J. D., 135
Satellites, Soviet, *map* 12-13, 108, *map* 109, 117-118; Soviet exploitation of, 106, 165, 166; unrest and revolt in, 116, 119-123; in Warsaw Pact, 176
Sergei, Grand Duke, 42
Shub, David, on Lenin, 68, 76
Silone, Ignazio, 85
Smith Act, 174, 175
Social Democrat, Marxist journal, 78
Social reforms, 11, 28, 177; Marx's view, 28
Socialism: definitions, 10-11; roots of, 20, 22; Soviet, 11, 117-118; utopian, 22
Soviet of People's Commissars, 67-68
Soviet of Workers' Deputies: of 1905, 42, 43; of 1917, 47
Soviet of Workers' and Soldiers' Deputies (1917), 47, 48, *49, 51
Soviet Union, *see* U.S.S.R.
Spanish civil war, 90, 91-92
Stalin, Joseph, 56, *66, 68, 76, *79, *105; characterization, 77, 81, 105; boyhood and early life, 76-77, *78-79; party secretary, 76, 79; conspiracy against Trotsky, 79-80; at Lenin's funeral, 80; Lenin on, 80; eliminates rivals, 81; and socialism in one country, 81, 88, 89; Five-Year Plan (1928), 82; terror regime, 83-88, 118, 179; economic achievements, 92; pact with Hitler, 94, 95, *96; at Teheran Conference, 97, 98; at Yalta Conference, 98, *100; violates Yalta pact, 101-104; postwar economic, scientific, political goals, 104-105; postwar purges, 107, 112; and Tito, 116; administrative inefficiencies under, 136; death of, 112; body in state, *114-115; downgrading of, 115, 118-119, 162; quoted, 81, 104-105, 143-144, 175; mentioned, 49, 78, 95, 113, 114, 115, 123, 126, 130, 133, 144
Stalin, Conversations with, Djilas, 104
Stalingrad, Battle of, *97
Stalinism: Soviet departures from, 117-118, 130; in Red China, 162
Stolypin, Peter, 44, *57
Suez Canal crisis, 118, 126
Summit Conference (1955), 116, *118
Sun Yat-sen, *88, 89
Surplus value: concept, 24; higher under Soviet exploitation of workers, 144

Teheran Conference, 97-98
The Future Is Ours, Comrade, Novak, 140
Tito, Josip Broz, 103, 116, *117, 118, 119, 164
Tkachev, Peter, 33
Tomsky, Mikhail, 78, 81, 86
Trotsky, Leon, *42, 67, 76, *81, 86; given name, 77; career of, 77-78; in 1905 revolt, 42, 43, 77; joins Bolsheviks, 51, 78; People's Commissar, 68, *72, 75; conspiracy against, 78-80; critical of party leaders and policy, 79, 82; murder of, 81
Truman, Harry, 108, 111, *112
Truman Doctrine, 108, 112
Tukhachevsky, Mikhail, 74, 75, 87
Turgenev, Ivan, *32, 36
Turkey, U.S. aid to, 108, 112

Ulyanov, Alexander (Sasha), 33, 34-35, *38
Uncommitted nations, *map* 12-13; Soviet policy on, 117
Underdeveloped nations, aid to, 171, *172, 177-178
Unions. *See* Labor Unions
United Nations, 107, 111-112, 122-123
United States, social reforms, 11, 177; utopian communities, 22; relief aid to Russia (1921-22), 71, *75; and Russian civil war, 73, *74; Communists in, 88, 90-91, 174-175; labor movement, 90-91, 174; and Spanish civil war, 92; in World War II, 94, 96, 98, 111; wartime aid to Russia, 96, 99, 104; forgo capture of Berlin and Prague, 101; "containment" policy, 108; economic aid to Europe, 108; and West Berlin, 108, 111; and China, 111; and Korea, 111-112; aid to Yugoslavia, 116; economic comparisons with U.S.S.R., *diagrams* 136-137, *graphs* 138, 139, *diagrams* 142-143, 146, 147; trade policy, 171; anti-guerrilla forces, 172, *173, 174; internal subversion, 174-175; military defense, 175-176, *177; democracy in, 178-182; education, 181
U.S. Peace Corps, *170, *172, 178
U.S.S.R. (*for events before 1922, see also* Russia): suppression of truth, 9, 19, 129; departure from Marxist ideals, 11, 27, 28, 67, 103, 140; named, 88; New Economic Policy, 75, 79, 81; 1923 strikes, 79; party and army purges, 84-86, 87-88, 118; show trials, 85-86; 1936 Constitution, 86; foreign

opinions of, 86, 87, 92, 94, 123; relations with Communist parties abroad, 88-89, 105, 108; secret collaboration with Weimar Germany, 89; relationship with Hitler Germany, 89-90, 94; and Spanish civil war, 92; and Czech crisis (1938), 92, 103; labor unions, 92, 129; Soviet-German pact, 94, 95, 96; strives for world domination, 94, 95, 103; in World War II, 94, 96-98, 101; Allied aid to, 96. *99, 104; and Poland, 96, 98, 101; war losses and devastation, 104, 132; postwar economic reconstruction, 104; exploitation of satellites, 104, 106, 165, 166; scientific advances, 105, 132-133, 175; postwar persecutions and purges, 105, 107, 112; control of culture, 107, 114-115; and Marshall Plan, 108; strained relations with Red China, 110, 162-163; Khrushchev's foreign policy, 116-117, 126; change of Stalinist policies, 117-118, 136; and Hungarian revolt, 122-123, 176; leadership upheaval (1957), 125-126; population, 128; size and geography, 128-129, *map* 130, 149; winters, 129; life in, 129-136, 138-140, *148-152; communications, 129; individual freedom, 129-130; education, 129, 131-132, 133, *145, 180-181; elections, 130; religion, 130, 133, 134; military service, 132; space achievements, *132, 133, 175; nuclear industry, *133; Regional Economic Councils, 136-137; "blat" and economic crimes, 137-138; income and taxation, 138, 140, 142; housing, 139-140, *152-153; government organization, *chart* 141; purchasing power of day's pay compared to U.S., *diagram* 143; movies and theater, *154-155; armament, 175; and disarmament, 118, 176; in Warsaw Pact, 176. *See also* Agriculture; Industrialization; Russian Communist party; Russian people

Utopia, More, 22

Utopian systems, 22

Versailles, Treaty of, 89

Vietnam: U.S. military aid, *173; North, 172; South, 95, 172

Voroshilov, Kliment, *114, 118, 123

Voznesenski, N. A., 106, 107

Vyshinsky, Andrei, 86, 101

War, threat of, 8, 126, 163, 172

Warsaw, 164; uprising (1944), 98

Warsaw Pact, 176

West Berlin, 9; agreement on access to, 104; blockade of, 104, *106-107, 108, 111. *See also* Berlin wall

West Germany, 104; change of U.S. postwar policy toward, 108; in Free World alliances, 171, 176

Westphalen, Ludwig von, 18

What Is to Be Done?, Chernishevsky, 34, 35

What Is to Be Done?, Lenin, 40

White Army, 73

White Russian government, 73

Wilson, Woodrow, 73, 74

Winter Palace, capture of, 52, *62-63

"Wobblies," 88

Wolfe, Bertram D., 84

Workers, working and living conditions of: Western Europe, 19th Century, 15, *16, 17; Russia, turn of century, 36-37; Soviet Union, 138-139, 144

World revolution, 9-10, 88; Lenin's aim, 31, 66, 88; *vs.* Stalin's socialism in one country, 81, 88, 89

World War I, 44, *45, 46, 50, *61

World War II, 89, 90, 94, 95-101, 111, 182

Yalta Conference, 98, *100, 101; Stalin violates agreements, 101-104

Yugoslavia, 13, 102-103, 109, 116, 164-165

Yusupov, Prince, 46, *59

Zhdanov, Andrei, 105, 106-107, 112, 114, 115

Zhukov, Georgi, 97, 114, 116, 125-126

Zinoviev, Grigory, 71, 78, 79, 80, 81, 82, 85, 86, 118

CREDITS

Credits for pictures from left to right are separated by commas, top to bottom by dashes.

Cover—Designed by Marc Ratliff, photo by Walter Daran. 6—James Whitmore. 8,9—Bild Zeitung. 12,13—Maps by Clifton Line. 14—The Bettmann Archive. 16,17—Picture Post Library, Gustave Doré, The Bettmann Archive. 19—Sovfoto. 21—Left, from Louise Dornemann's *Jenny Marx*, published by Volksverlag Weimar; right, Sovfoto, from Louise Dornemann's *Jenny Marx*, published by Volksverlag Weimar—Culver Pictures. 26,27—Culver Pictures. 28—From *The Red Prussian* by L. Schwarzchild, Scribner's, 1947. 30—Sovfoto. 32—Historical Pictures Service, Chicago. 33—United Press International. 37—Culver Pictures. 38—Sovfoto. 39—Courtesy Leningrad History Museum, Sovfoto. 40,41—Brown Brothers. 42—United Press International. 43—Culver Pictures. 45—European Picture Service—Preslit. 48—Museum of Modern Art. 49—Sovfoto. 50—European Picture Service. 51—Brown Brothers. 53,54,55—Paintings by Alton S. Tobey. 56,57—Paintings by Morton Roberts. 58—Paintings by Rudolph F. Zallinger. 59,60—Paintings by Morton Roberts. 61, 62,63—Paintings by Carroll Jones. 64—Painting by Rudolph F. Zallinger. 66—Margaret Bourke-White. 69—Culver Pictures. 72,73—Monkmeyer Press Photos, Brown Brothers, United Press International. 74—European Picture Service. 75—Brown Brothers. 78,79—Sovfoto except left. 81,82—United Press International. 83—Wide World Photos. 86—*Histoire des Soviets,* Jacques Makowsky, publisher. 87—United Press International. 88—*The New York Times.* 90—Official U.S. Army Photo. 92—Drawing by Matt Greene. 94—Harold L. Valentine from Wide World Photos. 96—United Press International. 97—Sovfoto. 99—Walter A. Curtin by courtesy of The Trustees of the Imperial War Museum, London. 100—Official U.S. Army Photo from Wide World Photos. 101—Free-lance Photographers Guild. 102—Illustration by John Tenniel from Lewis Carroll's *Alice's Adventures in Wonderland* and *Through the Looking-Glass,* Macmillan Co., 1929. 105—Sovfoto. 106,107—Walter Sanders. 108—Ministry of Food. 109,110—Maps by Clifton Line. 111—William P. Gray. 112—United Press International. 113—David Douglas Duncan. 114,115—Sovfoto. 116—Eastfoto. 117—United Press International. 118—Hank Walker. 120—Wide World Photos. 121—United Press International. 122—House of Photography. 124—*Paris Match.* 125—Michael Rougier. 128—James Whitmore. 130—© Rand McNally & Company, R.L. 62 S 103. 131—Jerry Cooke. 132, 133—Sovfoto. 134—Jerry Cooke. 135—*Der Stern* from Black Star. 136,137—Charts by Matt Greene. 138,139—Charts by Lewis Zacks. 141—Wide World Photos. 142, 143—Charts by Robert Reilly. 145—Jerry Cooke. 146,147—Howard Sochurek, Dan Weiner for FORTUNE. 148,149—Left, Howard Sochurek; right, Greg Shuker—Marilyn Silverstone from Nancy Palmer Agency. 150—John Launois from Black Star. 151—Howard Sochurek. 152,153—John Launois from Black Star, Jerry Cooke. 154—Marilyn Silverstone from Nancy Palmer Agency. 155—Edward Clark. 156,157—David Douglas Duncan. 158—Jochen Blume. 159—Brian Seed for SPORTS ILLUSTRATED. 160—Marc Riboud from Magnum. 161,162, 163—Eastfoto. 164—Dan Weiner. 165—Marilyn Silverstone from Nancy Palmer Agency. 166—Stan Wayman, Francis Miller. 167—Fraser Hale for the *Miami Daily News,* Larry Burrows. 168—Wide World Photos. 170—Charles Cooper. 172—Don Uhrbrock. 173—François Sully from Black Star. 177—Don Uhrbrock. 180, 181—Paul Schutzer.

xx